1992 PGA Championship, Bellerive Country Club

1994 PGA Championship, Southern Hills Country Club

1994 British Open,
Turnberry.
Practice round
with Watson,
Norman, and
Nicklaus.

Final round, the
winning eagle

Victory

Shinnecock Hills

St. Andrews

Back in Africa

THE SWING

Mastering the Principles
of the Game

by NICK PRICE

with Lorne Rubenstein

ALFRED A. KNOPF   NEW YORK

1   9   9   7

THIS IS A BORZOI BOOK
PUBLISHED BY ALFRED A. KNOPF, INC.

http://www.randomhouse.com/

Grateful acknowledgment is made to the following for permission to
reprint previously published material:

Cover photograph: Copyright © 1997 Stephen Szurlej/*Golf Digest*
Pages 160–64 and 166–67 (bottom row): Photographs of Nick Price
copyright © 1997 *Golf Digest*
Pages 178–80: Abridged from "What You Can Learn from the Greatest
Players I Ever Saw" by Sam Snead, from the February 1984 issue of
Golf Digest

PHOTOGRAPHIC CREDITS AND ACKNOWLEDGMENTS

For the color section in the front of the book:

page one: Simon Bruty/Allsport; page two: Michael C. Cohen (top);
Allsport (bottom); page three: Gary Newkirk/Allsport; page four:
Stephen Munday/Allsport (top); Michael C. Cohen (bottom); page five:
Michael C. Cohen; page six: Stephen Munday/Allsport; page seven:
Stephen Munday/Allsport; page eight: David Cannon/Allsport

Stephen Munday/Allsport: page 2; Chuck Brenkus: page 31 (left); Horst
Koch: pages 31 (right), 38, 155–59, and 166–67 (top row)

All other images in this book were derived from photographs by Scott
Halleran and taken at the Floridian Golf Club, whose hospitality is grate-
fully acknowledged. (Thanks, too, to the Redtail Golf Course, where
work on this book was begun.)

Library of Congress Cataloging-in-Publication Data
Price, Nick.
    The swing : mastering the principles of the game / by Nick Price
with Lorne Rubenstein.
        p.   cm.
    ISBN 0-679-44670-2 (alk. paper)
    1. Swing (Golf).   I. Rubenstein, Lorne.   II. Title.
GV979.S9S75   1997
796.352'3—dc21   96-52267
                                                                CIP

Manufactured in the United States of America
First Edition

To my wife, Sue,
and my children, Gregory, Robyn, and Kimberly—
for I could not have achieved what I have
without them.

contents

While playing the golf circuits of the world, it is very hard to form meaningful relationships with one's fellow competitors. It takes a unique kind of personality to bridge that gap between a rival and a fellow competitor.

Nick Price is one of those rare individuals. He is loyal, supportive, and a great friend to sit down and have a few beers with, without our respective golf careers ever getting in the way. He is someone I have the highest regard for and would consider one of my closest friends. We derive as much pleasure out of each other's victories as we do out of our own. Nick is always leaving little quips and messages to boost me on, cheer me up, or congratulate me, and vice versa. I am proud to call him my friend. I believe he is one of the great players of the Tour. When Nick is on a roll, look out, because he is a fierce competitor and a man of awesome talent.

I am sure you will find in this book a reflection of this great human being, a man who is loved and respected by all in the golfing community.

—*Greg Norman*

Having known Nick Price since he was ten years old, I have strong recollections of his aggressive swing—even at a young age. His fast tempo has always been a trademark. With the great improvement in his swing over the years, Nick has always been able to maintain his natural tempo despite the criticism that he would be better off if he swung slower. The proof of the pudding has been his tremendous results over the past few years.

When we first started on swing changes in the winter of 1981, Nick had a lot of wasted motion; combined with excessive leg action, this produced a lot of inconsistent shots. Since those early days, it has been a matter of continually refining his technique based on those early faults. What this has shown is that certain tendencies in one's golf swing are always there—you just have to keep working on them.

Since a lot of the work was trial and error, it has been a real learning experience for both of us. I know that working with Nick has enhanced my overall teaching ability. His great talent and undying search for perfection have brought great rewards, and it is no mean accomplishment when his peers say he is one of the best ballstrikers of all time. When he is on his game (which is frequently these days) Nick hones in on the pins, and strikes the ball in such a way that the contact sounds like a bullet being shot out of a gun—a sound only a few great players can claim to own. His book will help golfers of all levels understand just what it takes.

—David Leadbetter

by Lorne Rubenstein

One of the reasons golf is such a fascinating game is that it offers every golfer legitimate hope of improvement no matter his or her age. As Nick Price shows in these pages, a golfer can be better at age sixty than fifty, fifty than forty, or forty than thirty. In golf, older can really mean better simply because we can learn about our swings, and by thoughtful practice and application we can gradually reduce the influence of our bad habits. This is not to say that those habits won't always be with us. David Leadbetter, with whom Nick worked to improve his own swing, believes that traces of the first swing remain throughout the golfer's lifetime. But this only means that we need to be on guard against our particular mistakes and to understand that these faults will tend to creep in when we least expect them. There's no taking anything for granted in golf; this is certain.

But a golfer can be confident of improvement if he or she takes a long-term approach to change. And that is what caught my interest when I first watched Nick play golf during the early 1980s. I remember a chat we had during a tournament when he was frustrated because he was not winning on the PGA Tour but said with conviction how he felt that one day the gates would open wide for him and he would win. He was speaking a fundamental truth here, I think. Nick was saying that his swing was improving and that this progress would result in lower scores. He was becoming more consistent: His shot patterns were more to his liking, the ball flight was more uniform. Maybe he wasn't shooting the low numbers consistently enough to win, and maybe he was shooting too many

73s and 74s, which always hurt during a tour event, but the significant factor was that Nick was progressing.

Through his own trials, Nick learned a great deal. He learned that the golfer who wants to improve—to really improve—needs a sense of humor, because things do not always go according to plan. Having a long-term plan that makes sense and that incorporates sound principles is no guarantee that there won't be obstacles. Golfers, like anybody engaged in a discipline of refinement, must be able to laugh at themselves, to take the good with the bad. Happily, Nick has been able to do that. The life of any professional golfer is full of unusual happenings that help ease the way, as long as the player can see situations with some humor. In the course of following Nick over the years, interviewing him for articles, and then working on this book, I learned that his ability to take things in stride and to appreciate the lighter side of the golf professional's life has quite a bit to do with his play on the course.

In this regard—taking the bad with the good and appreciating how very little works out exactly as one wants—I think of something Robert Frost told the writer Roger Kahn. Kahn was in Vermont, where he was interviewing Frost for an essay he would write. During one exchange he asked Frost if his method of writing had changed over the years.

"If I'm not in shape so I can strike it out, like a good golf stroke or a good stroke of the bat, there's not much I can do," Frost told Kahn. "Oh, you get so that some days you can play a beautiful game, but there are always days when you can't. Those days, I can't redo them. They're done. Down the sink.

"What some seem to do," Frost continued, "is worry a thing into shape and have others worry with them. Not to say I don't have the distress of failure, but the worry way isn't for me. There are the days you can and the days you can't, and both are training toward the future days you can."

I have often thought of those last words: "both are training toward the future days you can." Nick knew this when he was working in those dry days of no tournament wins from 1983, when he won the World Series of Golf, until 1991, when he won the Byron Nelson Classic. Nick was sticking to what he knew was best for him; he had seen the improvement in the flight of his golf ball, in the way it was taking off more often exactly down the line he aimed, in the way it penetrated through a strong wind. Power, accuracy, control: Nick was on the right track and was not straying from the path he had chosen. Never mind the days when he couldn't, or even the days when he could. He was thinking about the long run; he was looking to the future.

One of the reasons I was excited about helping Nick with this book was precisely that he takes a sensible and practical approach to improvement. He does not fool himself. He never felt that good golf would come easily or that he could learn one special trick and suddenly, overnight, his game would be transformed. But don't many of us—golf dreamers all—often feel that we can become better golfers *just like that*? I have certainly deluded myself into believing that—into thinking the latest swing tip or theory was *it* and would give me the golf game I knew I had inside me. What a powerful idea; what a grand illusion.

Then I started noticing Nick's gradual improvement, and that over time his scores began to reflect the changes he had made in his swing. Nick had taken a courageous stand in the early 1980s when he decided to change his swing—grip, address, arc, and plane. Just about everything, that is. Most of us think about doing something similar because what we have isn't working over the long term. We fool ourselves by shooting a low number one day, but forget that we chipped in a couple of times, or holed lots of putts, or that we just had one of those days when our timing was on. We had the feel.

But eventually every golfer realizes he shouldn't depend on feel or timing alone. If he accepts the highs and lows that come with a reliance on feel and timing and decides not to take on a long-term program for betterment, he will continue to have his bad days while waiting for the feel and the good day it will bring. This peak-and-valley golf does not offer much security, and so I suspect it isn't enough for most of us.

Neither, I think, is reliance on a strong mental game. Although I completed a graduate degree in psychology and during my studies spent hours in the library reading about the fascinating psychology of golf, I came to see that such factors as visualization and a positive attitude were not enough to offer me lasting improvement. Golfers need decent mechanics to play well over the long run, and they must complement this with sound thinking and strategy. Every golfer needs an understanding of the swing in general and his or her own swing in particular, and of what the top golfers do well—what the majority have in common. Then, with some well-thought-out practice, every golfer can improve.

There's no magic, just good old enjoyable hard work. And isn't the promise of golf, perhaps the quintessential lifelong game, that we can lower our handicaps by working intelligently, given a program that makes sense, that is logical?

Nick offers here just that program, and is proof himself that long-term improvement is possible. We don't have to tee it up wishing and hoping that our timing will be on, or that we will hole some long putts. We can chip away at our problem areas and little by little replace them with good swing habits. And inch by inch, stroke by stroke, we will find our games significantly improved. Nick improved to where he won the 1992 and 1994 PGA Championships and the 1994 British Open, to where he was the game's number-one-ranked player for much of 1993 and 1994. During one stretch he won sixteen tournaments in fifty-four starts. No wonder Ben Crenshaw said that Nick was a golfer "in full flight."

I think that is what we all want out of our golf and through our golf—we want to become golfers in full flight. But "in full flight" will have a different meaning for each and every golfer. For Nick it meant getting to the point where he could contend regularly in, and win, major championships. For another golfer it might mean reaching a level where he or she can earn a PGA Tour or LPGA Tour playing card. For somebody else it could be qualifying for a national or state amateur championship, or for the quarterfinal matches of a club championship, or simply enjoying one's golf more on a regular basis with friends. It all amounts to trying to play to one's potential. This is the wonderful challenge of golf; this is the beauty of a beautiful game.

Some years ago when I was having one of my first conversations with Nick—this was when his shelves were bare of championship trophies, but also when he was seeing improvement in his swing—he said that for years he played without knowing much about the golf swing. As he put it, "I was like a salesman who had sold as much as he could, and who needed to take a course. I didn't know what else to do."

What Nick did was work out his own course over the years, with the help of such instructors as David Leadbetter and his then-associate Robert Baker. He also took the opportunity to speak with many others about golf, including Simon Hobday, the colorful South African with whom Nick traveled for some time on the European Tour after turning professional. He studied, he asked questions, he examined swing sequences of the best players, took his own swing apart, and rebuilt it. Now it is an efficient, handsome swing, with no extra moving parts. Nick's is the swing pared down to the essential, to what he considers the principles of the game. And that is what you will learn here. You will learn how to cut away excess and get to what matters during the swing.

"My bad shots are not as bad as they used to be, not as destructive," Nick said during our conversation those many years ago. "I don't hit as many off-the-wall shots. I just don't seem to go birdie, birdie, double bogey anymore."

Nick was becoming more consistent and so was able to be patient; he knew lower scores would follow, and then he would win, and win, and win. But that did not mean that he would always be at the top of his game; this is just not possible in golf, a demanding sport in which one can get out of synch at any time. It's important at such times, as Nick writes, to persevere, to keep working on the things that brought improvement. In the long run this strategy is the most useful approach to a better golf game.

It's also a strategy that Nick embodies in the way he goes about his business. Or maybe it's not correct to use the word "business," for to Nick golf has remained a game. Of course, he makes a very good living at it, but it has always been apparent to me that he enjoys working at his game and also playing the game. Of the many examples I could cite that demonstrated his passion for golf as we worked on this book, I would like to relate just a few.

There was the hot afternoon in Florida when Nick was hitting golf balls for a couple of hours. I was doing the same off to one side, and every so often I wandered over to watch Nick. "Watch this one," he would say. "It's going to be just a little lower than the last one." A few minutes later he added, "I'm trying to get my grip just a little stronger." Change never stops, even for the best players in the world. After a hard practice session, Nick was only warmed up. "Let's play nine holes," he said. And off we went into the early evening.

Then there were the two days when Nick and I started to work on the book. He had been in Toronto for a skins game and was on his way to Flint, Michigan, for the next PGA Tour event. Driving along, we turned the tape recorder on and began the sessions that led to this book. Halfway to Flint, we stopped at the Redtail Golf Course near London, Ontario, to spend the night. Soon after we reached this golf retreat, Nick borrowed some clubs—he had sent his on to Flint—and was out on the course. Playing in street shoes and using a variety of clubs not his own, he put on a clinic of shotmaking. I recall with particular delight the three different shots he hit into the eighth green: a high, floating nine-iron, a long pitch-and-run with a seven-iron, and then a punched eight-iron that flew low and landed just short of the green, took a bounce or two, and spun itself out near the hole. Here was a three-time major championship winner who was taking simple pleasure in hitting different golf shots. This was a man who loved golf as a child loves sport; he was in his element.

I also remember an evening on a beach in Florida. Nick was giving me a lesson and demonstrating how I ought to keep my lower body quiet; like many tall golfers, I tend to move my legs and hips too much. Nick told me to dig my feet into the sand and then swing the club so that I would feel what it was like to maintain a stable lower body. Sensations: A golfer must develop the proper sensations, and a capable teacher will show him how to feel the swing, not only how to understand it intellectually.

Months have passed since that evening on the beach, but as I sit here writing I can summon up the feeling of quiet legs and hips. I imagine myself on that beach, turning around my legs, sensing finally what it means to develop torque and resistance during the swing. And I think of Nick himself, working hard for many years to rid himself of his own swing faults, or at least to subdue them. He is just like you and just like me: He wants to get better and will feel this way until he no longer plays golf.

"I told you things were coming together," Nick said to me a moment after coming out of the scoring tent after winning the 1991 Canadian Open, his second win of the season and a harbinger of the next season, when he won the PGA Championship, his first major. I thought of how much I wanted to feel that confidence in my own game, feel that things were coming together. And as we worked on this book, I thought how all golfers want the same.

But how do things come together? They come together only if you recognize your own particular problem areas, understand the quirks in your own swing, and then work toward a more reliable swing that incorporates more of the common factors that all fine golfers share. This isn't to say that Nick wants every golfer to swing as he does; not at all. He emphasized very early on to me that he wanted to do this book so that he could provide what he calls a "directional map, a frame of reference."

"This is a guide to help the reader swing better and enjoy the game more, to help simplify his thinking," Nick said one afternoon in his office. "Nobody has written and nobody ever will write a book that will enable a nongolfer to go out and shoot 72. But the more fuel or food for thought a person has, the more options I can give him to work on certain things in his game, the better off he will be. Then he can try different things that may work for him. The person who is out there shooting from the hip, shooting in the dark, will find the road difficult. The golfer must be able to whittle his swing down and be more specific about what he is doing, and what he needs to do.

"I think a real misconception that people have when they read a book is that it will improve their very next game of golf," Nick added. "That may happen, but it isn't likely. I wanted to do this book more than anything so that it would help people measure their swings and games from the time they read it forward. If a person can say after reading the book the first time that he improved the next day by a shot, good. But I will feel I have accomplished something if he can say after a year, 'I've stuck to what Nick is trying to tell me and I've actually come down four shots in my handicap.' That to me is solid progress. It's like the guy playing the stock market to make a profit the next day. He's going to come up short many times. But if he plays the market over a long period of time and goes about it in the right way, he will make money at it. In the same way, how often does it happen that somebody buys a house and turns around the next day and sells it for twenty percent more? That might happen once in your lifetime. My point is that rather than try to get it all done overnight, just make the commitment to yourself and to progress. The reader will hear this idea many times in this book. If he thinks that the book will turn him from a twenty handicap to a ten overnight, I would suggest he forget that notion. It won't happen. What will happen is steady, sure progress."

Think about "steady, sure progress" and "things coming together" as you read about Nick's road to his own best game and as you apply his ideas to your own game. You will take your own road, and things will come together for you as well as you hit better and better golf shots, time after time, month after month, year after year.

THE SWING

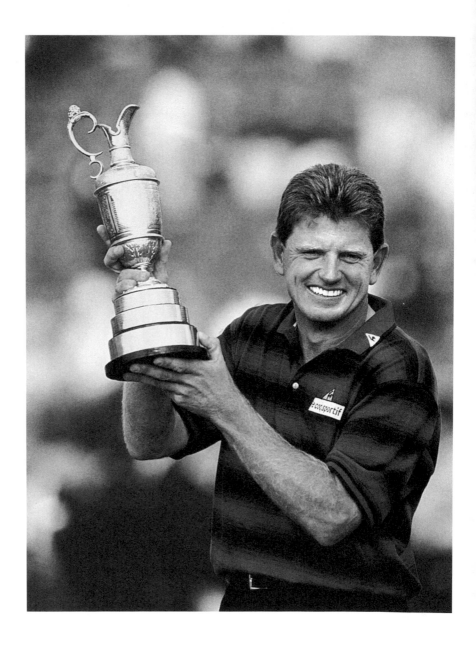

chapter one

THE ONE ESSENTIAL: PERSEVERANCE

How weird is golf? That's the question I was asking myself when I arrived at Turnberry in July 1994 to play the British Open. I had spent the previous week at home at Lake Nona near Orlando practicing for the championship. Every session had been exciting, because I was hitting the ball better than I ever had before. I genuinely felt that my game was reaching a new level. I had won my last tournament, the Western Open, and generally my game and overall sense of well-being could not have been better going into a major championship.

But this game is often bewildering. That sense of well-being can dissipate in an instant—and for no apparent reason. During my first practice session at Turnberry, all the good feelings I had at Lake Nona mysteriously left me. Monday was bad, Tuesday was awful, and Wednesday's practice on the range was only slightly better. But I worked on the same things as always. These elements had helped me win on the PGA Tour twice in 1991 (after not winning since 1983) and then to win the 1992 PGA Championship—my first major. I won one other tournament on the 1992 PGA Tour, and then in 1993 and 1994 won seven more times on the PGA Tour prior to my arrival at Turnberry. By sticking to the same things I had emphasized for years, I slowly but surely began to get my game back on the practice ground at Turnberry as midweek came and the tournament began.

How do you explain the dramatic reversal from Lake Nona to the early part of the week at Turnberry, from feeling so confident about my game to feeling so worried? It's easy. It's the game of golf. The experienced player does not panic in this situation. And although I was close to panicking, I didn't, because there was a huge difference from the late 1970s and early 1980s. I could easily remember my inconsistent and inefficient game then and even in 1982, when I led the British Open at Troon in Scotland by three shots with six holes to go but then dropped four shots coming in to lose to Tom Watson. In March 1982, after some dismal play on the European Tour, I had decided to revamp my swing and make a long-term commitment to improving; my swing was not reliable enough to win major championships. I worked with David Leadbetter for five weeks that first visit at Grenelefe near Orlando, where he was then based, and noted in my diary before I left that I had taken a huge step in the right direction. The entry reads: "These five weeks spent practicing with David were well spent! The smartest thing I ever did!"

I continued to refine my technique day after day, year after year, and finally started winning regularly in 1991. Sure, I had won the 1983 World Series of Golf on the PGA Tour, a win which, like my play for most of the 1982 British Open just a few months after starting to work with David, was a sign that I had made the right decision to change. But then it took another eight years for all the hard work to really pay off.

Now, at Turnberry, all my efforts came to fruition. I knew that the swing changes I had made were correct. I was having trouble simply because of human nature. There was no reason to shift focus from what I had been working on to something new. I firmly believed that eventually my body would adjust to the cooler conditions in Scotland and also to the time change. The swing was still there. I just had to trust it, a policy that was proved correct when I went out after my practice session Wednesday for a round in which Greg Norman and I played

Jack Nicklaus and Tom Watson. It was indeed an honor to play with two past winners of the British Open at Turnberry, Norman and Watson, and with Nicklaus, probably the greatest golfer ever. I shot 67 and Greg shot 66, but we lost the better-ball match to Jack and Tom, who each shot 64. But I felt I would be ready the next day.

Thursday I opened with an encouraging one-under-par 69 that was full of solid shots. The week got progressively better, but I was beginning to wonder if things were going to work out. Then in the final round I was three shots behind with nine holes to play. I still felt I had a realistic chance to win. Jesper Parnevik was clearly playing the best golf of the day and up to this point was making it difficult for anybody to catch him. Yet I knew that Parnevik had never been in this situation before—leading at the British Open during the last nine holes—and thought perhaps he would make a mistake or two coming in. But I would also have to make something happen.

After missing the thirteenth and fourteenth greens and chipping and putting for pars on both holes, I had my first birdie chance on fifteen but missed from fifteen feet. A lot of people still look at the long eagle putt I made on the seventeenth as winning me the championship, and it did, but the sixteenth was also extremely significant. After a good tee shot there I decided to use a ridge to the left of the hole and past it to bring the ball back to the hole. The hole was cut so close to the front edge of the green that anything short by as little as six feet would roll back into a stream in front of the green. That's why I decided to use the slope. The shot came off perfectly. The ball pitched just past pin-high, ran up the slope, and spun back to fifteen feet from the hole. In 1982 I wouldn't have played the shot that way. Since then I had learned not only about my swing but also how to think my way around the course and manage my game. I rolled the putt in and walked to the seventeenth tee two shots behind Parnevik.

The seventeenth that day was playing downwind, and I knew a good tee shot on the par-five would leave me a long to medium iron into the green. I hit a really solid drive but pushed it slightly. The ball flirted with the fairway bunker on the right, but because I had hit it so solidly the thought of it going in the bunker never entered my mind. The ball ended up in a patch of light rough just off the right side of the fairway. The hole was cut on the front right-hand section of the green just over a series of humps and hollows. I could probably have gotten a five-iron to the hole, but I decided to cut a four-iron, because if I slightly mishit the five-iron the ball would likely come up short and to the right of the pin. And it would be very difficult to get up and down from that position.

I remember watching a video of the 1977 British Open when Watson and Nicklaus had dueled at Turnberry. Watson had won in the end, shooting 65-65 the last two rounds to Jack's 65-66. Jack had hit a weak second shot to the right on seventeen and had a difficult chip over the moguls. I wanted to be past the hole, because the easiest putt was from beyond the pin. I put such a good swing on the four-iron and struck it so solidly that the ball refused to cut and headed for the left edge of the green, where it took a slight bounce to the right and ran up approximately fifty feet from the hole. Although it would appear that I was playing negatively in aiming left of the hole and beyond it, I felt as I walked onto the green and saw my ball that I had an outside chance to make the eagle putt. The putt had only about six to eight inches of elevation to it, which over fifty feet is nothing.

I picked out a spot on the crest of a ridge between me and the hole and ran my putt right over the top of that spot. As soon as the ball started tracking and running at that little mound I got excited. I had hit the putt on the line I had picked, and it had the perfect speed. When you're playing at this level of pressure your senses become amazingly acute. You can get so into a putt that you know it's going to come up one roll short. But I knew this one had the right speed, and it broke exactly as I thought it would going over the ridge. Then I started running on the green, trying to follow the putt's progress. The scene unfolded so slowly I could see every roll of the ball. About three feet out of the hole the ball hit a spike mark and wobbled. I held my breath for an instant and thought, "Oh no, don't knock it off line." It dropped. I can still see myself standing there watching the start of the putt, running to the right as I felt it had a chance, then jumping high in the air and hugging my caddie, Squeeky Medlen, who wanted the British Open as badly as I did.

I don't know if I will ever be able to again do something in my golfing life as significant as holing that eagle putt on the seventeenth. It was like holing a shot on the last hole when you had to, fairy-tale stuff. Now I had made the eagle I needed. The crowd was going berserk, Squeek was hugging me, and my playing companion, Ronan Rafferty, appeared as excited as I was after witnessing the turn of events. Then I learned that Parnevik had bogeyed the last hole. I couldn't hear myself think, but I knew one thing: I had to control my emotions, because the round wasn't over. Back in 1982 at Troon I had awarded myself the championship on the thirteenth tee, when I quietly said to my caddie and friend Kevin Woodward, "That's it, we're going to win this thing now." That was a big mistake, one that haunts me to this day.

Of course, by the time I got to Turnberry I had also won a PGA Championship, so I knew what it was like to bring in a score at a major. The highlight of my run of fifteen victories around the world since 1991 was undoubtedly the 1992 PGA Championship win at Bellerive in St. Louis, my first major. Although I played extremely well for sixty-three holes of that championship, it was the way I played the last nine that won it for me. I used all the experience I had gained over the previous years and put the lessons into practice. I had learned how to be patient and stay away from mistakes. In those concluding nine holes I was the one who had the most experience. Things had changed since 1982 at Troon.

By the early 1990s I finally felt that the changes I had tried to incorporate into my swing were part of me. My swing was now sound; the proof was there, as I was hitting the shots where I aimed them. My game had evolved to the state where I could rely on it; my swing wasn't just going to fall apart at any given time. I actually felt that if my short game was in good enough shape, I could never shoot over par. This is a strong statement, but true.

Still, this did not mean I was bulletproof. Far from it. No matter how well you are swinging, you will still have the odd period where nothing goes as planned. All you do then is go through the same routines. Don't panic; don't go from one swing theory to another. Usually you will find that you have taken some aspect of your swing for granted and fallen away from something that is a key in your game. Or maybe you simply have erred because you are human. Accept this and get back to the basics that worked for you in the past.

Doing just that had brought me to the seventy-second hole at Turnberry with a chance to win. I wasn't going to make the mistake now that I had made on the thirteenth tee the last day at Troon; there was no way I was going to take anything for granted. But the situation was heart-stopping, and I had to gather myself. I had gone into the seventeenth two shots behind Parnevik and had emerged one shot ahead with one hole to play.

The eighteenth at Turnberry is a dogleg left par-four. To add pressure to the situation I had bogeyed this hole in rounds two and three. I took a three-iron to make sure I hit the fairway, and I killed it, although I wasn't trying to hit it hard. I pulled the shot maybe two yards off line—that's how defined my targets had become—and when the ball bounced forward I thought I would have a five-iron to the green. One last iron, two putts, and I would win the British Open. I got up to my ball and had only 157 yards to the flag. It was a perfect seven-iron for me; with the pin being left of center I had plenty of green on the right to use.

First I assessed the shot as I walked up to the ball. At that stage I noticed a "D" on a sign in the grandstand behind the green and told Squeek I was going to aim there. Squeek, who is always positive, said, "Split it, Nick." Then I went through my normal routine, as if this were any shot at any time. I was feeling aggressive and wanted to get the shot over and done with. But experience helped me there. I held back and went through my preshot routine bit by bit, and although it only took five or six seconds it felt like a minute, because I was slowing myself down. The routine is important, and I think that if you go through it correctly at a crucial moment, the adrenaline you are holding inside comes out at the right time. I made sure I did that. No longer would my routine vary from two or three seconds to fifteen seconds depending on the shot, as it used to. I had learned how important a routine was to efficient golf, particularly for getting into a nice comfort level. I was at that level as I stood over the shot from the last fairway at Turnberry.

I flew that shot straight at the "D," splitting it. The ball finished in the middle of the green, twenty-five feet right of the hole and just past pin-high.

But still the championship was not over. I misread the speed of my first putt and it came up a couple of feet short. Just before me I had watched Ronan hit a putt of the same length from the same point, and it broke. The last thing I needed at that moment was anything but a straight putt, and I don't mind admitting that I had the wobblies on my putt to win the British Open. But I stuck to the putting routine I had so meticulously developed in the same way as I had refined my swing, and holed the putt. It went in very slowly. I was not going to jam that putt in. I was under control and put the right speed on the putt.

Even now I get choked up when I talk about the final three holes at Turnberry. The calculating precision of my play was the culmination of years of working at the game to which I had dedicated myself more than twenty years ago halfway around the world in my home country of Zimbabwe. I was in the middle of quite a streak at Turnberry, and in fact won my second PGA Championship and my second Canadian Open later that summer. I might not have thought it possible to continue the successful run I had been having since 1991, but by then the victories were only the result of my previous years of commitment to improving. The streak could not last forever, but it was proof to me that it *was* possible to make dramatic changes to one's game.

I had played my first British Open as an eighteen-year-old amateur at Carnoustie in 1975 after qualifying at the Old Course in St. Andrews, and I fell in love with the championship. Maybe I would never win it. Who knew? But I was going to play in it as often as I could to give myself the best chance. To do so I had to master the principles of golf and develop an efficient swing, meaning one that I understood and that worked under pressure. For too many years I had a long, flowing swing, full of extraneous hand, arm, and leg movement. That swing could not withstand the demands and pressure of the last nine holes of major championships. I built my whole theory about golf around efficiency and consistency. I wanted to be able to hit one rock-solid shot after another. It didn't have to be a perfect shot, just something that would keep the ball in play—put it in a place from where I could continue. That's what I felt I had now, and that's what I still feel I have.

You too can achieve an efficient game—efficient in your swing, short game, putting, and thinking—and can reach your potential in golf. If you want to improve and are willing to commit yourself to a program of developing your game, you will reap the rewards of more reliable golf. In this book I will take you through some of my background in Africa, to show how I learned the game—bad habits and all. Then I will explain my theory of the efficient swing based upon what I have learned. Finally I will present what I believe are the essential principles of an efficient golf swing and game and offer drills that will help you integrate the swing changes and feelings as you gradually become a better ball-striker. Work with this program, give yourself time, and you will be well on your way to getting the most out of your golf.

There is no reason you cannot improve, although this will not happen overnight. It didn't with me and I can't imagine it does with anybody. Change takes time, and while we live in a hectic, get-it-done-now society that often seems to preclude long-term programs—we all would prefer instant gratification—I still believe that the most intelligent plan allows for slow but sure progress. Persevere with a plan and you will progress—that's my theme.

I have been keeping a diary since I started professional golf, and you have read the entry I made after spending time with David Leadbetter in 1982. But the most important notation is the one I make at the back of every diary that I begin at every new year. There are three words, each followed by an exclamation mark.

Those words are "Persevere! Persevere! Persevere!"

chapter two

OUT OF AFRICA

Although I have had the opportunity to play on the top courses in the world and in the best tournaments, I frequently have to pinch myself. I often think back to how it all started when I was eight years old back in Rhodesia. Being the youngest of three brothers by seven years, I went through some difficult times but was fortunate to be able to draw from their knowledge and experience. Both of my brothers, Kit and Tim, were and remain extremely talented sportsmen. They set standards and examples that I still follow.

My father, Ray, loved sports. Cricket was undoubtedly his favorite, and most of our Saturdays during cricket season revolved around school and social cricket matches. Sundays, however, were always family days, and it was not uncommon for all of us to get up at dawn to go fishing. You can imagine the competition among the three brothers. We were always trying to outdo one another by catching the biggest or the most fish. Although my mother, Wendy, enjoyed fishing and the days out, she always seemed to work the hardest preparing for our family outings. She would do the breakfast and pack the lunches, and I am sure she was happy when Monday rolled around. Then she could pack us off to school and work and finally have the house to herself.

My mother and father, who were British, met in India, where my dad was serving as a major in the Indian army. My mother had joined the nursing corps and went to India just after the outbreak of World War II. They were married in 1944, and my eldest brother, Kit, was born in Karachi in 1946. My father retired from the army and the family moved to Durban, South Africa, where Tim was born in 1950. I came along seven years later, and still haven't gotten it out of my mother whether I was an afterthought or a mistake! My father worked in the clothing business until his death in 1967.

We had moved in 1961 to what was then Salisbury (now Harare) in Southern Rhodesia (now Zimbabwe). Southern Rhodesia was still under British rule. On December 31, 1963, the Federation of Northern Rhodesia, Southern Rhodesia, and Nyasaland split up. Southern Rhodesia became Rhodesia, Northern Rhodesia gained independence from Britain and became Zambia, and Nyasaland became Malawi, which also gained independence from Britain. I grew up during the Unilateral Declaration of Independence era, a period after November 11, 1965, when Ian Smith, the deputy prime minister, along with his cabinet, declared independence from Britain. But Britain didn't recognize the UDI and imposed economic sanctions on Rhodesia. At the same time, Smith refused to turn Rhodesia's government over to the African majority; a protracted period of unrest followed, along with a civil war to which I was conscripted. Smith attempted, though unsuccessfully, to secure legal independence from Britain during this war, and at the same time sought a political solution to the civil war with African leaders. This led to the creation in 1979 of Zimbabwe Rhodesia, but did not stop the civil war, which continued until April 18, 1980, when a policy of one-man, one-vote was installed. It was at this time that Rhodesia became Zimbabwe and Salisbury became Harare.

Although this is not a political story, it is impossible to separate who I became from the circumstances under which I grew up. Clearly as a white person I had advantages that black people did not have. I was never comfortable with these conditions nor did I understand them.

Shortly after the family settled in Salisbury I started my education at Belvedere Junior School and began playing sports. Sports were an important part of our lives, and all of us were encouraged to participate in as many as possible—not that we needed any encouragement. Cricket, soccer, swimming, field hockey, and of course rugby were the main sports. Because of the year-round beautiful climate we could play these sports twelve months a year. To this day I believe that Zimbabwe has the best climate in the world, and I'm sure this was a factor in my becoming a golfer.

My eldest brother, Kit, had an outstanding record academically and in sports during high school. He always passed his exams with distinction, and in sports he received his colors for being an outstanding batsman in cricket. Kit has always been the perfectionist in the family. This is not to say that he is the most adventurous, but when he decides to get involved he does so with a thoroughness that I envy. Tim, on the other hand, has always been an adventurer. He was never afraid to try new sports and break ground in any direction. It was Tim who introduced me to golf.

I can clearly remember the day Tim arrived home having spent twelve shillings and sixpence (approximately $3.50 then) on a secondhand set of golf clubs—if you could call it a set—from a pawnshop in town. I had no idea of golf at this stage of my life and was fascinated at this amazing array of utensils in an old canvas bag full of holes. Soon after Tim got back to the house, we were outside on the lawn taking divots deep enough to bury the family's dog in.

As I became more aware of golf I was eager to see what a course looked like, especially as I had heard Tim and his friends talking about fairways and greens and how the grass was manicured to perfection. The only playing surfaces I had seen were rugby fields and cricket pitches, which are standard shapes and sizes and have hard surfaces, particularly in winter. No wonder I couldn't wait to walk onto a proper golf course, and finally the day arrived. Tim and two of his friends planned for days how they could sneak onto nearby Sherwood Golf Club and play a few holes without being seen. I didn't realize at the time that because I was seven years younger than the three fellows I was the designated caddie. In any case, we hopped on our bicycles and rode the three miles to the holes farthest from the clubhouse. I was there to caddie, but after seeing the fellows swat a few balls I decided to have a go. As I recall, it was at the monstrous 340-yard par-four fourteenth hole that I took my first swing at a ball.

Until that time I had always played any two-handed sport left-handed. My father was a left-handed batsman in cricket, and to me it was just natural to follow his example. In Tim's hodgepodge "set" of golf clubs I was lucky to find one left-handed club. It was a Robert Forgan five-iron, from the Scottish manufacturer of the same name, with a plastic-coated steel shaft; the club had a grip so slippery that I was terrified it would come right out of my hands. (This is probably the reason I grip the club tightly to this day.) I was a little disappointed, though, with the state of the fairways, because they were clearly not as good as the rugby fields and cricket pitches I had been playing on. Still, I couldn't believe how beautiful the grass was on the greens. I had no idea that you were supposed to use a putter. Around the greens I went, trying to chip the ball into the hole. But I did have enough common sense not to gouge out divots.

It wasn't long after this that we decided it was best to pay our green fees and play a full round of golf. Warren Hills Golf Club was really where it all started for me. The club did much to encourage junior golf, a policy that was apparent in its green fees. It cost us $1.50 for a year's junior membership with green fees of ten cents for eighteen holes. Of course, we were allowed to play only on certain days and at certain times, but the important thing was that we now had access to the game and opportunity to learn the basic rules and etiquette, which came quickly. We had to learn these basics because the members scrutinized us and often wrongly accused us of not raking bunkers, replacing divots, and fixing ball marks on the greens. This criticism didn't bother me, because being on the golf course was a golden time for me; none of my friends knew anything about golf, and here I was venturing into new territory.

We soon learned that during the school holidays most of the golf clubs would hold junior tournaments (eighteen holes, medal play) on weekday mornings, for an entrance fee of twenty-five cents. The first tournament I played in was on a Friday morning at Warren Hills, and I can remember it clearly. There were many new faces, the clubhouse was teeming with activity, and I was going to play with guys I had never met before, which frightened me. I was so nervous I decided to lock myself in the toilet in the locker room and not even go to the first tee. Tim came running in to find me when I failed to appear. It took a fair amount of coaxing, but I came out, and with serious anxiety made my way to the first tee. I cannot remember with whom I played that day or what I scored. But I do know that I had a great day and that I was hooked on this game of golf.

As I became more involved in golf I realized how refreshing it was to meet other young people outside school. I felt that school always regimented us in one way or another, but that was not the case in junior golf, where we all learned from one another in pleasant circumstances. Each of us felt he was doing something independent, in that no teacher was overseeing his progress. We could be ourselves, although the other side of this individual game of golf was that if you missed a shot or a putt you had only yourself to blame, because there were no teammates. This aspect appealed to me, as I could practice, play, and improve without having to wait for ten or fifteen other guys to compete as well. Golf allowed you to compete against a course, yourself, or another competitor. It allowed a person to go down his own road.

I had been golfing for only about two years when my father died. We had played a couple of games together, including a round at the Police Golf Club one Sunday that I remember well. As usual, the entire family was out that day. Little did I realize that this was to be the last game I would play with my dad. His death left a huge hole in my life, but as time went on my mom and my brothers were always there for me. I often wish, however, that my dad were around to see what I have accomplished—not so much to see my accomplishments on the course, of which I am obviously very proud, but to see the person I am and how golf has, I believe, made me a better person.

I honestly believe that the greatest benefit to playing golf is that it teaches you from an early age to treat others with respect. The nature of the game instills in you a basic common sense. It's so simple: Be considerate of your opponent because it is the only way to play the game, and also remember that whatever you do to your opponent he can do to you. Maybe I am from the old school, but to me there is nothing lower on the ladder than gamesmanship. I have lost respect for a few individuals over the years who have tried it on me, some of them exceptionally good players too. But the tactic does not work. I get more fired up when such shenanigans are going on, and usually play better in response.

In the late 1960s it was extremely difficult for juniors to get onto a golf course, with the exception of a few courses. However, we were allowed to practice and could hit balls on the practice tee as much as we liked. My mom, who had started playing since my dad's death, would play on Sundays with a few of her friends, and I would go along to the club. On one of these Sundays I met Geoff Cannings. He and I were both obsessed with the game and started a friendship that day which is still going strong. Golf was a good game for Geoff, because he was overweight and not very athletic, which meant that he couldn't be as competitive as most of us in rugby and cricket, the sports in which most kids participated. Over the years we played frequently as both partners and adversaries. The competition was always there, and although my golf was always a notch or two ahead of his, golf allowed us to compete against each other.

Most of the houses in the area in which I lived had fairly good-sized gardens, and it wasn't long before Geoff and I were destroying our mothers' lawns. Golf around the garden was born. We sank a series of tin cans into the ground at strategically chosen areas. Normally, we put the holes in prime lawn areas so that the whiffle balls we used would putt better. It was not unusual, however, for the next tee to be under a tree or near some other obstacle that would force us to invent or create some kind of shot. We played and bet on everything, with the loser making the sandwiches for lunch or running to the store to get Cokes. We played mainly seventy-two-hole championships for a cent a shot on occasion, and if you lost ten cents you had really played poorly. It was always preferable to play right after it rained, as it was easier to take the divots that we loved to see flying away. Our mothers learned of these activities early and soon insisted on some limitations. We were told not to hit any shots over the roof, as the divots we took eventually landed against the painted walls and turned them a red clay color because of the turf we had.

We played so much golf in those early days. If I play thirty-six holes a day for the rest of my life I will never play as many holes as I did around our gardens. We would play all day, only stopping briefly for lunch or a quick drink. Of course, we did this only during school vacations or after school. Round and round the garden we went, sometimes playing 144 holes a day. Some days Geoff would come over to our house at nine o'clock in the morning or spend the night at our house so that we could get out early. This was golf for the pure fun of it, and out of it came the desire to get the ball in the hole any way I could. I was going to get the job done somehow.

Getting the job done has to me always meant having an imagination that you feel free to use because you know you have a sound method that lets you hit creative shots. Golfing in the garden helped me develop that imagination and to trust it. The more fun we had, the more vivid our imaginations, the better we played. Every putt we had was for the British Open or the Masters. I would pretend I had to make a thirty-footer to win a championship. And later when I wasn't making the progress I wanted, this element of fun kept me going—not that it was always easy to see the fun during the times I struggled, but the idea helped me return in my mind's eye to those days in the garden when the only thing that mattered was being out in the fresh air with my friends.

That thought, that image, made it easier for me to handle the times when I felt I was working hard but getting nowhere. I kept thinking golf would be enjoyable again if I could understand my swing and find out what I needed to do to improve over the long run. And every so often that kid who banged the ball around the garden showed his face. It might have been just one shot at some tournament that didn't even matter, but it made me glow inside with the realization that I might yet realize my dreams in golf. And I needed that feeling, because I had made the commitment to myself that I was going to play golf professionally and do the best I could. I would remember golf in the garden and my friends who still lived in Zimbabwe, and think that maybe we were all still kids at heart playing a game. Yes, I was playing golf for my livelihood, which meant that I could not always escape the anxiety I felt when I didn't do well. But I learned to draw on the early days. It didn't take me long to realize that my love for the game and not a craving for money or trophies had decided me on becoming a professional and trying to reach the highest levels of the sport.

I try to think that way even today, when I have achieved some of my goals in the game by winning major championships and tournaments around the world. But golf will always humble you. I went from leading money-winner in 1993 and 1994 on the PGA Tour to lesser seasons the next two years. Those two seasons were disappointing, no doubt about it. But my family—my wife, Sue, and our children, Greg,

Robyn, and Kim—was still in great shape, and I still enjoyed my life immensely. The challenges always were there and always will be there.

My pleasant feelings about the early days also figure in another way. When I get to the course today wherever I am playing a tournament, I look around and see that I have a beautiful surface to putt on, a nice fairway to hit from. I don't have to hit a shot out of the daisies in the flower patch, where my mates would never allow a drop when we played. There was no such thing as a free drop, even against rocks or a wall. You would have to turn the club around or play some sort of chop shot. When you're a kid your friends are ruthless, and so you play from anywhere. Now I play off fairways I hardly knew existed as a boy growing up in Africa.

But if we didn't have immaculate conditions we did have fantastic opportunities to compete. In Rhodesia we had school year-round, three terms with three vacations ranging from four to six weeks each. During the school vacations the four provinces in the country (Mashonaland, Matabeleland, Manicaland, and Midlands) would hold junior tournaments. Salisbury was in Mashonaland, and because we had the biggest population we usually had the strongest golfers. Tournament prizes were never more than two or three balls or perhaps a one-dollar gift voucher, but we didn't care. We were not out there to win prizes but to beat each other and be the best we could. The biggest prize would be to get your handicap down as swiftly as possible. We were given a junior golfer's passport in which all scores were recorded. Handicaps were adjusted immediately. It was simple and it worked well. The passports meant a lot to us, as they were like school report cards. Every time you played, you had the passport attested; we carried our passports with pride and were careful not to lose them.

The daily tournaments we played during the holidays took place at Royal Salisbury on Monday, Chapman on Tuesday, Country Club (in Salisbury) on Wednesday, Sherwood on Thursday, and my home course, Warren Hills, on Friday. It took a while before we could play these private clubs on weekends, and then we had to be on our best behavior. The breakthrough came at Warren Hills when a few of us were given permission to play on weekends there and to enter club competitions.

But even before that happened, we managed to get some weekend games in. I wanted to play Saturday afternoons, because I often played rugby, field hockey, or cricket in the morning, but there was no way. Bob Burnell was club manager and secretary at Warren Hills, and while he sympathized with those of us who wanted to play Saturday mornings he had to say no because he was the voice of the members. And so I had to figure something out. Luckily I got some help from Roger Bayliss, a friend then and now.

Roger and his wife had just emigrated from England, and he couldn't understand why the club would not allow me to play on weekends. He decided to get around this by booking a time for Saturday afternoon and putting four names down. He knew that one of his mates was unlikely to show up or be available, and I also knew that. The plan was that I would be practicing at the club and having a meat pie and Coke about fifteen minutes before Roger's starting time. Roger would ask the secretary if he had seen so-and-so, and would learn the fellow simply was nowhere to be found. Poor Roger would say the guy had stiffed him again and so would get the secretary's sympathy. Burnell would look around for a fourth and see me sitting there eating my meat pie. He wouldn't have much choice but to ask if I wanted to make up the foursome.

But real golf was not the only way I involved myself in the game. Sometimes it seemed that every single game we played as kids had a golf derivation. There was even a game of golf darts that I still enjoy. The rules are that you take a step back from the standard throw line and then must keep the dart inside the treble, or first inside circle. Throw the dart outside that and you score a bogey; outside the double, or outside, circle and you score a double bogey. A bull's-eye is an eagle, while next is a birdie and then a par. We usually threw three sets of three consecutive darts, and then your opponent would play his nine holes; one more time around for each player and you would have finished your eighteen holes. Do that four times and you have completed a seventy-two-hole tournament. Each tournament was on a different course, or so we would pretend. We told ourselves that a winning score at the Masters was 276, twelve under par. That was one of the ways we kept our eyes fixed on the big tournament each April.

We even had golf games in cricket. Hitting for four runs scored a birdie, hitting for six an eagle. If you just hit the ball you made a par; if you missed, it was a bogey. Bowl out and you scored a double bogey. We also played a "golf" game around cars. For example, three popular cars in Rhodesia were the Mazda, Toyota, and Datsun. Each player would choose a car and an equivalent score for the next eighteen cars that would come down the road or that we would pass. I might have picked Mazda for birdie, Toyota for par, and Datsun for bogey, while trucks did not count. The guy who got the lowest score for the eighteen holes was the winner. These games were symptoms of how crazy we were about golf.

Back on the course with real golf, my game improved rapidly in the beginning, and I reached a single-figure handicap before my thirteenth birthday. I could shoot in the 70s fairly regularly, but getting to the next level of shooting around par took another two years. I needed to grow, and when I did the strength made all the difference in my being able to shoot par on a more regular basis.

Although we were all fortunate as juniors in being able to play on different courses and in experiencing tournament play, one thing was missing. That was good instruction. I do not mean to be disrespectful to any of the golfers in our country at the time, but we did not have access to sound basic instruction, and so most of us were self-taught. I learned through trial and error, from the other good players in Rhodesia, and also from my junior golf buddies. I also had no idea that golfers played for money, because the only tournament we would see was the British Open, which came our way on sixteen-millimeter film after the tournament, and I would see Gary Player holding the

British Open trophy, not being handed a check. The first time I realized that golfers were playing for money was when I opened a U.S. magazine and saw that the winner of a tournament received $25,000. I was shocked. After all, my mom was dropping me off at the course with fifty cents in my pocket.

The fact that I was essentially self-taught as a youngster has led to my thinking from time to time about what the smartest strategy is when introducing a youngster to golf. For instance, when do you start a kid with a teacher? And when do you cut off instruction so that the youngster can learn to rely on himself with his teacher as support? I think that a new golfer should certainly be instructed in the basics of the grip and stance, perhaps be given some information about the swing plane. Then it's time to let him go, at least until he has incorporated the basics and learned to have fun with the game. Too much early instruction can hinder a kid from using his own creativity, and he more than likely would resent being molded anyway. Only very special youngsters can take the important bits and pieces of instruction and while working with a teacher allow their own flair to develop as well. I am sure that Jack Nicklaus, Phil Mickelson, and Tiger Woods were able to do that.

However, I should add that a new golfer before he or she is far along ought to begin using the video camera. In my day in Rhodesia we were looking at still photos if we had any references at all; we did not have access to video, which would have enabled us to see the swing in motion, to stop it in places, and also to view it from a variety of angles. But kids today have easy access to so much information and equipment, including the video camera. There is a danger that this can become confusing, but the young golfer who learns what the swing plane means—to cite one crucial element of the swing—can accelerate his development. He could learn in a month what it took me ten years to understand.

A good teacher is also of paramount importance, as I came to realize many years after trying to learn the swing on my own. For example, if you give one hundred schoolchildren a book to read, they will probably come up with one hundred different interpretations. But an effective teacher will probably put fifty of them on the right track and help them come to an understanding of the book. The other fifty kids might eventually understand the book, but it would take them much longer to get there without having the road map the teacher would provide. There is a parallel in golf, in that a player might, if he is lucky, hit on a productive method for himself without instruction. But we all need some help along the way; otherwise we go off track. There are many ways, to use another analogy, of driving from New York City to San Francisco. But the person interested in making good time takes the most direct route. It can also be enjoyable to take many side trips if that is your choice, but there may be complications along the way.

While it was exciting for me to finally play with older golfers at Warren Hills—once Roger Bayliss figured out the strategy for getting me on the course on Saturday afternoons—the main thing was still the junior tournaments. It cost each of us twenty-five cents to enter the weekday tournaments, for which the prizes were the two or three balls I have mentioned. It was good that we weren't offered lavish prizes, for then we might have concerned ourselves more with what we could win than with playing our shots.

We learned early that putting a score on a card counts, because all the weekday tournaments were eighteen holes. Waste a couple of shots and you felt you were out of it; it was important to get your score in as best you could and see where you stood. And get that score any way you can; even if you aren't swinging all that well you still have to resort to the fundamentals and find a way to get the ball around. As a junior in Rhodesia I didn't have much of an idea about the principles of the swing and had not even given them much thought; golf was just simple sport to me, not algebra. That couldn't last if I meant to make the sort of progress I was beginning to want, but the seeds of an idea that have lasted to this day were planted: Don't give up. Get the ball in the hole, somehow. Keep trying to hit the right shots and maybe some good things will happen.

Back then our thirty-six-hole one-day provincial championships were scheduled throughout the school holidays, and also the only seventy-two-hole tournament on the schedule. We were allowed caddies, but I pulled my own cart until I was fifteen. After that I usually took a caddie, because my mom came to understand the importance of having one in a tournament and offered to help me out with the cost.

I was about sixteen when my mate Thomas Makanda started caddying for me. His dad worked for the people who lived next door to us, and sometimes I used to hit balls from our garden into their garden. Thomas would be playing there while his dad worked, and he would watch me through the fence and toss the balls back. Eventually he told me he wanted to come to the course or to caddie for me. I said sure, and we've been great mates since. We would go fishing or camping together, and although at that time many people frowned on a black boy and a white boy spending time together, that didn't worry me. At school you were even afraid to tell some white friends that you had black friends, and some parents could be really nasty about whites having black friends. I didn't care, nor did most of my friends. Still, Thomas wasn't allowed to golf except on Mondays at Warren Hills, which was a problem for us. But we got around that whenever we were far enough from the clubhouse that we could not be seen. Then Thomas would hit some shots with my clubs.

Thomas caddied for me in the 1991 Zimbabwe Open, and burst into tears when I lost the lead I had coming in and did not win the championship in the sudden-death playoff. I told him that it wasn't the end, and that he shouldn't worry, because I would win the tournament one day. I did win it at Royal Harare in 1995, and Thomas was carrying my bag. It was rewarding for both of us to win the premier golfing event in our country; our friendship went back many years, and we both felt very good about the win.

Thomas has been a big part of my life, simply because the friendship we forged in the early days through golf was a strong one. Thomas was right there with me when I was learning how to play in tournaments. I often think about him when I'm off playing in some part of the world. And I also miss Zimbabwe; it's my home; my heart is there. As the saying goes, once you have Africa in your blood it's always there. I often feel the call to return, to fish in Mozambique or on the Pungwe River in the Eastern Highlands along Zimbabwe's border with Mozambique. Undoubtedly, though, my favorite spot at home is the Zambezi River; it is Africa in its purest form, with an abundance of wildlife. Anyone who grew up there knows that it is the wildest continent in the world. We have many different snakes in Zimbabwe that can kill you, and crocodiles that will eat you if you swim in the wrong rivers. Even now I can be sitting in a hotel room in Manhattan or London reading a good novel about Africa and can feel exactly what the author is writing about. Something will spark a memory and I will feel I want to be back on the river. Often, watching a documentary on Africa, I will feel transported. My life has moved to golf courses and cities around the world, but somehow I still never feel very far from Africa.

Besides Thomas, another great friend and caddie is a South African, Tiger Lekhulene. He caddied for me in the first pro tournament I won, the Asseng in South Africa in 1979. I met Tiger at the Rand Park Golf Club in Johannesburg, and he has caddied for me in every tournament I have played in South Africa. Although I haven't known Tiger as long as I have Thomas, still we formed our friendship early on. The highlight of our times together was my 1993 win in the Million Dollar Challenge at Sun City, South Africa. Together we blew the field away. We enjoyed further success in early 1997, when I finished second, first, and first in three consecutive tournaments. It was particularly gratifying to win the South African PGA Championship, because I had placed second there four times.

So it is, as with Tiger, that my core friendships are from those school days when we played junior golf. And it wasn't like I was the top dog or anything in tournaments; there was always a large group of guys who vied for the tournaments: Denis Watson, Mark McNulty, and Tony Johnstone, just to name a few. It was rarely clear who was the top player.

Long before I won any pro tournaments, however, I made a change that had a significant effect on my development as a golfer. I made the decision at age sixteen to switch from playing the small British ball that was popular then to the bigger ball that American golfers were using. I felt that I wanted to become a professional golfer and knew that the small ball was being phased out, although that took a few years in Rhodesia. If I was going to have a future in the game, then I had to learn to play the big ball. Making the change to the big ball helped, because it was harder to use. The big ball didn't go as far as the small ball if you mishit it, for one thing. It was more subject to being blown about in the wind because it didn't penetrate as well, and so it required better ball-striking. Hooks and slices were exaggerated with the big ball. Perhaps I sacrificed some wins at the junior and amateur levels because I was often competing against players who used the small ball. But that was okay, because I knew that down the road my decision would benefit me. I wanted to learn the hardest way I could, and I also knew that I could revert to the small ball back home if I wanted to. But something inside me made me want to challenge myself. I don't know why this was so, but it made sense to me to make the game as difficult as I could.

One way I did this was always to go right to the back tees, all the way to the very back. I'd stretch the course out to its absolute limit and always try to play the course at its toughest. If I shot 72 or 73 I could go to my older brothers, Tim and Kit, and tell them that I had posted a good number. I didn't tell them that I had played from the tips, but I knew that because I did the game would be easier if I played from the forward tees during a tournament. Where I had hit a five-iron from the back tees before I would now be hitting a seven-iron.

There was something else I did as a junior at home that later had quite a lot to do with my decision to change my swing and make it as efficient as possible. As a teenager I didn't think it was smart to play creative golf—that is, to hit low draws, high hooks, and pitch-and-run shots. I could play them if I had to, but I preferred to hit standard shots. My thinking was that if the shot was simple and straightforward, then the swing would also be conventional. I felt that if the swing was simple, I was more likely to be able to reproduce it. If it had a huge, complicated twist or turn to it, then it wouldn't work under pressure.

Looking back, I can appreciate that I was right in many respects, and my swing today is a much-refined version of what I was thinking years ago but could not produce. Long, flowing swings often don't work under pressure. If my whole theory of the golf swing eventually was built around the desire for consistency, a large part of the reason for this can be traced to my thinking as a youngster. The major difference is that I thought only about consistency in those days. But I had no idea how to go about attaining that objective, how to eliminate the wasted motion in my swing.

Now, though, I understand that creativity is a very important part of golf. You simply must be able to hit all sorts of shots that fit all sorts of situations in tournament golf. You must know you can create them even if you don't use them. The game is also much more enjoyable if you are confident enough to try these shots. It became clear to me over the years that I had to develop a standard, reliable shot—be it a fade or a draw—*before* I could embellish and become a shotmaker, a creative golfer with flair. And as I have indicated, had I remained a golfer who played entirely by feel, even if I could hit interesting-looking shots, I don't believe for a minute that I would have won major championships or turned into a relatively consistent golfer. But at the same time I know that shotmaking is critical to championship golf.

Here's a story to illustrate what I mean. Michael Campbell, the superb young New Zealander, was leading the 1995

British Open at the Old Course after three rounds. He had never been in such a position, and he asked me on the practice tee the morning of the final round if I could offer any advice. I said only one thing: "Michael, hit the shot you feel comfortable with. If you have 150 yards to the green and you want to hit a low five-iron up there, go ahead. You don't have to hit the perfect-looking shot that you believe Jack Nicklaus or Greg Norman might hit. That's not your job today. Just be Michael Campbell and use the easiest way you believe you can get the ball on the green." In the end, Michael did not maintain his lead, but he did finish third, just one shot out of tying for the lead with John Daly and Costantino Rocca. I like to think that I gave him a useful tip whose genesis was in the days I played junior tournaments in Rhodesia.

But the other side of the story is that I had to spend nearly twenty years from my junior days before I could combine consistency with creativity. It was worth the wait. When that putt went in at Turnberry in 1994 I could have jumped seven feet high, as flat-footed as I am. I'll remember the magnitude of that putt for the rest of my life. It had its origins in Rhodesia, so far away in time and distance from Turnberry.

In July 1974, when I was seventeen, I traveled outside Africa for the first time. My destination was the South course of the Torrey Pines club in San Diego, where I had been invited to participate in the Junior World Championship. I had been playing the big ball for over a year and so was quite comfortable with it. I was excited about making my first trip outside Africa, and I felt good about my game. But I had little idea of what to expect in America.

Shortly before I left for America I ran into a little problem when I picked up a flu virus and had to spend a week in bed. Naturally enough, my mom was worried, because I was going on my own to San Diego. I was also concerned because it was taking a long time for me to feel better. My mom decided at the eleventh hour to come along, which made me feel better on a number of counts. For one thing, I thought she knew something about flying. Having flown just once in a small-single Cessna plane when I was thirteen, I was a bit nervous. But she didn't know anything about flying either.

We had quite a journey, first flying to Johannesburg, where we caught a 707 to New York, which took about eighteen hours. I had never been confined like that, and can still remember the uncomfortable seat. Then we flew from New York to Chicago and on to San Diego, arriving one morning just before noon. Two hours later I was on the practice tee at Torrey Pines. I wanted to see what American golf was like. It felt strange. I had never been exposed to country club life before. My first impression was that Torrey Pines was beautiful.

At the Junior World I competed against 256 golfers from twenty-eight countries in the fifteen-to-seventeen age group. Having arrived four days in advance of the tournament, I had gotten over my jet lag by the time the first round started. I wasn't thinking about winning, just putting up a good show. The best anybody from Rhodesia had done was to finish in the top twenty-five. I was hoping to finish in the top ten.

An opening round of three-under-par 69 tied me for the lead with two U.S. players, Graham Cowan and Clyde Rego. I followed that round with two 72s to take a three-shot lead into the final round. In the end I won by four shots after a final-round 74, but not before I had some problems. On the seventeenth hole I drove into a bunker, hit my second up into a tree, where the ball stayed, and went on to make a triple-bogey seven. I had hoped to finish better than that, but, fortunately for me, I still came out on top. My mom wasn't able to come out to the course at all; she was too nervous.

The win was a big deal at home. I had won against some top young players, such as Gary Hallberg, John Cook, and Hal Sutton, and also some top juniors from Great Britain. It was the strongest international field of juniors you could play against. When I got home, people made such a big thing of it that I was actually embarrassed. I was introverted in those days and didn't know how to handle the hoopla.

My win certainly boosted my self-confidence. Yet when I look back on pictures of my swing then, I see a youngster who stood up and merely swung hard on every shot. I was competitive, no doubt about that, but the seeds of my later inconsistency were there already; the bad habits that I still fight were visible. If you study the photo on the left you will see that I finished in the reverse "C" position that can compromise balance and promote inconsistency as well as cause serious back problems. Moreover, I could be a streaky putter at times, and in fact still am, although I'm much steadier day to day. My posture over the ball while putting was far too cramped; I had a very difficult time in those days maintaining my steadiness over the ball, in large part because I put myself in a tense, congested position from the start. This cramped posture is also apparent in my address position of years ago.

But still I had won in San Diego. I had managed to get the ball into the hole by accepting the ups and downs I was experiencing. In my second-round 72 I had made five bogeys, three birdies, and an eagle—clear evidence that just about anything could happen when I was on a course. This pattern would remain and would trouble me for years until I gained consistency. But I did stick to a game plan in San Diego. I knew coming in that it was important to accept any bad patches; who knew what might happen on the next hole? I made enough birdies to offset the bogeys and the triple bogey on the 71st hole, and did not mind getting excited about the good holes then. It's important to maintain one's composure in golf, but there is nothing at all the matter with allowing one's feelings out at the appropriate moment. A woman who was living in San Diego but had been a teacher in Salisbury followed me at the Junior World and commented on how I had a habit of jumping up after holing a good putt and spinning myself around in midair. This must have been a personal trait, for it is exactly how I reacted when I holed the putt that won the 1994 British Open at Turnberry.

Upon my return from San Diego I continued to play tournaments at home and to progress. Gary Player hosted a tournament that I won, and at the end he gave the golfers some good advice. "Make sure you can play really well before you become a pro," Gary told us. "There are three hundred professionals trying to win tournaments in America, and most of them are eating beans." Gary encouraged me and felt I could become a very good player. He did point out a couple of problems that he saw. At the prize ceremony he noted that I had been on the fifteenth green the last day when the fellow with whom I was playing had a putt on a similar line to mine. Instead of watching how his putt broke, I was off on the sideline talking to a friend. Gary said, tongue-in-cheek but still making his point, that I ought to have been watching the line. I was embarrassed, because I was expecting some praise and here he was pointing out an error I had made. But I listened. Gary also pointed out later what he felt was a defect in my shoulder position at address. The way in which I use my shoulders would eventually become a cornerstone of how I think about the golf swing; I came to understand that the golfer who uses his shoulders properly ensures that the right things happen during his swing.

My win in San Diego continued to give me self-confidence, and in 1975 I reached the quarterfinals of the British Amateur at Royal Liverpool in England, or Hoylake as it's known. That year I also qualified for the British Open at Carnoustie after shooting 150 at the Old Course in the thirty-six-hole qualifier; at Carnoustie my rounds of 77-77 did not make the halfway cut. In any case, my daily golf activities were soon to come to an end, for in 1976 I began my eighteen-month national service in the air force.

The service taught me that golf wasn't the be-all and end-all in life and that I was fortunate to do something I loved. A couple of my friends were killed while doing their service, and sometimes golf seemed very far away. But I remained hungry to compete, and I turned pro in August 1977 after completing my service. I was soon invited to an exhibition match that took place at West Nicholson, a course with sand greens just south of the city of Bulawayo in Matabeleland. The three players who I joined were Simon Hobday—the amazing, eccentric, lovable Simon, who would go on years later to win the United States Senior Open Championship and kiss the green after holing out for the title—and George Harvey and Teddy Webber. We were given five kilograms of game biltong, which is basically flavored strips of dried meat, a staple of Rhodesian cuisine that we eat as if it were candy. When we went fishing we took biltong along with us as a snack. The five kilos of biltong at West Nicholson constituted my first reward for playing as a professional.

After that enjoyable affair at West Nicholson my first professional tournament was the South African PGA Championship in November 1977, in Johannesburg. Although I didn't wow the golf fraternity, I did finish a credible twenty-first and received a huge check equivalent to $277. I was in heaven. It doesn't sound like much now, but I had been getting only $102 per month in the air force. Now here I had earned nearly three times that salary in one golf tournament.

But I was soon to learn how difficult professional golf could be. I started the European Tour in 1978 and struggled for some years, although I did make slow and fairly steady progress. I qualified for the 1978 British Open at the Old Course and finished thirty-ninth. To me the British Open was the tournament to beat all tournaments; I really wanted to win it one day. I had been beside the eighteenth green in 1975 at Carnoustie when Tom Watson won, and again in 1978 I was there in the same area at the Old Course when Jack Nicklaus won. I could see the emotion and tears on Jack's face and realized how important the British Open Championship was to everyone.

But my game wasn't sharp for the most part in my early years as a professional. I hit the ball too high too often in the wind on the European Tour, even though I did come close to winning a couple of times. In 1978, Bob Byman, an American player on the PGA Tour, one-putted the last three greens to beat me by a shot in the Dutch Open. And the Irishman Des Smyth holed a putt against me to win the 1979 European Matchplay Championship. Maybe I was destined to be a late-bloomer.

I finally did win, in 1980 at the Swiss Open. For some reason that win came easily; every so often my game would fall into a slot, but there was no reason for it. The change for the better was a mystery, and I always wondered what I would do the next week. Still, I was improving. I went from fifty-first on the Order of Merit in Europe in 1978 to thirty-first in 1979 and to fourteenth in 1980. But then I hit a wall. My season in 1981 was terrible; I went backward and finished thirty-eighth on the Order of Merit. I was practicing four times harder than I had in any of the other years and devoting my entire life to trying to improve. The search for a better swing occupied my time off the course as well as on it. I was obsessed with getting better but was getting worse, and had no idea what was going on. I actually considered walking away from the game because I was so frustrated.

I never really understood my swing in 1978, 1979, and 1980, when I relied on natural talent alone. It was inevitable that this reliance would catch up with me, and it did. That's

why in 1981 I did something I would not recommend to anybody who does not understand his own swing, tendencies, and
faults. I tried to change my swing on my own so that I could
hit the ball lower. But my game went haywire, and by the end
of 1981 I was so vulnerable I would listen to anything anybody
said about my game. Although I didn't want to give up, I knew
I could not continue like this. Just the fact that I was considering leaving the game told me that it was time to go to an
extreme, time to make real changes. But I had exhausted my
own ideas. Having played the European Tour for more than
four years, I was going backward. I knew that I had to make
changes, but this time I would not make them on my own.

Something had to be done, or my career was in jeopardy.
For one thing, I determined to go to America in early 1982
after spending time at home in the hot African summer.
Maybe I could get into some PGA Tour events, although I
would have to qualify for them. But I needed a change, and
immediately felt better as I looked forward to playing in
warmer weather both in Africa and then in America. I told
myself not to get too upset over my performance in 1981; I had
to learn from it. I wrote the following in the back of my 1981
calendar: "In short 1981 has been a terrible year for me. I am
very happy that it is now over. I look forward to 1982 with a
whole new incentive. I have set new goals to achieve higher
than before because of the past year. If it takes me forever I will
be in command of myself and this game. I am not going to let
it get the better of me. I am far too strong mentally and I have
more faith in myself than ever before."

It was not long after I made that entry that I decided to see
my good friend David Leadbetter, who had made the break
from Europe to America. David is five years older than I am,
but I had known him in Rhodesia from when I was ten years
old, and we had played a lot of golf together, including during
our junior days, in Africa. David was born in England but
grew up in Rhodesia from the age of about five. He was a student of the golf swing, and as far back as I can remember he
had his nose in golf magazines and instructional books. I also

enjoyed reading and studying about the swing, but I always did it in bits and pieces. I could see the problems of other guys with whom I played frequently. But you can't see what you're doing yourself in this game, because you are supposed to be looking at the ball and 70 percent of the swing happens behind you. Consequently I did not have a clear understanding of my own faults or of the basics of the swing. I had depended on little Band-Aid ideas for my game, a tip here and a tip there, one-a-day pills to get me through the round. But now it was time to learn; now it was time to go from tidbits of a few words here and there to a complete approach that tied all the bits together in a way that made sense to me.

The result was that I committed myself to making the changes required to have a career in golf. By the end of 1981 I had spent the greater part of my golfing life trying to do well. It had been difficult and frustrating, but I didn't want to fail. It had become obvious that the short-term methods I had been using led to short-term answers and short-term success. But long-term success demands methods that stay the course. I felt dedicated now in a way I had not been before, perhaps motivated by my own frustration. By dedication I don't mean that I was running ten miles a day to stay fit and hitting balls hours and hours a day and talking to a variety of teachers. But I do mean that I was thinking about the swing when I put my head on my pillow at night, and that, for better or worse, I would find myself checking my hand position during my swing while I was stopped in my car at a light or when I was fishing. The swing was never out of my mind.

The result was that I decided to seek a teacher with whom I could work closely and over a long period. I was making a decision to place my trust in somebody. Who could I work with who would build my understanding of the swing? I had seen how David had improved Denis Watson's posture and swing in 1981, and because I knew I could trust David, he was an obvious choice. I couldn't just call up Bob Toski or any of the other famous teachers and say, "Hey, my name is Nick Price, I've won one tournament, and my game is going nowhere." But I had known David for a long time. So my decision was easy—he was the best person for me to consult. I called him and said, "David, my game is so bad. Denis told me you've helped him, and I wonder if you would see me." He was delighted that I had asked and told me to get over to see him in Florida. I told him that I would finish the 1982 South African Tour at the beginning of the year and would then come over.

I budgeted five weeks to spend with David. It was like wiping the slate clean. Now, of course golf is my livelihood, my chosen career. I would not ask an amateur player to devote so much concentrated time to change. And yet I do believe that any kind of change, no matter how minor, requires a firm commitment, one that does not waver every time a shot flies off line. The idea is to work a program into your schedule.

The first thing David did was to put my swing on video. This was the first time I'd seen my swing. I nearly threw up after seeing my swing slowed down, it was so bad. It was clear that I had far too many moving parts and that there were two distinct shaft planes in my swing: severely steep on the way back and far too shallow on the way down. Ideally, as I would learn, it would be great if the backswing and downswing shaft planes could be mirror images of each other. I would also learn that it is difficult and all but impossible to achieve this, and came to prefer a backswing that was slightly steeper and a downswing that was slightly shallower by comparison. But my shaft planes years ago were far too exaggerated. I had too much wasted motion. Until I saw David I hadn't realized how many sources of error there were in my swing.

My work with David proved of immense value. In the end I incorporated elements of what David suggested along with ideas of my own that began to develop with his encouragement. New ground was being broken, so David was also learning from my situation and enhancing his knowledge. David helped me achieve a much better understanding of the swing than I had had; he gave me a foundation I could build upon. In the years since I have continued to refine these ideas and to simplify my swing as much as possible. It's a never-ending

**Too steep a backswing
(also note the exaggerated gap
between my knees)**

Too shallow a downswing

process that stimulates me as much as it ever did. It is also true
that I can fall back at any time into my old bad habits, although
they will never be as severe as they used to be.

My play in the 1982 British Open just a few months after
spending time with David confirmed that I was definitely
moving in the right direction. Only six months previous, I had
thought my career was in jeopardy and that perhaps I did not
have a future in golf. But my play at Troon made a great difference in my outlook. For the first time I felt I could win a
major tournament, even as I knew that it was no easy matter to
make wholesale changes in one's game. My old bad habits
would return with no warning; I couldn't get them out of my
system totally, just as you may have trouble ridding yourself of

your swing faults. They will always be there in some form or fashion, which I am sure you will see is evident in my swing sequences. But the satisfying feeling that comes from making a commitment and seeing improvement is unequaled.

That became apparent to me at the 1983 World Series of Golf in Akron, Ohio. I had qualified for the PGA Tour that year by finishing third in the qualifying school tournament in November 1982. That was followed by my winning the South African Order of Merit. I was the first person to win it without winning a tournament, which showed that I was playing consistently week in and week out. In America, in my first full year there, I felt steady improvement but could still lose my game overnight. By the World Series of Golf—for which I had qualified by winning the South African Order of Merit—I had played seventeen PGA Tour events and missed the halfway cut in seven of those. In fifty-one rounds I had scored in the 60s only once, and stood 117th on the PGA Tour money list. These were hardly the sort of outward positive signs that would demonstrate I was improving; hardly signs that I had made the changes David and I had worked on nearly a year and a half before I came to the Firestone Country Club for the World Series. But I knew that I was improving, slowly but definitely.

Then, what do you know, I won the World Series with rounds of 66-68-69-67 to beat Jack Nicklaus by four shots. All week I aimed for the middle of the fairways and greens, didn't try to do anything special. It was just solid golf that rewarded me with plenty of birdie chances. Suddenly I had won a significant event on the PGA Tour, for which I received a ten-year exemption from qualifying for tournaments.

Yet I did not win on the PGA Tour again until eight years later, in 1991. I did win elsewhere, which was encouraging, but I was frustrated that I couldn't win on the PGA Tour. I got into playoffs, I had many close shaves, but I couldn't get to the finish line first. I had to be patient, and I certainly learned the meaning of the word.

After winning the World Series I hoped I would continue to win on the PGA Tour. But that didn't happen. I still had much to learn before I would understand the principles that top golfers have in common. The practice tee was my laboratory, the golf course my proving ground, and my swing the subject matter under consideration. I wanted an efficient swing with no wasted motion.

Golf is all about patience. I said it earlier and I will say it again: Golfers who mean to improve, get the most out of their games, and reach their potential must make a study of the game. They must study what the top players have always done well, must understand the swing in a logical manner, and then must stick single-mindedly to this approach. It takes time to sift through the many theories about the swing, but such study does help one perceive the similarities in what may appear to be quite different approaches. The beauty of golf is that the flight of the ball and the results on the course tell us all we need to know.

chapter three

THE THEORY OF THE EFFICIENT SWING

An efficient golf swing incorporates the fewest moving parts while producing maximum results in terms of direction, distance, and ball flight. These factors add up to control, and to me the ultimate art of golf is in controlling the ball. It is an attribute of all the top ball–strikers. It is the factor that adds fulfillment and pleasure to any round. It is the factor that makes a golfer feel secure. He comes to know that he can go out day to day and play consistently, within reason. I say "within reason" because we are, after all, human and subject to making errors despite our best intentions and understanding. We may feel ill, lose our timing, and so make errors. Our bodies, and therefore our swings, may betray us no matter how sound our understanding.

But if we develop an efficient swing, we can be all but certain that our games will return, that our poor rounds are the aberrations. By understanding and constantly refining our swings through applying the basic elements that make up an efficient swing, we will forever be on a graph of improvement. Our peaks will be higher and more frequent, our valleys shallower and less frequent.

Developing the golf swing is like controlling the temperature of water through hot and cold faucets coming out of one spout. Sometimes the water is slightly too cold, sometimes too hot. We fiddle with each faucet until the mixture is just right. That's when we feel our best. That's when we swing our best. The grand plan is to find the right temperature and to maintain it. Not every person likes the same temperature in the shower or bath, nor the same temperature every day—this is the human element. Yet we all want to reduce the variations in temperatures so that, day by day, round by round, we are operating within a narrow range. This also applies to the short game and to putting, where efficiency is critical because the margin of error is less.

I have always been fascinated with the golf swing. I can remember very well as a young lad the different swings of all the good players at my club, their mannerisms, their rhythms, and of course how far they hit the ball. Most of these fellows and a few women as well were single-figure handicaps—but to me they were professionals. I tried to copy little things from each swing, the areas in which I thought each golfer was strongest. I always wanted to be different, and I figured if I could take the best of everyone then I would have the perfect swing. This sounds familiar, doesn't it? In fact, I should have been looking for what the good players had in common. The kind of swing I was looking for wasn't possible, since we are all built differently and have varying rhythms and tempos. Then there is what I believe to be a most critical factor: that we all vary in suppleness.

As I got older I tried to learn more and more about the swing by getting my hands on as many instruction books as I could. Oddly enough, my first instructional item was a long-play record album that Arnold Palmer did in the mid-1960s; it included an instructional booklet sandwiched between the foldout and the double LP. Like most kids I was more impressed with the sound of the club hitting the ball than with any of the instruction.

Among the many books I read were Ben Hogan's *Five Lessons: The Modern Fundamentals of Golf,* Jack Nicklaus's *Golf My Way,* Dick Aultman's *The Square-to-Square Golf Swing, Bobby Locke on Golf,* Bob Toski's *Touch System for Better Golf,* and a book by Henry Cotton. This was quite a diverse group. Except for Aultman, a journalist, each writer was a winner of major championships. Yet each had a different explanation of how he gripped the club, addressed the ball, and swung. This was also true when it came to magazines, which I studied with as much fervor as instructional books.

It just did not occur to me then that the best swings incorporated common factors. Maybe this is because all swings look different to the naked eye. You can really see only the beginning and the end rather than the significant parts that happen along the way, and it is at the start and finish that golfers appear to vary so much. Fuzzy Zoeller looks cramped over the ball but hits very good golf shots with, apparently, little effort, given his gentle tempo. Lee Trevino sets up well left of his target as if aiming far afield from where he wants the ball to finish. Tom Weiskopf is a tall player who stands majestically to the ball and looks the picture of grace. George Archer is two inches taller than Tom, yet chooses to crouch over the ball. Sam Snead stands easily to the ball and finishes like a Rolls-Royce humming into its parking spot. Jack Nicklaus addresses the ball in a deliberate fashion that suggests he is preparing himself for battle; he looks so rooted to the ground, so determined. Ben Hogan stood to the ball with a posture that in my mind is unrivaled. It was relaxed, it was natural, it had poise and grace and exemplified fundamental athleticism. Phil Mickelson and Tiger Woods, two exceptionally talented young players, are also poised as they stand to the ball, yet they seem looser than Hogan from start to finish. By loose I don't mean without the necessary connections that efficient swings demonstrate, but that they appear so flexible they could be strands of spaghetti. All of these swings and so many more belong to highly accomplished golfers. And each player is as recognizable by his swing as by his signature and fingerprint, and each is easily distinguished from the others. Yet all these swings work well.

Now I see that I was missing a great deal in regarding only the external components of the swing. Perhaps this was because while growing up in Rhodesia I missed out on two things. First, I was unable to watch golf on television at all. We would only get sixteen-millimeter films of tournaments played the previous year that my club, Warren Hills in Salisbury, would show on weekend evenings. Second, there was the lack of video cameras, to which I have referred; these only became available in the late 1970s and early 1980s for me. I believe the video camera has had a huge impact on golf teaching over the last fifteen years. Players have more understanding of their swings because the video camera allows them to stop their swings at any time and analyze specific segments. Today's cameras allow you to examine the clubface clearly at any stopped point of the swing, and in this case seeing truly is believing.

The result is interesting to me. Often I am working on one aspect or another of my swing with David Leadbetter. Let's say that I am trying not to make as steep a backswing; I often work on this because I have always tended to make too steep a backswing. I'll hit balls on the range and feel I am exaggerating a move to shallow out the backswing, and it usually happens that eventually I think I am getting the proper backswing plane down. But then when I study the swing on video I see that I'm not even close. This is why I recommend specific drills where appropriate. These are the keys to accelerating your progress and to helping you *feel* the proper sensations. Once you understand what to look for, nothing enhances your chances for improvement like proper drills combined with use of the video camera and, from time to time, a teacher who knows your swing.

Growing up without a video camera, I could only consider the external, visible components of the swing. Increasingly, there is a strong sentiment *against* breaking the swing up into its component segments, as if to do this is to compromise the integrity of the single unbroken motion. But how else is one to understand the swing except by breaking it down? This to me is the essence of learning the swing. Only after I felt able to dissect the swing and comprehend its parts was I able to grasp the elements the top players had in common and then put the pieces together. These elements make the swing work. Only after you have broken the swing down can you understand it. Then and only then, for instance, did I begin to understand the significance of the setup in making it more likely that good things would happen during the swing. Hogan broke the swing down into the first part—to the top—and the second part—through to the finish. He analyzed very carefully what was going on, piece by piece, from start to finish. Most top golfers have broken the swing down in order to develop a better understanding.

Here's an analogy. Look at a beautiful house. From the outside one sees what the architect has created, but it is a myriad of details—the wiring, plumbing, heating, and air-conditioning—that make the house function smoothly. Don't let aesthetics fool you into believing that a good-looking swing, then, is necessarily fundamentally sound. The golf swing is a chain of events. If there is a weak link anywhere in the chain, you will need to make compensating moves or else lose efficiency. I will take you through the sequence of events that compose an efficient swing and help you understand the elements that create power and control.

There are endless examples of how one weak link can compromise efficiency. To pick one, think of a golfer who stands open to the ball at address. The effect of this is that he restricts his hip turn in the backswing, because he has farther to travel—from open at address through square and then turning away from the ball. He therefore makes it difficult for himself to make a 90-degree shoulder turn—where the golfer's back is facing the target—which is a principle of technically sound golf. Should he try to reach the 90-degree position from a beginning where he stands open, he will put serious strain on his lower back. It is no surprise that for one reason or another nine out of ten golfers experience back problems at one time or another. They set themselves up for possible problems in a variety of ways from the start. Lee Trevino and Fred Couples are examples of enormously talented golfers who set up open. Both have suffered from back problems. I won't argue that you should not set up open if that is your firm preference; but please understand that your back may not like it.

Another example of a golfer who can run into problems is the one who makes a poor takeaway to begin his backswing, throwing the club either out of alignment or off plane. He too will have to make compensatory moves during the downswing in order to hit the ball accurately with distance. The secret in golf is to have a backswing so sound that on the course you don't think about the downswing. Of course, that does not happen too often. And yet I have experienced many moments in my career when I have only thought of a position in my backswing and the ball has come off the clubface properly. The correct backswing will set up the conditions that make it much more likely that the right things will happen later.

The more complicated you make the swing or the further you get from the fundamentals, particularly early in the setup and the backswing, the harder it will be for you to reach the correct position at the top. The last thing you want to be doing in a pressure situation is to be thinking about a move in the downswing when you should be thinking of where you are aiming and visualizing the shot. You want to leave method or how-to on the practice ground. Once you get to the course, your objective should be to make a score, and so you should be concentrating more on strategy than on your swing. However, we are all human and so it is not surprising that we often need to think about a key in the address or backswing; I'm like this myself, especially when for one reason or another I am just not feeling quite right with my swing. At these times I need something to think about, which makes it that much more important to know the few things that are essential to my swing. And I rarely become preoccupied with a swing key while I am over the ball; the thinking takes place before I step into my address position. Once you are over the ball the only things on your mind should be your target and how you want the ball to get there.

I was helped immensely in my studies by sequence photos of my swing and of other swings. Beauty may be only skin deep, but another beauty lies hidden to the untutored eye. That is the beauty of the technically sound swing. As I began to understand this and to become interested in swing technique, a whole world of exploration opened to me. And I felt the stirrings of an excitement I had not known before; it was the thrill of the search, the quest, that was imbuing me with its power. If I could come to appreciate what made golf swings work, then I could move toward making my own swing function efficiently.

When I could identify what was happening during the swing it became possible point by point to assemble the pieces into a coherent whole. There were times that I incorporated too many pieces, but that was part of my learning process. As I became more familiar with the video camera and what I was looking for I started to clarify in my own mind what made swings work and endure.

Surely, I thought, there were reasons that some swings stood the test of time, still the most significant measure of a method's soundness. The method that stands up does not break down. Bobby Jones, Ben Hogan, Sam Snead, Jack Nicklaus, Lee Trevino, and Tom Watson maintained their form over long periods. It was important to learn why they could do so. We all know that short games are critical parts of performing well week in and week out, but I also believe that you will be able to play longer and, if you choose, compete longer with a sound swing grounded in the common principles that all top-class players employ. You will derive more pleasure from the game.

As my confidence in analyzing swings matured, I also became more confident about adding personal interpretations.

These led me to the swing that I work on; in fact, little if anything has changed in the way I approach the golf swing since 1986, by which time I had a solid understanding of what I was trying to accomplish from start to finish. That meant not necessarily that I would win tournaments or that I had developed the controlled swing I wanted, but that the flight of my golf ball was much more often than not providing me with the feedback I wanted. The flight was telling me that I had incorporated into and grafted onto my swing the elements I had sought when I initiated my study some years before. And even when I didn't flight the ball the way I wanted, I had a good understanding of what had happened. It became a matter of refining the swing and constantly working to eliminate sources of error, and, of course, developing an efficient short game and putting stroke. Then I would win.

Now I believe that I can recommend an approach to the swing that will give any golfer lasting enjoyment. I see no reason that a golfer cannot reach his potential as long as he works diligently and steadily on the program that I present in this book. Ben Hogan advised golfers to groove the fundamentals, and certainly that is also my advice. I wrote down those important three words—*groove the fundamentals*—time and time again in my diary.

Remember, however, that we will all look different though we work on the same principles. But inside that space from start to finish, where the measure of the swing is taken, the component parts will work similarly from one golfer to another. Human beings all look different and are built differently; but inside, our hearts beat the same way, our muscles contract and expand in the same manner. The activities that go on in our bodies are involuntary for the most part, and so here the analogy breaks down. Yet this is all to the good of golfers: The parts of the swing *are* amenable to our voluntary control. The difficulty in golf—the challenge—is that we have to initiate the motion and create a reaction. Golf *is* a reaction sport, just like tennis, soccer, rugby, and baseball. But because we begin from a fixed position and are facing a stationary ball, we must find a way to start the swing. The key is to react to the target rather than to the mechanics or details of your swing; yet you can only do this once you have assimilated the principles of the swing and made them second nature. Then you become less of a thinker on the course and more of a player.

Once you are able to do this, because you are confident of your backswing the downswing becomes an instinctive reaction. However, if you have a bad backswing you have now created a poor move on the downswing. You would have to do something unnatural on the downswing to compensate for the inefficient backswing.

**The position at the top:
A good backswing goes a long way
to make the downswing instinctive.**

A further example: The golfer who reverse-pivots in the backswing—whose weight for the most part stays on his front foot while he takes the club away—now has to move his weight back on the downswing in order to square up the club-face at impact. And so his weight is falling backward while his club is going forward. He ends up in poor balance and the ball usually goes right with a huge slice. But if I show that person the correct backswing after the years of his reverse pivoting, he will have no feel for the correct way to move once he gets to the top. If he does what he has been doing all his life—the downswing ingrained in his body—he will hit six inches behind the ball. This fellow must work on a correct down-swing motion until it does become instinctive.

Now, elements in the setup and also in the backswing can create a reverse pivot. You cannot cure the person of his reverse pivot by simply telling him to do the right thing in one area. You must go where the problem is and work bit by bit, drill by drill, day by day.

Be aware, then, that you cannot undo years of an incorrect down-swing just because you have improved your backswing. It takes time and effort before your body will trust enough to let go of the past. Then and only then will you reach a higher level on the learning curve.

My Own Learning Process

Until 1982 my swing was characterized by excessive leg and hip action; the motion in my legs and, as a consequence, my hips exceeded what was required to move the club into a sound position during the backswing. But the books and mag-azines I read in the 1970s taught us that to create speed you have to use your hips and legs aggressively. I was a product of my reading and thought I had to clear my left hip as fast as pos-sible from the top of my backswing to create speed. But the left hip moves only about four inches in the backswing, whereas your hands move about six feet and the clubhead fourteen or fifteen feet. It's very easy to move that hip back the four inches to its address position in a split second, but it takes a long time for the clubhead to catch up, especially because you will have to increase your hand and arm speed so much; this can lead to all sorts of disconnections.

I did not appreciate that my excess hip and leg movement was a primary source of inefficiency and made me swivel and slide all over the place. I lacked a fixed position from which to operate and from which to rotate my upper body. My legs moved out, back and forth, and so my swing was on shaky footing and I frequently lost my balance. I was like a house that lacked a firm foundation.

Yet I continued to use my legs emphatically. It appeared to my untrained eye that effective golfers shoved their legs forward through impact; I figured this was because they had moved them backward first and now were simply generating an equal and opposite reaction during the forward swing through impact. I misinterpreted what the term "weight transfer" meant. I thought it signified that you consciously and conscientiously transferred the weight of your lower body to the right foot going back and to the left on the return portion of the swing. It did not occur to me that the legs should provide a brace, a relatively still point within motion. Instead my floorboards were wobbly.

In 1982 I started to see the error of my ways. David Leadbetter showed me videos that indicated I had little in the way of body dynamics in my swing. This lack of body dynamics is very evident in the early swing sequences in Chapter 10. Because my legs were moving quickly and erratically, they were not synchronized with my hands, arms, and shoulders. The solution to the start of my swing was to settle my legs down so that my upper body could work more in tandem with my legs. My lower and upper halves had been out of control, not synchronized. It was as if they were a couple of dancers on the floor, neither of whom knew whether to lead or follow.

After starting to work with David, I was able to focus my attention more clearly on the parts of the swing where I had been going wrong. For the first time I wondered why the legs should be considered so important in golf. We weren't running or kicking a ball. I could not have played field hockey, as I did as a youth in Rhodesia, with less than active legs. This is obvious. But, conceivably, one could hit a golf ball without legs, using only the upper body. I had read Ernest Jones's book *Swing the Clubhead,* but did not take proper notice when he wrote of his ability to drive a ball 250 yards after losing part of his right leg while fighting for the British army in 1915. I might also have thought about Douglas Bader, a World War II pilot who lost both his legs in an aircraft accident but could still hit the ball over two hundred yards. I had also pretty much dismissed the central thesis of Jones's ideas. He wanted the golfer only to swing the clubhead, and argued that the body would necessarily follow.

I didn't give that idea much credence, because I believed my swing already had too much hands in it, and to me swinging the clubhead meant using the hands aggressively. How could you generate clubhead speed by swinging the clubhead alone? Clubhead speed comes from three main sources: arc or length of backswing, retention of the set or cock in the wrists until pre-impact, and body rotation. Tiger Woods and John Daly do all three of these extremely well and therefore hit the ball an awfully long way. When these movements are combined with the correct weight transference, more power is added. Otherwise how do golfers such as Ian Woosnam and Gary Player, the one five feet four, the other five feet seven, hit the ball farther than guys a foot taller and substantially heavier? It's simple: more efficiency of movement. The point is to use your body in a way that will maximize power and control. Why use only one part of your body?

As I have mentioned, the swing is in two halves: upper and lower halves of the body. I separate the body at the hip line. Because we are stationary, the lower body doesn't have as much movement as the upper body. We are looking to synchronize the two halves and thereby create the most amount of speed in the body rotation. There has to be a coordinated

**Separating the body at the hip line:
the swing in two halves**

movement between the two halves that creates an efficient delivery of the clubhead on the ball.

During what I think of as my fledgling days as a student of the swing, in the early to mid-1980s, I read and reread Ben Hogan's superb book *Five Lessons: The Modern Fundamentals of Golf.* Even today I carry a copy of the book with me. My copy is full of notations I have made, sections I have highlighted, my agreements and disagreements with Hogan's ideas. (I agree with this ball-striker of ball-strikers far more than I disagree with him, but I do disagree in some critical areas.) I refer to the book often, as I do to the notes I keep in my journal, a selection of which is included later. These notes represent passages I made along my route to understanding the swing.

Hogan had problems hooking the ball for much of the first

part of his career, and then turned himself into the most reliable ball-striker the game has known. It has been said that he hit the ball so accurately, and the same way swing after swing, that he had his own channel in the sky. Bobby Jones is another one of my favorites, and since his videos came out in the mid-1980s I have spent countless hours watching his instruction. He was an absolute genius who probably had a better understanding of his swing than many great players have of theirs. His swing and Hogan's had a lot in common, although each player explained and illustrated his ideas differently.

Jones had an old-fashioned backswing in which he took the club inside and had it pointed to the right at the top. He let the club go past parallel at the top, to the point of overswinging. But the club was in perfect position after he started his downswing, and it returned through the parallel-to-the-ground position with the shaft pointing down the target line, which indicates an on-plane swing. It was on line there and remained that way through impact. He explains his backswing simply in the videos that have been put out in recent years, but I think it would be difficult to emulate it because it's complicated and has many moving parts.

Hogan, on the other hand, was more efficient in his backswing. Over the years many players have tried to copy Hogan's swing, but I would not recommend this. As a notorious hooker of the ball early on, he built into his swing a variety of anti-hook corrections. It was interesting to note what happened to his golf after his near-fatal car accident in 1949, which damaged his legs extensively. Hogan had to spend many months in bed but began to work on regaining some strength in his legs by walking in his living room, then to the mailbox, and eventually around the block. Only after his accident and this recovery period did he play his best golf. I think this is because his legs were not as strong as before the accident, and so he could not move his legs or hips as quickly.

The Hogan example shows that you have to take into account a person's circumstances and background when studying his swing. I have also found it interesting that Hogan had extremely supple wrists and, I am sure, a double-jointed left thumb, which allowed him to retain the angle between his left arm and the shaft deep into the downswing like nobody before him. This was one of the key sources of Hogan's power.

While I have a better understanding today of what Hogan said in his book and what he did with his powerful swing, I did misread much of what he said. I emphasized certain elements and effectively ignored other aspects that turned out to be significant. For instance, Hogan writes that we do nothing consciously with the hands and arms. But he does go on to say that when he hits the ball he wishes he had three right hands. However, I misunderstood his observation. I took him to mean that nothing happens with the upper part of the body, and that the lower body moves the hands, arms, and shoulders. That suggested to me that I get my legs into the swing, but good. If they *really* moved, then my upper body would travel along, all the more powerfully.

The natural consequence of my flawed reasoning was that I felt justified in emphasizing my leg motion, or at least in willfully underestimating the role of the upper body. I would later learn about the proper use of the lower body and better understand what Hogan meant when he wrote about the legs and also what Jones meant when he spoke about the use of the hips. But earlier I was far too interested in having fast legs.

Then, however, I looked closely at swing sequences of the top players, Hogan included: *Their lower halves were invariably quiet.* Their legs played a supporting or weight-bearing role and rotated only when the hands got to just in front of the right hip on the way down. Then they rotated, creating the speed in the upper half of the body just at the right time. The most consistent ball-strikers were turning their upper halves against the stability of their lower halves. Make no mistake, however: There is turn in the lower body, but its speed alone does not create power. The rotation of the upper body against the relative stability of the lower body is one of the key sources of power.

This began to seem reasonable to me, especially as I reconsidered the very nature of golf. I have said that we don't move out of our place or zone—the one we have created at address—when we swing. Lines drawn up from the tops of our feet represent the outer limits of the space we occupy during the swing; we don't cross those lines. Remember, this is looking from a face-on position. The legs and hips *are* active in the swing, but in their support and positioning, not by any excessive motion. When I realized this I began to control my distances more consistently. Why need the legs move in any active way then? And we don't hit the ball with our legs or swing the club with our legs. We hold on to the club with our hands and swing it with our hands, arms, and shoulders. I felt I was on my way to building an efficient swing when I realized and accepted these ideas.

Staying Within the Zone
We Have Created at Address

Control Through Plane

Still, it was obvious that you just could not swing the club anywhere with your hands, arms, and shoulders. There had to be a means of governing the path it traveled on during the swing. The clubhead had to move in an organized, stable manner. By "organized" I mean that there should be a minimum of variation from swing to swing in the way the club goes back and through the ball to the finish. Clearly, the most reasonable way of achieving this was to develop a method whereby the shaft and clubhead were linked to the upper body. In this way I could avoid my hands flipping the club around and altering the path of the clubhead. That is, I could keep the club on plane.

Over the years the swing plane has been the subject of much controversy. For me, at least early in my career, it was the most difficult aspect of the swing to understand. I so misled myself through an improper understanding of swing plane that I can

Note in the third image, the power and momentum of the downswing have forced my right shoulder just past the line. This is acceptable because it occurs well past impact.

trace many problems in my early career, and even occasionally now, to not understanding this correctly. The concept can be tricky, and I find that a complete understanding of it is elusive.

The plane represents the path either the shoulders or the shaft travels on, and there are two distinct planes in the swing. There is the path the shaft travels on and the path the shoulders travel on. I can remember early in my career as a professional reading Hogan's and also Gary Player's descriptions of the plane, in which they visualized a pane of glass running from their shoulders to the ball. I became confused here because I was under the impression that this was the plane the shoulders rotate on, whereas in fact the shoulders rotate on a much flat-

Note that in the image at right I have turned more around my body and kept my leg movement to a minimum.

Backswing   Downswing

ter plane. The pane of glass actually represents the correct left arm plane at the top of the swing.

The result was that I began to try to swing my shoulders on a steeper or more vertical plane than required. To compensate for this I had to flatten the plane out tremendously on the downswing in order to create any power. If you refer to the black-and-white photo taken of me in 1981 you will clearly see what I mean. Contrast this with the swing plane I've worked to achieve. Also note that the left knee used to shoot out as the right knee straightened and almost locked. But in the later photograph, the knees are working together because of my improved swing plane.

Shaft Plane

We must at this stage appreciate that the length of the club and the distance we stand from the ball determine the shaft plane, which changes with each club. Suffice it to say that the driver plane is much flatter than the shaft plane with a nine-iron, when one is standing closer to the ball. The shoulder plane also changes from club to club but not nearly as much as the shaft plane. The more efficient both planes are, the more consistent your delivery of the clubface to the ball.

There is also a distinction between the shaft plane on the backswing and on the downswing; your backswing plane is going to be slightly steeper than your downswing plane. Remember, as I have said, that it would be ideal if the planes were mirror images of each other, but that this is all but impossible to achieve. This shallowing out on the downswing plane, or the path the club travels on, occurs because of the slight lateral move that you make with your hips from the top of the backswing to create speed in your downswing, as you will see. On the other hand, the shoulder plane—because of this flattening or shallowing out of the swing plane—is slightly steeper on the downswing than on the backswing. This steepening occurs because the right elbow drops into a position near the body on the downswing in an effort to keep the club moving from an inside, on-plane path onto the ball. This is a common occurrence in all sound ball-strikers' swings.

Shoulder Plane

The shoulder plane is visibly flatter than the shaft plane. A line drawn through each shoulder joint at the top of the backswing points to a position well beyond the ball. As you approach the impact area the shoulder plane steepens slightly but then releases back onto its correct or original plane through impact. Make no mistake about this: *The shoulder plane is a result of the shaft plane, although in time you will emphasize the former rather than the latter. The angle or lie of the club determines the shaft plane.*

**Shaft plane (on backswing) and
shoulder plane**

But as you begin to change to become a more efficient golfer, be mindful of swinging the shaft on the correct plane. Your shoulders will follow correctly.

Some people might feel it's easier to be conscious of the shoulder plane than of the shaft plane. I certainly feel that way, but I only work on my shoulder plane when I am convinced that my shaft plane is correct. The better player you are, the easier it is for you to work on the shoulder plane as opposed to the shaft plane. As you progress and feel you have the shaft plane under control, you will be able to do this.

Over the years I have given a lot of thought to the shoulder plane, because my confusion about it led me down many side roads from which I had trouble emerging. But eventually I came to understand the shoulder plane quite clearly, although I am still learning about it.

Here's how I picture the shoulder plane now, and I like to think of a particular diagram. If I drew a line from my sternum to the ground at 90 degrees to my chest, then drew another line from the base of my neck parallel to the chest line—that is the plane my shoulders should rotate on.

By all means work on your shoulder plane if you feel it's easier for you to do so. But please remain conscious of the shaft plane at all times. Conversely, if you prefer to work primarily on the shaft plane, please be aware that there is also a shoulder plane. Don't make the mistake I made when I was starting out.

A Cautionary Note

You will notice in the full swing sequences in Chapter 10 that my early misconceptions of the swing plane are still apparent in my swing today. I am constantly working on my swing plane, and if you compare the old black-and-white photos to the recent sequences you will see how far I have come. But there is still room for improvement. Our old tendencies are always there, to some degree.

Spine Angle

You have probably heard this term, as it has become quite popular in modern instruction. It is the angle at which you set your spine at address and is a very useful visual aid when analyzing swings. Try to maintain your spine angle as long as you can, but realize that the degree to which you can do so is dependent upon your suppleness. It may be difficult for some people to maintain spine angle through to the finish, but every golfer should try to maintain it through the halfway point of the follow-through. The critical path along which you want to maintain spine angle is from the start of your swing through

Maintain spine angle throughout the swing

that halfway point. If you can get nearer the finish with your spine angle intact, wonderful. But it isn't all that critical.

The Importance of the Shoulders

I have indicated that I have always had too steep a shaft plane going back. This comes from my misreading of the meaning of swing plane, and, consequently, from trying to keep the club too square for too long in the takeaway. I swing the shaft too straight up, or vertically, in the backswing. When my timing is on I do reroute the club to get it back on plane on the down-swing, and so can play reasonably well then, if not as consistently as I would like. But I have always been looking for something that would add consistency to my shaft plane.

That, I discovered, is possible through thinking more about my shoulder plane. As I progressed and came to understand the shaft plane, I realized that it was now important to think about my shoulder plane. The shoulders are an important key to maintaining an efficient plane, because to move them is to move the club. To move the shoulders properly is to move the arms and hands, that is, and hence the club. The shoulders move on a relatively flat plane through a smooth arc, and permit the shaft to move on its steeper plane through its own arc that is at the same time synchronized with the upper body.

Golfers often start the club back with the hands alone, because this feels natural. But this can cause many problems: picking the club up and restricting arc and turn, keeping the weight on the left foot, reverse pivoting, casting the clubhead from the top just to get back to the ball, a steep clubshaft plane going back, and other difficulties. You can be sure that if you pick the club up with your hands you will never be as consistent a golfer as you would be if you involved your shoulders and subsequently your entire upper half.

Try this now. Stand with a club in your hands and assume your address position. Now, keeping your shoulders still, take the club back with your hands alone. Notice that you have lifted the club only by using your wrists. But you want your bigger muscles and joints to control the smaller ones. The more you involve your hands, the harder it will be for you to play consistent golf. There is just too much rotational ability inherent in your hands and fingers for you to be able to rely on them. Use them excessively and you will create little if any shoulder turn, little if any power storage at the top.

Now, however, feel as if your hands, arms, and shoulders move back together, in a unit. Notice how this makes many good things happen. You feel some turn, and your weight moves to your right foot without your having consciously transferred it or done anything with your legs or lower half. And best of all, the club has moved back as if it were on a track. That track represents your shaft plane. And you have made it go there simply by introducing your shoulders into your back-swing. Move your shoulders correctly and everything will follow. Move your legs and hips without focusing on your upper half and you will never create the dynamic position required in the backswing. Remember that solid ball-striking requires a completed backswing. This is a prerequisite: *Complete your turn.*

We do not want to compromise the plane in any way. The shoulders have become a key for me and can become a key for you in helping to achieve a better shaft plane. Imagine a swing that went back and forward only twelve inches each way, or a swing with a driver in which you were trying to hit the ball only sixty yards. That's not difficult to do. But the difficulty is hitting the ball 275 yards and straight. The difficulty is adding power. The trick in golf is to maintain control of both direction and distance.

Adding the requirement of distance means you must move the club through a bigger arc. The bigger the arc, the greater the chance of moving the club off plane and introducing an error from which you will need to recover. The chance of doing this increases because we must turn our bodies as the club moves through a bigger arc. Rotary motion when added to straight-line motion as in the sixty-yard swing multiplies the chance of error.

But you lessen the chance for error when you tie in the

movements of your hands to the mass of your upper half. You then create a favorable situation where the clubhead will remain on track.

The use of the upper half is a central aspect of the way I think about the swing. While the legs are undoubtedly the strongest part of your body, the fact is that we hold the club with our upper body. Because the big-muscled legs and hips move the least in the swing, it is very easy for the rest of the body to get out of whack; this can result because of too much or too little use of the lower body, and is why it is important that the lower body be in the correct positions right from the address position in order to generate overall speed.

If you are going to walk somewhere, you move by pointing your shoulders in the direction you wish to go. You lean in the direction you want to go, and your shoulders and then your legs follow. If you start with your legs you will look as if you are making a goose step, and will appear stiff.

For example, if you do start the swing with only your legs, you may reverse-pivot because your left shoulder will dip instead of staying high and pulling your upper body behind the ball.

Staying on Track

In some ways it is counterintuitive to swing the club back not with your hands alone but with the shoulders as well. We are not accustomed to thinking about what our shoulders do. Yet after studying the swings of many top players I concluded that the one thing they had in common was the way in which they used their shoulders. The shoulders are generally the widest segment of a person's upper torso. Link the movement of the shoulders to the arms, hands, and clubhead and one ought to have a reliable way of moving the club. I began, then, to work on involving my shoulders; the shoulders moved my arms, hands, grip, club shaft, and clubhead.

At the same time, I recognize that it is difficult to feel that your shoulders are initiating the swing and moving the club.

This is why I suggested earlier that if it is easier for you to think of your shaft plane than of your shoulder plane, fine. Most people who emphasize the shaft plane are also thinking about their fingers, hands, and arms as the primary movers of the club. Fair enough; but understand that as you progress you will become a more efficient swinger as you develop the feeling that you are starting the swing with your shoulders. You will gradually learn to control the swing with your shoulders while at the same time allowing your hands and arms to take up their more passive but still significant roles. In my early days, because my leg movement was so furious I had to back this up and compensate with too much hand movement. This was the only way I could keep the clubface square through impact. But now I feel that my hands are very passive throughout the swing until impact when they unload the power. They are passive because my upper body is controlling the clubhead.

We will get into the details of this more shoulder-conscious swing as we go along into the separate segments of the swing. For now, simply appreciate that you will improve your ball-striking dramatically as you learn to subdue the overuse of your hands throughout the swing and allow your shoulders and other big muscle groups—primarily your hips—to exert the major influence during your downswing. Your hands will be active—make no mistake about that—but they will be responding to your body motion, not the other way around.

Begin to think of the swing, then, as one turn back from the ball and another turn through. I suggest this because it is the ultimate goal. You transmit the energy latent in your body through the shaft of the club into the head of the club by using your entire body properly. Many elements go into this, to be sure, but it's the destination we are hoping to reach. It's the way to an efficient swing, one that will allow you to play to your potential and hit quality golf shots time and time again.

chapter four

THE GRIP

A good grip will make efficient golf easier, since your hands are the only parts of your body that come into contact with the club. You can always find players who have unconventional grips, and many of them do well. But these golfers must build idiosyncrasies into their swings to compensate for their poor grips. A player who has a sound grip and who checks it regularly will never have to worry about it hurting his swing; the proper grip can only help his swing. Certainly most golfers would be able to swing more efficiently if they gripped the club correctly.

Most great players over the years have had grips that I would call *conforming*. They place their hands on the club in a neutral position, with neither hand influencing the grip unduly. By neutral I mean that you place your hands in neither a strong nor a weak position; neither hand is turned too much to the left or the right, neither hand is too much underneath nor too much on top of the shaft. Get your hands correctly on the club and your grip will allow you to hit the ball solidly and drive it on its intended flight. Remember, we are speaking here of a neutral grip, not a neutral hand position. When the clubface is square to your intended target you should be able to see two to two and a half knuckles of your left hand; this represents a neutral grip.

**From above, two or two and a half knuckles show
on the left hand.**

Oddly, perhaps, the effect of a correct grip is to minimize the influence of the hands and fingers; or to put this another way, to allow them to perform properly. Overactive hands and fingers can wreck your swing by flinging the clubhead this way and that. Underactive hands and fingers can inhibit their correct functions in the swing. A grip that allows you to present the clubface to the ball squarely without manipulating it with your hands will also go a long way toward ensuring that the body and shoulders are controlling the clubhead. This is the objective.

A weak grip—for instance, one in which the left hand is turned to the left too much and the right hand is also turned to the left too much—will invariably lead to your flipping the hands over too sharply through impact. This will occur because you will sense that the club is open as you come into the impact area and will want to square it up. Often the result will be a glancing blow. To make solid and square contact you will need exquisite timing. It's asking a lot of yourself to expect such precise timing shot after shot.

A strong grip, with the hands turned clockwise too much, or bearing to the right, will mean that you will have to use your legs and lower body with extreme precision and plenty of force through impact. This is the only way you will be able to hold the club square to the target line and will invariably lead to fatigue in your legs as the round progresses. If you are not feeling 100 percent, you will tend to draw or hook the ball.

All the same, there is no rule that says that you cannot play with a weak or strong grip. Just understand the difficulties involved in each choice. Corey Pavin uses a weak grip, but he is such a remarkable shotmaker and manipulator of the club-head that he is able to do so. Bobby Locke gripped the club very strongly with his left hand and hooked the ball most of the time. When asked why he gripped the club strongly with his left hand, he liked to say that he was quite happy to collect the money from his playing partners with his right hand.

Ben Hogan gripped the club in a slightly weak position, although he described it as neutral. I prefer a grip that is a bit stronger than Hogan's. We must understand that one of the reasons Hogan went to a weaker grip was that he fought a hook all his life. I also like a modestly stronger grip because it is easier to recover from a shot that is well struck but hooks a little than from one that is struck but a glancing blow and goes to the right, or slices.

My point is that there is an ideal grip that will make your life easier, but there is also more than one way to hug your children or hold your glass of wine. If you use other than the ideal grip, then the compensations you make will probably lead to inconsistencies and unnecessary injuries. I've noticed in tennis, for instance, that a weak grip puts strain on the elbow and can lead to tennis elbow. Bear in mind that we are looking

for a benchmark from which you can work. You must understand the effects that either a strong or weak grip has and then
factor these in when making swing changes. Changing your
swing without considering your grip can lead to problems.
You must practice and experiment so that you can find out
whether you feel more comfortable with a slightly stronger or
a slightly weaker grip. Always remember that the golf swing is
like a computer. If you feed in the relevant information it will
calculate and give you a response based strictly on the data you
supplied. We are seeking the relevant information so that we
can generate a valid response.

There are two players I have seen whose grips always made
it look as if the club were molded to their hands. I'm speaking
of Arnold Palmer and Roberto DeVicenzo, the fine Argentine
player best known, unfortunately, for signing an incorrect
scorecard after the final round of the 1968 Masters and thereby
losing the opportunity to get into a playoff with Bob Goalby.
Let's not forget, though, that he won the 1967 British Open at
Hoylake in Liverpool. I only saw DeVicenzo once, but his grip
was so powerful yet so composed that it stayed with me as a
vivid image; he set his hands on the club beautifully. As for
Palmer, he never looks as if his hands are working against each
other. Sometimes you see players who have one hand on the
club nicely but the other in a strong or weak position; their
hands then work not in unison but in competition. The
unusual grip with one hand is invariably compensating for a
particular move in the player's swing. Palmer sets his hands on
the club so that they are partners, not opponents. I should add
that I also like Ben Crenshaw's grip, particularly with the
wedges and putter. He fits his hands so comfortably on these
touch clubs.

Molding Your Hands to the Club

Left Hand

The club in your left hand should run across the hand from
the cup in your forefinger through the base of the pad (the

fatty part) of your left palm and into your pinkie finger. There is a good way to ensure that you are doing this properly. It is best if a friend helps you. First, stand erect with your left hand at your side. Keep your left arm straight. Have your friend put a club in your left hand, and grab hold of it while you keep your arm straight and at your side. Hold the club 90 degrees to your body, or parallel to the ground, without bending your left arm. Make sure that you are pointing the club directly in front of your left shoulder. Now look down while moving your head as little as possible. Simply glance down. You should see two full knuckles on your left hand, with a trace of a third; or, to put it in golfing vernacular, you should see two and a half knuckles.

When you put the club in front of you, the V or line formed between the thumb and forefinger of your left hand should split your chin and right shoulder. Use this neutral left-hand position as a checkpoint. A further checkpoint is to ensure that your left thumb is on the right side of the shaft. It is always advisable to use a club that has a line or a point of reference down the middle so that you can check the relationship of the clubhead to your hands. You then don't have to look at the clubhead and need only consider your hands. Be certain that the person who puts the marking line on the club's grip makes it absolutely square to the clubhead.

Another way to do this is to position the line on the shaft so that it runs down where you want to place your left thumb. I like to do this, as I then simply place my left thumb so that it runs down that line. Then I know it is in the correct position and that I have my left hand on the club correctly with the clubface square. Grips that incorporate a line running down the middle are commonly available.

Right Hand

The shaft of the club should sit in the base of the fingers of your right hand so that the pad of the hand actually is in position to drive the club through the ball. This is a position of

Hit the ball with the pad.

maximum power and control and is something that you help set up at address. (The pad of the hand is that portion below the index finger.) You want to hit the ball with the pad, or at least feel as if that is what you are doing. After all, the pad is the strongest part of the hand. If I were to push you, it would be with the pad.

The lifeline of your right hand should fit directly over your left thumb. The V produced by the right thumb and forefinger should point to the same place as does the V formed by your left thumb and forefinger. This is a neutral right-hand grip. Try to get the V's running parallel to each other between your chin and right shoulder.

If these V's point to the right of your right shoulder, you have a strong grip; if they point straight up the grip, you have a weak grip. These are very useful checkpoints.

The significance of forming the correct V in your right hand especially is that it will allow you to set the club on the correct plane at the top of the swing. If the V is in a weak position, your club will probably point to the right of your target at the top of the swing. If it is in a strong position, your club will probably be "laid off," or point to the left of the target.

Weak Grip   Strong Grip

The ideal (neutral) grip is right between the two.

These effects apply to the vast majority of players, but of course there are always exceptions to the rule.

Having been careful to get your hands on the club so that they are primed for action, you should also be careful about how you overlap the fingers of your left hand with the pinkie finger of your right hand. The finger should slot in almost automatically between the index and middle fingers of your left hand (assuming you use the Vardon or overlapping grip) if you have the aforementioned details right. It will slip in nicely to a position where the tip fits just on top of the junction between the index and middle fingers of your left hand.

Grip Pressure

I have always preferred to hold the club firmly. This may be because of that first club I had with its slippery grip, or perhaps it's the fear of losing control of the clubhead. Or maybe it's just an idiosyncrasy. But although I grip the club firmly, I try to keep the tension out of my arms and shoulders. The firmness is in my hands, nowhere else. The result is that on a scale of one to ten I grip the club at seven or seven and a half. The ideal is a five, but always related to your strength. Let the speed of your swing dictate your grip pressure. Larry Mize swings the club slowly, and his lovely rhythmic action allows him to grip the club on the light side. Lanny Wadkins swings quickly and as a consequence grips the club on the firm side. If he gripped lightly he could lose control of the clubhead as he comes through the ball.

Every golfer, no matter his strength, will automatically firm up his grip through impact; it's an instinctive response to holding an implement that is about to collide with another object. It makes sense to me, then, that you should if anything grip the club more toward the firm than the soft side. This is also advisable if the transition from the top of your backswing to your downswing tends to be fast. You don't want to lose control at this vital time, so ensure that you grip the club from the start with your left hand at about a six on the pressure scale. I emphasize the left hand because it carries the greater load in the transition from backswing to downswing.

One of the keys when it comes to grip pressure is that you require enough flexibility and strength in your wrists during the backswing so that you can load the club effectively for the downswing, when all the energy you have created will expend itself at the ball. In general, people who have strong, big hands, thick fingers, and large wrists are not as flexible and supple in those regions as people who have thinner hands, fingers, and wrists.

What does it mean to load the club, and how does this requirement of the efficient swing bear on grip pressure?

Loading the club means setting up a situation where power is stored in the clubhead and shaft. You do this by setting the club at the top, which a sound grip enables you to do correctly. To set the club or cock your wrists means to create an angle between your left forearm and the shaft of the club. Ideally you want to create a set of 80 to 100 degrees at the top, assuming you are of normal range of motion. I will explain this in more detail when discussing the backswing.

A weak grip will tend to lessen the set if you keep the clubface square to the target, while a strong grip will increase the set. Power in the swing is dependent in large part on retaining the angle from the top of the backswing until just prior to impact. The club is then released subconsciously because of the centrifugal force of your body rotation and the angle dispersed through the ball at impact; this happens as a

Set the club at the top

result of the rotation of your upper body. Again, the proper grip will allow you to use your body to advantage here; the body rotation will square up the club at impact while your wrists give up their hinge.

Please understand that there is a trade-off of clubhead speed and control in the loading action I am describing. If you increase the set to 120 degrees (assuming your wrists are supple enough to allow that) and rotate your body at the same speed as the golfer who has a 90-degree set, you will hit the ball farther. But you will also increase the speed of your hands and wrists at impact, which may create problems, especially with the short irons. There you need some finesse, and it is not easy to hit finesse shots when you have so much hand speed through the ball. Again there is a trade-off.

Conversely, if your set is less than 90 degrees it will be hard for you to generate clubhead speed through impact without rotating your body quickly, thereby losing balance and compromising control. It becomes difficult in these circumstances to keep your upper body moving at a rate fast enough to square up the club, which can lead to too much of an arms-and-hands swing. It is all too easy to have the club open at impact, or to compensate by snapping the clubface closed with your hands.

Grip Thickness

A thicker grip on the club will give you more control, because it will lessen the play of your fingers—but I believe that you will lose power. A thinner grip will allow you to create more clubhead speed, because the club is more in your fingers. But you may lose accuracy, because you don't have as much to hold on to. The law of the trade-off applies, as always. You can't have it all in golf. You are searching for the best combination of control, power, and balance.

One more word about the grip on your club, a small but important point. Take a club in your hands now and observe the cap at the top of the grip. You always want to have the farthest part of your hands—the top of your hands, that is—below

Correct   **Incorrect**

that cap or ring. If you hold the club higher up, you will weaken your left hand because part of it will not be on the club.

Don't worry if you modify your grip from time to time to change the feel; I like to do this, because it is easy to get stale with one's grip. Changing grip pressure or even hand placement just a fraction can often introduce a revitalizing element to your game when it sags. Inevitably you will come back to your standard grip, because you have not veered all that far from it. You have a benchmark to work from, which is important. You will return to it with renewed feeling for the club in your hands.

Work on your grip and you will be well on your way to building a lifelong approach to good golf. It is the very foundation of the swing, the very stuff of controlled power. A sound grip simply makes the rest of the game much easier. As I have explained, there are unusual grips that do the job well enough, but to me you will find long-term happiness and consistency much more readily if you build an orthodox grip and stick with it.

Practice your grip whenever you can and you will soon find it much easier to make the changes on the course, as you will feel more comfortable with any new positions you have to incorporate.

While practicing your grip, monitor the position of the V's. Be aware of how the club is sitting in your hands. Monitor grip pressure. A little work with your grip on a regular basis can do wonders for your game, and there is no better place to begin working toward an efficient swing.

chapter five

THE SETUP

While the grip is the beginning of the setup, here we consider how you actually position yourself to the ball. In trying to simplify the swing we want to simplify the setup. It is all too easy to make mistakes here, and there is no reason that this should be the case, because there is a very simple formula to follow. And, of course, we can control the setup because we place ourselves into a position prior to making the swing. The idea is that you learn a few principles, alternate practice with a mirror as a check and without one to learn the feelings you want on the course, and soon you will be well on your way to a more consistent setup. It also helps to have a friend check you from time to time, but make sure he or she understands what you are trying to do. Best of all is to use a video camera.

It is true that the more a person looks like a golfer over the ball the easier it will be to make the correct start to the backswing or takeaway. If you don't start with faults you will find it much easier to make the initial start to the backswing or takeaway. The swing is a chain reaction, and the golfer who gets the first links in the chain—grip, stance, and setup—right has a much better chance of getting the later links right.

And yet many golfers still question why the setup should be so important. I have often heard the argument that the truly significant part of the swing occurs when we are coming into the ball, that nothing that happens prior to this is all that crucial. Golfers I speak to at pro-ams and even tour professionals argue that if setup were really critical, we would not see so many different ways to do it. But remember that we are trying to create a standard base from which to operate. Sure, you can stand open or closed, but you will have to make compensations somewhere. I believe it is extremely important to integrate a proper setup deeply into one's game and well worth taking the time. If you adopt a consistently simple setup without complicating matters, then all you need do is maintain that setup to keep the club synchronized with your body.

Ball Position

Before we discuss the finer points of the setup, I would like to mention ball position, which has been a huge source of controversy for years. I'd like to deal with it quickly.

It has been fashionable to move the ball backward or forward in one's stance depending on the length of the club: forward for the longer clubs and farther back for the shorter clubs. I do this only when I am trying to alter my ball flight. If I want to hit the ball higher than usual, I move it toward my front foot, and if I want to hit it lower than usual, I move it toward my back foot.

Other than in these circumstances, I am a strong believer that the ball should be placed in the same relationship to the golfer's shoulders right through the bag. This position is right in front of the left breast. You can see that as my stance narrows when the club gets shorter, my ball position does not change in relation to my body. The only thing that is happening is that my right foot is moving closer to the ball and my left foot is opening up as the clubs get shorter. My stance gets more open, that is, because I do not need as big a turn with the shorter clubs as I do with the longer irons and woods.

Stance width varies from wedge to driver.

Stance Width

Here, as always, the middle road is the wise road. With a driver one should stand so that the feet are placed apart the width of the shoulders as measured from outside the shoulders to the inside of the feet. Lines drawn from just outside the shoulders will intersect the ground at the insides of the feet. The stance width diminishes as the club gets shorter to the point where with a wedge the feet should be clearly within the shoulders. We have moved from a point where the feet are outside the shoulders to one where they are inside the shoulders.

Alignment

Alignment is associated with ball position and target awareness. I generally try to keep my feet, knees, hips, and shoulders square to my intended target from my driver through my six-iron. From the seven-iron through the pitching wedge I like to stand progressively more open. By standing open you restrict your turn and consequently eliminate excess movement of the lower body (legs and hips). You really don't need to hit the ball far with the shorter clubs, so by minimizing the use of the lower half you are now focusing more on accuracy than power. The less of a turn, the more precise I can get. If I miss the center of the fairway by thirty feet, it's normally still a good drive. But if I miss my target with a shorter club by thirty feet, I have generally hit a poor shot.

There is one more important factor in alignment, and this is the matter of eyeline. We all too often neglect our eyeline, which should be square to the target line; you do not want to cock your head left or right. Many golfers could help themselves simply by checking their eyelines. Any tilt can cause problems, because you will feel you must compensate to return the clubface squarely to the ball. If you swing according to your eyeline you will have a predominant flight pattern one way or the other, but rarely straight or close to straight. Just the slightest tilt of your eyes away from square will throw your body off. Be careful about this.

Stance and Posture

Bobby Jones wrote that the average golfer's stance is too wide and that the average golfer holds the arms too far from the body. I agree with these views and have tried to develop my own thinking along the same lines. There is no reason to set up to the ball in any extreme manner.

The first consideration in the setup is the manner in which we stand to the ball. Remember that we want to keep the lower body quiet, the better to enable us to use the shoulders to start the swing. This is just another indication of how one element can influence another. One might not think immediately that how we stand to the ball will influence the takeaway, but it does.

For this reason I think that the swing should begin with some sort of slight move to stabilize the lower body, to concentrate your attention on the fact that you intend to keep it quiet. I like to feel that there is tension in the inner muscles of my legs, which gives me a braced feeling like someone could push me from the front or behind and I would not topple over. However you choose to create this feeling, it is obvious that you must have a solid base to work from.

Right away I want to emphasize that it is preferable to stand to the ball with as straight a spine as possible, then lean over from the hips and allow your arms to hang naturally. Your height will obviously determine your spine angle. If you are short, it will be more vertical than if you are tall. The lower back should be straight, or flat, while the shoulders should appear powerfully poised for action. You don't want a round-shouldered appearance; this is something I fight, because I am by nature round-shouldered. The result is that in trying to square up my shoulders I sometimes get too much out on my toes at address. This occurs because I reach forward in an attempt to square up my shoulders. In guarding against this I must watch that I do not get too far from the ball and my weight too far over my toes.

The more curvature you have in your spine, the more likely it is that you will encounter back problems along the way in your golfing life. It is inevitable that you will place some stress on your back during the swing, simply because you are turning around your spine. But you can minimize the stress and strain by standing correctly in terms of posture and, also, parallel to your target line.

The posture I advocate, then, is one in which you are relaxed and not standing to the ball all that differently than if you simply reached down with a club and started swinging at grass clippings or an object in your way. I'm sure that you, like

The upper body turns behind the ball toward a line in the middle of your stance.

me, have been out for a casual stroll, picked up a stick, and begun to swing at a stone on the path. You didn't flex your knees unduly or reach far forward to take a swipe at the stone. Instead you instinctively measured the distance you were from the stone and let yourself swing away at and through it. Remember, however, that you are putting yourself into an unnatural position anytime you lean forward from an erect position. There are many ways to lean forward, but if you have a bend in your knees, keep your lower back straight, and bend from the waist, you will achieve the correct position.

When you stand to the ball you want to feel your weight right down the middle of your feet, not too much to one side or the other, not too far forward toward your toes or too far back toward your heels. It is also a good idea to sense your weight in the middle of your body, in the area of your navel. It also may help you to imagine a vertical line from the ball position at address because to complete the backswing you want to get the upper half of your body behind that line. Your ability to do so will depend on your flexibility.

As far as sensing your weight in the middle of your body, imagine also a line extending from a point midway between your feet. This is a useful reference point because you will effectively turn toward that line at the top of your backswing; doing so will ensure that the shoulders and upper body are turned behind the ball line. Some people believe this is swaying or moving off the ball, but you will see at the top of my swing that I have stayed within my stance. Turning as I suggest will ensure that you avoid reverse pivoting.

If you distribute your weight evenly at address you will feel poised to swing. I could come up and try to push you over but I won't be able to topple you if you are settled into the ground nicely with your feet and standing tall at the other end. Try it now. You can easily achieve the feeling of being both grounded and tall. They go together, the one counterbalancing the other.

In assuming the stance, stand erect with your feet shoulder-width apart. Bend at the waist, all the while keeping your lower back straight and allowing your knees to bend.

The stability I have suggested will encourage just the right amount of flexibility in your knees. You will produce a slight angle in each knee with the kneecaps pitched forward ever so gently. You will also feel a stretch in your upper body as your lower back straightens and your rear end sticks out slightly.

Because you are about to *do* something—make a swing, that is—you will automatically gear up for the activity. Your body will react to the task it is facing, and you will generate some tension. I don't particularly like the word "tension," because it suggests stiffness, rigidity, or anxiety. By "tension" I mean a sensation of dynamic poise. You are about to engage in a physical act, and so you want to feel ready to spring to life. You want a posture that feels dynamic as opposed to static. It's the difference between standing in a line for a ticket at the movies and suddenly springing to attention when you notice an old friend who has just joined the line. A feeling of energy goes through your body. I'd like you to feel that energy as you stand to the ball. The correct position at address will help put you in the appropriate spirit for golf; this is what I mean by feeling energetic as you stand to the ball.

I have found that it is important to stand with the hips and shoulders square to the intended line. This is because I advocate a swing in which the shoulders and to a lesser degree the hips during the first part of the downswing, as you will see, are the primary motivating factors for power and direction.

Keeping the hips and shoulders square is more critical than keeping the feet dead square, although if there were no rotation during the swing—if we were constructed so that we could swing up and down in a perfect pendulum motion—dead-square feet would be ideal. However, there is rotation in the swing, and so it is okay to have the feet turned out slightly from square.

As long as you keep your hips and shoulders square to your intended line, you can stand with your feet probably 20 to 30 degrees open or shut without any noticeable effect on the efficiency of your swing. That said, I would rather have golfers stand slightly shut if they are not going to stand square, because this will get them into the backswing. Moe Norman is a very good example of this; he's one of the most consistent ball-strikers we have ever seen, yet he stands quite closed to his target line. It is also worth noting that as we age we lose flexibility, and so it doesn't hurt to stand slightly closed as we get older. I would also strongly suggest that younger people who may not be very flexible stand in this manner. But be careful not to close your shoulders even though you are standing closed with your feet. When I speak about "closed" I am speaking about the relation of your feet to your target line.

If you stand open to the ball it is more difficult to get into the backswing, because you must turn more; you have to force a backswing in this situation. I really don't like people to stand open. Having said this, I want to emphasize that standing closed is the lesser of two evils. If you're not going to stand square, that is, I would prefer that you stand closed rather than

Open stance   **Closed stance**

Square stance

open. As I have indicated, such gifted players as Lee Trevino and Fred Couples stand open to the ball, but they can develop back problems. It is also true that to stand open to the ball for most players is, I believe, to invite inconsistencies in ball flight. Even Trevino would be the first to tell you that his extremely open stance makes it difficult for him to hit the ball high. If you have a look at his left wrist, it is always shutting the club-face down through impact. But he understands this; he knows that if he wants to hit the ball high he has to hit a five- or six-wood. And he hits even those clubs low by comparison.

Couples, meanwhile, can be prone to hitting a big hook or a block to the right. Because he stands open to the ball and lifts the club up to start, he can sometimes drop it too much on the inside coming down and hit a serious hook. Again, he would be the first one to tell you this.

Still, there is no way I would ever suggest to Trevino or Couples that they change their setups. That would be preposterous. But I am saying to all golfers that if there are departments in which they lack consistency, perhaps by modifying the things that lead to inconsistency they might eradicate some of it. The important thing is that the golfer be aware of where he or she departs from standard form.

My preference after much experimentation and study is to turn both my left foot and right foot approximately 10 to 15

10° 90°   90° 10°

degrees from a 90-degree position to the target; I point my left foot toward the target slightly and the right away from it. I advocate this position because it creates more balance in the swing.

Although it has been fashionable in the past to keep the right foot at 90 degrees to the target line, I think that this is more restricting than helpful for many golfers. Unless you are extremely supple it is harder to make a full turn because your right foot placed in such a way will effectively block the turn. You can still build up the necessary torque or resistance in your right side by having the foot turned to the right 10 degrees.

I certainly agree with the principle of turning the upper body against the resistance of the lower body. But we are also trying to increase the arc of the swing, a major source of power as long as it is under control. The longer the arc—the *wider* the swing—under control of the plane, the more powerful and penetrating the ball flight. And here's the benefit of turning the right foot out: *It allows for an increase in swing width, as it makes it easier to take the club back a greater distance, to stretch back farther.* It is also easier to create a bigger shoulder turn this way, *as long as your lower half remains stable.*

Everything you have done during your setup is meant to ensure that you give yourself the highest probability that these positive attributes will be part of your swing. There is no substitute for these details as you work over the long term to build an efficient swing.

Pointing the right foot out will not compromise lower-body stability. I originally felt it might, but practice proved otherwise. I came to understand how important it was to create width in my swing, and so I gradually realized how much sense it made to turn the right foot out as I do now. But I never would have gone ahead with this had it reduced control of lower-body stability. It did nothing of the kind. My lower body was as quiet as I wanted it to be—a stable support to my upper body. And I had also set myself up to increase the width of my swing. I might add that if you point the right foot out you will also get the added benefit of your right knee rotating ever so slightly during the backswing; it does not lose its flex or stability, but it does rotate slightly in association with your upper-body rotation.

Now that we've considered the lower half of the body at address, what about the upper half? First, of course, ensure that you have the correct shoulder tilt in your posture, which is influenced by how far you stand from the ball and the club you are using. There will be more shoulder tilt with a driver than with the irons because you have more weight on your right foot at address with a driver—whereas with short irons there is more weight on the left foot, which lowers the left shoulder. With the driver you want 60 percent of your weight on your right side. With your five-iron you want your weight 50-50, and with your short irons you want your weight 60 percent on your left side and 40 percent on your right. Allow your arms to hang naturally. You will notice that you create tension in your shoulders if you raise the hands at all. You want your shoulders to be as relaxed as possible. Also think to keep your chin up because this will enable your left shoulder to pass underneath your chin at the top of your swing. I've always tended to have my chin down. It's something I've fought during my career. Ensure also that a line drawn across your shoulders is square to your target line. This will dramatically increase your chances of making a shoulder-conscious swing that at the same time generates the proper plane.

An efficient setup can do so much for your game. Pay attention to it and you will be well on your way to much-improved ball-striking. Stand in front of a mirror and concentrate on the key points below while visually confirming that you are incorporating them. Then gradually ignore the mirror so that you can acquire the sensations of the proper setup. Have a friend check you from time to time.

Key Points

1. Feet planted so you can feel them braced on the ground.
2. Slight flex in knees.
3. Feet turned out 10 to 15 degrees.
4. Lower back straight, tilt from hips.
5. Arms hanging freely, no tension in shoulders.
6. Weight evenly distributed.
7. Chin up.

chapter six

THE TAKEAWAY AND BACKSWING

David Leadbetter and I worked for many years on the takeaway and backswing, and we agree that these segments of the swing occur, actually, in three parts: the first move from address to a position where your hands, arms, and shoulders have moved the shaft together in a unit to what I like to call the eight o'clock position, allied with some slight forearm rotation; the second part, to the ten o'clock position, where you have introduced more rotary motion; and the final segment in the series, where you complete the backswing by turning your shoulders 90 degrees to the target. This is the classic "back to the target" position at the top of your backswing.

The Takeaway

To the Eight O'Clock Position

In the ideal takeaway, the hands, arms, and shoulders together move the clubhead for approximately the first three feet. Nothing else moves; your lower half remains in place as it supports the motion in your upper half. You maintain the relationship between your hands, arms, and shoulders that you had at address—the triangle set up there—and move the clubhead back those three feet.

I like to think of the angle or slight cup that I create with the back of my left hand at address as staying constant to this eight o'clock position—in fact, throughout the backswing—and also to think of the back of my left hand as representing the clubface. The toe of the clubhead starts to open up during the takeaway, but I do this not with my hands but by rotating my shoulders. A useful checkpoint is that you must maintain the angle your arms and shaft form at address to the eight o'clock position. Notice also that if you keep your left hand in the same position as at address, you will have introduced a slight rotation in your left arm to get the shaft on plane. This forearm rotation encourages the constancy of the left-hand position.

Notice also that your hips and legs have remained static through the eight o'clock position. They will do their part shortly, but they have little role during the initial takeaway other than supporting your upper body.

This first move should be done as smoothly as possible. Even though I have an upbeat tempo and my takeaway appears quick, I always try to make it smooth. Here is where video can be of such immense assistance. Examine my swing at this stage and you will see that I have simply moved my hands, arms, and shoulders back together. My move is relatively quick, but it is also smooth. You can further confirm the integrity of this takeaway move by examining swing sequences of most tour players; we all make this first move fluidly, although there are always slight variations to it.

To the Ten O'Clock Position

Having reached the eight o'clock position you will find that your arms and torso begin to pull the hips and then the legs with them while you maintain a good right knee flex. It is important to be conscious of the right knee flex at this stage and to maintain it, because losing the flex by allowing the right knee to straighten can cause many problems. You must remember that you turn around a flexed right knee. There will be movement in the knee—the rotation I spoke of in the previous chapter—as it must not be rigid. But you do maintain its flex as you move to the ten o'clock position. And because your

Correct rotation around the knee   **No rotation**

upper body is pulling your lower body, you will feel that your left knee is being pulled behind the ball.

As your arms and torso pull the legs and hips, you will be rotating the club onto plane with your left wrist still in its constant position. You should at this stage start setting or cocking the wrists. When the left arm is at the interim nine o'clock position, or parallel to the ground, the shaft of the club should be almost vertical but obviously still on plane. Somebody standing behind you should be able to draw a straight line from your hands through the sternum to your target; this is an excellent checkpoint that, as you grasp the picture, will help you attain the proper ten o'clock position.

To the Top of the Backswing
At the ten o'clock position of your left arm, the club should be fully set, or the wrists fully hinged. The shoulders should be at about 80 degrees to the target. From here you will feel that the whole left side of your body is being stretched.

I would like to say something here about the width of the backswing, an aspect that I found increasingly important as my thinking about the efficient swing matured.

I had grown up thinking that you wanted to keep the right elbow tucked in during the backswing, and that this would help control the club and body. It also made some sense when I was swinging the club on a more upright or steeper plane, as I could have hurt myself by allowing my right elbow and arm to follow that plane. It was easier on me, and more orthodox, I thought, to keep the right elbow folded in during the backswing.

But around 1988 I changed my thinking. By this time I was playing steadier golf, if not yet winning. I saw that keeping my right elbow in restricted my arc, making it too narrow, and it didn't add to the feeling of a controlled swing that I was seeking. On the contrary, I felt bound up and under a hold, not free. It was strange, because I had swung the club almost wildly in my early days, up high and steep, but at the same time had restricted the motion in my right side. I realized that I was not balancing the use of my left and right sides; I had curbed

**Freedom in the right
arm and elbow**

**Restricting the right
arm and elbow**

my right side too much. This made no sense to me after I improved the shape of my shoulder plane, and it was about then that I began to think about letting my right arm move with some freedom.

Just that single idea has made a vast difference to my ball-striking. My arc widened considerably, and so I had that much more time to generate clubhead speed. Equally important, I felt my swing was more robust. Another positive effect was that by letting my right arm go I brought my right shoulder more into play, which was in order because I was building a more shoulder-controlled swing—a swing controlled by both shoulders, that is, not one more than the other. Now I was able to rotate not only my left shoulder but also my right shoulder.

Allowing myself to widen out my right side also made it easier to turn my shoulders to the 90-degree-to-the-target position and complete my backswing. And once you've reached the ten o'clock position, the only thing left to do to complete the backswing is to turn your left shoulder under the chin and make sure that you get to the 90-degree position. Stay shoulder-conscious and allow the left shoulder to move behind an imaginary line that runs out from your body halfway between your feet. By moving your left shoulder in connection with the right knee that stays flexed, you will create the tension—the stored-up power—that you will release through body rotation on your downswing.

Make sure that the left shoulder stays high, that it does not lose its height. If you do this correctly you can be certain that your weight will transfer correctly from your left to your right side and that you will never reverse-pivot. You will notice that you have transferred your weight from 50 percent on each side at address to 5 percent on your left side and 95 percent on your right side at the top of the backswing. This ratio that I am describing occurs with the driver and the longer clubs, but as you progress down through the clubs to a nine-iron, for instance, you only require maybe 40 percent on the left side and 60 percent on the right at the top. This is because you aren't trying to hit the ball a long way with your short irons. You are more concerned with accuracy than power here.

Now you are wound up and ready to spring into action on your downswing. All that power—the arc of fire—that you have developed during your backswing has to be released. Now that you have assembled the materials, it's time to let the package do its work where it counts—on the downswing and through the ball. You have created a powerful, athletic position from which you will reverse direction and start the downswing.

Backswing Drills

Takeaway Drill

Place two clubs or shafts on the ground parallel to each other and assume your normal address position with a third club (I like to use a five- or six-iron to practice this drill). One of the clubs on the ground should be pointing to your target and right on your toes. The other club should be exactly on the line that you will draw the club you are using back on. Another way to look at this is that the club on that line will be underneath the head of the club you are swinging.

Take the club away to the eight o'clock position. Notice that the clubhead at the eight o'clock position is inside the farther shaft on the ground. A common problem here is that the golfer keeps the club square too long. A good checkpoint is that a measurement of the distance of the butt of the club from your body at address will be the same when taken as the club passes your right thigh as you hit the eight o'clock position.

Do this drill as often as you can. It will be of value in helping you feel the correct positions to hit on the takeaway.

Preset Drill
Place two shafts where we have placed the lines. One shaft should be three or four inches outside the ball, the other between your toes and the ball. Address the ball. Bring the

club parallel to the ground only by cocking your wrists. You should feel a stretch in your right wrist. Make sure your left wrist is in the same cupped position as during your normal address. Your hands should be at a point between the ball and your feet, while the shaft of your club should point to your target.

From this position, turn your shoulders behind the afore-mentioned imaginary line, keeping in mind the plane at the ten o'clock position. Then swing smoothly through the ball. Please don't try to hit the ball too hard in this drill or as far as you would normally with the club in your hands. I have always done this drill with a seven- or eight-iron. When I started working with David Leadbetter I hit eight hundred balls a day using this drill. It was a wonderful corrective to my faulty backswing positions and set me on the track of a proper plane.

Baseball Bat Drill

I often found it difficult to picture the plane of the backswing while using a golf club. This is because, like most golfers, I am more conscious of the clubhead and what it is doing than of what the shaft is doing. David and I had spoken when we started to work about the advantage of using a baseball bat to improve muscle tone, and I took the idea a step further. I now carry a baseball bat wherever I go. I painted the bat black on one half so that it would provide a visual image of my back-swing and help improve my shaft plane. The contrast between the painted or darkened part of the bat and the light part has been a tremendous help. I also found it helpful to have some-thing without a head on it so I would be more conscious of the shaft plane and not what the head was doing.

Set up in your normal address position and observe the two halves of the bat. As you go into your backswing from eight to ten o'clock, feel the bat rotating and also that when you get to the ten o'clock position the two halves are on plane. As you become accustomed to the bat you will be able to transfer the image when you are swinging a golf club.

Width Drill

In 1988, David Leadbetter and I noticed that my right elbow tended to stay close to my body throughout my backswing. In essence what was happening was that my arc going back was shortened because my elbow did not move correctly in the backswing. A narrow arc resulted, and I subsequently had difficulty in creating clubhead speed through impact. This led to a very steep angle of attack on the downswing, which left huge gaping holes in the ground that looked more like mortar craters than divots.

David figured that if we could stop the right elbow from folding too quickly in the backswing, I would get the feel of what we were looking for. The first gadget he came up with was an inflatable water wing normally seen on toddlers at the swimming pool, not on a Florida golf course. However, as I was David's number one guinea pig, I put this on and hit some balls. In a very short period my divots had shallowed out and my ball flight had lowered; the water wing was working. Not long after this, David invented (with the help of an engineer) a device that helps put the right arm into the preferred position. Although I own five of these, I still carry the water wing in my golf bag at all times. The device has very frequently drawn amused comments on the practice tee at PGA Tour events and at Lake Nona, where I did much of my work with David.

This, along with the right-arm drill I describe later, will help you develop a sense of what the right side should be doing in the swing—by helping you create width in your backswing while widening your arc and shallowing out your downswing.

chapter seven

THE DOWNSWING

As the backswing has taken you to a position where, as it were, you have made an investment in potential returns, the downswing is where you cash in. You have prepared yourself to move through the ball with commitment to your target, and everything you have done until now has made it easier for you to do so. In many ways the downswing is a reaction to the backswing. But it's a reaction with a difference.

The downswing consists, as I see it, of two parts. In the first segment you initiate the downswing with a slight lateral move and rotation of your left hip toward your target. This in coordination with the pull of the hands drops the club into what I feel is a slot, and, as you will see later in the relevant section, this is accompanied by a sitting or squatting onto the right knee. In essence what we are trying to do is to store the power we have created in the backswing. In the second segment the left hip and left shoulder now clear as hard and fast as possible. This allows the right side, that is, the hip, shoulder, and arm, to release powerfully. This in turn will let your right side explode through the ball at the correct moment, releasing all that stored-up energy that you have created in the backswing. Again these segments crystallize into a single fluid motion, even though it is helpful to think of them as two separate actions. You will see this when I examine more closely the moving parts of the body.

It may seem a controversial assertion to you that the downswing occurs in two parts, because we most often think of the downswing as one fluid motion. But in breaking the downswing down I think you will see that it does occur in two segments. I am not suggesting you think of these segments on the course; the drills I will provide are there to help you feel the sensations of the two-part downswing.

The downswing is not one continuous motion from the top; there is a certain amount of wait in the lower body before everything turns through the ball. The way to feel that wait is to keep the flex in the right knee while squatting onto it. The downswing is not a single, fluid "whoosh" from the top, then, but more of a pull and sit motion followed by a rotation and release. The secret is not to think that the downswing is just a blur of hips, legs, arms, hands, and clubhead coming down. It isn't. There is a sense of purpose from the top. You have to feel that the club is being worked down in the correct sequence even as you are letting it go on the course. To practice the downswing on the range is to get the feel of what should happen.

Step One: Left Hip Rotation

From the last chapter you know that you have reached the end of your backswing when your shoulders have turned approximately 90 degrees to your target. You will feel a nice stretch all the way down your left side and perhaps in the upper half of your left arm to the shoulder (depending on how supple you are). Your left shoulder will be touching or under your chin, while your spine angle, which you created at address, will remain as in your setup. The rotation of your upper body to 90 degrees will also have pulled your left hip to where it is rotated approximately 40 to 45 degrees (again, depending on your suppleness). I mention this again because while the efficient swing is one in which the upper body turns against the resistance of the lower body, still there is movement in the lower body. The important key is to maintain the flexibility in your right knee; move it too much or straighten it and you will lose the torque or dynamic tension. But if you keep it steady and allow your left side to work into your right on the backswing, you will feel your weight on the inside of your right leg at the top of the swing. You have stretched, and as you identify with the sensations you will come to sense when you have completed your backswing.

Now it is time to unwind the elasticity you have created. You initiate the downswing by making a slight lateral move toward your target; at the same time you rotate the hips back toward the target. Be careful not to do this violently, because it will lead to many complications, as I will explain. This is a smooth continuous motion that takes you from backswing to downswing and causes the chain reaction. Your torso will now respond, thereby pulling your shoulders at the start of the downswing. This is natural, and you need not think about the shoulder motion at this stage.

While we have said that the downswing is all but instinctive—a reaction to the backswing—still plenty is going on, as is apparent in swing sequence photos. I will speak of these details and have tried to understand them as they apply to my swing. But try not to think of the many details on the course. This is just to provide you with a better understanding in case you have any downswing faults. Remember, you need only do what we are highlighting; these are the essential principles of an efficient swing.

I have found it useful to break the swing down into each independent segment, and see the following segments as the major moving parts of the swing: the hips, the shoulders, the hands, and the clubhead. Here are the distances these parts travel to complete my full backswing; but remember, this is what I feel they do for me, and I am six feet tall. The same relationship applies to you whatever your height, but is also dependent on the length of club you have in your hands. In this instance I am describing a driver. To achieve a complete full backswing turn, the left hip will probably move or track four inches, and my left shoulder will track eight inches as I complete my backswing. My hands, meanwhile, will move approximately six feet (seventy-two inches) and my clubhead alone some fourteen or fifteen feet (about 180 inches). You can take these measurements yourself by having a friend help you or by using video stop-action. If you move the hips too violently and fast in the downswing—remember, they have only four inches to return to address—your hands and clubhead will never be able to catch up. It is for this reason that the hips are the controlling force in determining the speed of your downswing. Move them too fast and nothing can catch up. Move them too slowly and everything catches up too quickly.

As I mentioned, the left hip initiates the downswing with a slight lateral move. But the hip slows down after this first move and allows the hands and arms to drop into a position where the right elbow is in front of the right hip. You must feel

Hips, shoulders, hands, and clubhead

The major segments of the swing . . .

a slight squatting or sitting onto the right knee in this first part, as it is this sitting or squatting that slows the hip rotation momentarily and allows the hands to catch up. Sam Snead did this so beautifully in his downswing.

You want to get your left hip back to a square or semisquare position to allow your hands to catch up. The left hip then rotates, and the hands release. If I turn my left hip all the way right from the top of my swing, my hands cannot catch up.

In the late 1960s and early 1970s it was fashionable to use the hips and legs more than what I believe is required in the swing, and a player had to flip the club over with his wrists in

HANDS
6 feet

CLUBHEAD
14–15 feet

SHOULDERS
8 inches

HIPS
4 inches

. . . moving to the top

order to make square contact with the ball. This would result in inconsistencies and called for a lot of practice and feel. This also resulted in the high-hands, reverse "C" position finish that was a trademark of golfers then, putting an unnecessary amount of strain on the lower back. I tired quickly when I swung that way.

Here's an image I like to use that helps set up the entire move through the ball and also helps restrict too fast a left hip move at the start of the downswing: Picture and feel your spine angle at address and try to maintain it. Many golfers wreck their swings because of an impulse to get back to the ball too quickly, or hit from the top. This results in a spinning of the hips and a raising up of the body as the golfer tries to hit the ball from his full height. The shot that results is a huge mishit slice. It seems difficult, however, for many players to maintain their spine angle all the way through the swing. Working the hips too quickly is

**Squatting onto the right knee while
maintaining spine angle**

one of the many mistakes that golfers try to compensate for in the downswing. Along with trying to maintain my spine angle throughout the swing, I also try to picture the shaft of my club approaching the ball on the same angle that I set it at address.

Your chances of making this happen are dramatically enhanced when you make the correct backswing, as you will be in position to move the left hip just the right amount and speed. You don't want to spin the hip. You want to move it laterally and to rotate it slightly. There is a significant difference between rotating the hip and spinning it.

If you spin your hips, which I think of as rotating them too quickly—I say "hips" because when you rotate the left hip the right hip follows—it will be very difficult for your arms and hands to catch up; they will get stuck behind you. But if you learn to rotate the left hip the correct amount and at the correct speed, and then feel that you are slowing it down by squatting, you will give your upper body a chance to catch up and reach the position where your right elbow and right hand have passed the right hip.

Another way to look at the left hip move is that you turn it from its 40-to-45-degree position at the top of the backswing to about 5 degrees short of square. This goes a long way in enabling your hands and arms to drop down, and remember you have created speed by going from 40–45 degrees to 5 degrees. Although your hips may be slowing down, you still have a huge amount of momentum with the upper half. Now you are in a position to unleash that stored-up power in both halves through the ball.

By rotating your left hip you begin to turn your legs, especially the left knee, and to a lesser degree your upper body. I think of the left hip rotation as a modest but quick move to initiate the downswing. I have a quick tempo, which is natural for me. You will find your own best tempo, which will probably reflect the way you move about on and off the course. The important consideration is to know when to release the hip—not too early and not too late. It's all a matter of synchronizing the various elements in motion, which requires practice.

Another positive effect of rotating and then slowing the left hip is that you will be able to create a huge amount of clubhead speed at the bottom—at impact—because you will have waited just long enough for the clubhead to catch up. Had you overrotated your hips, then your hands and subsequently the clubhead would not be able to get to the ball in time. There would then be a huge dissipation of speed at this stage. Instead of accelerating as you hit the ball, the clubhead would slow down, and you would lose power. Conversely, had you not rotated at all and cast, or thrown, the club from the top, you would get a tremendous amount of speed at the top section of your swing, but then it would slow down well before you reach impact.

In the first instance—overrotating your hips—the club would be too far behind you, and you would have to come over the top of the ball with your shoulders to compensate. In the latter instance—not using your hips at all—you would get the club too far inside on the way down and have to use your arms and hands to flip the club over in order to get it back to square. Both of these examples are extreme. The extent to which a golfer falls toward either extreme defines him as being either a legs or a hands swinger. Let me expand on that briefly. Hands and arms swingers generally hit the ball flat-footed, while leg swingers are well off their right foot through impact.

You can see that I am advocating that you become a balanced swinger of the golf club by not letting your hips overpower or overcontrol your downswing. If your hips take over, you will lose the potential speed you created during your backswing. If you don't use your hips at all and ask the arms and hands to do all the work, again you'll lose speed. If you use the hips just enough, the clubhead will be accelerating right up to contact.

Now that we have examined both the constructive and destructive aspects of left hip motion, I would like to return for a moment to the relationship of the various parts I mentioned before. I think that most of us tend to use our hips too quickly on the way down, which as I have said is a problem. Some people do need to speed their hips up; they appear wooden, almost frozen in place. Generally, they have not reached the right position at the top or they have reverse-pivoted. They therefore feel they must spin their hips to make something happen. As ever, getting the backswing right will help you avoid these problems.

This matter of hip movement further shows that getting things right at the start—at address—makes it much easier for the correct things to happen during the downswing. Imagine, for instance, that you address the ball with a decidedly open or closed stance. You will then have to speed up or restrict your hip turn. But set up properly and you need only the minimum to gain the maximum.

Sometimes I find myself thinking of my hip movement in terms of miles per hour. I like to feel that my hips work at about three to four miles per hour—that lets me achieve maximum clubhead speed. If I move them in the range of five to six miles per hour, then the shoulders, hands, and clubhead lose speed dramatically. And if I throttle back to one to two miles per hour, I find that I become too arms-and-hands-oriented in order to compensate for what feels like a lack of body speed, and too much arm and hand speed when not synchronized with the hip motion can ruin the swing. Again, I'm looking for that balance . . . not too fast and not too slow.

It took some years before I understood exactly what the hips do. I watched tapes of Bobby Jones and studied Byron Nelson's and Jack Nicklaus's swings. While observing Sam Snead, I took note of the bow in his legs and the squatting position of his right knee when he started down, and realized that by bowing his legs he keeps his left hip from going too fast. Ben Hogan did it slightly differently but still maintained that powerful sit-down appearance.

The sit-down sensation also helps you stay lower through the ball but still with fairly level hips, another key to consistency. The best ball-strikers don't all have this sit-down look; they have figured out some other way to slow the hips down through this stage. For me, though, this sit-down position is a wonderful image and an easy one to explain. If you create this position while maintaining your spine angle, you will get the club coming in low as it approaches the ball. The result is a shallow, long divot, which is a superb litmus test for effective ball-striking. You lose much acceleration and power and have no control of your ball flight if you come in steeply. A deep, gouging divot will surely follow. Golfers who generate such divots are the ones the grounds staff get to know really well.

In my earlier days when I worked my hips too hard, I would lose my spine angle and thereby steepen my plane. I used to take divots so deep in soft ground that the irrigation pipes were never safe.

Spinning the left hip violently will have other harmful effects as well, of which leaving the club behind, as mentioned, is the most likely. You cannot catch up and will hit all kinds of bad shots ranging from a snap hook if your hands release too early to a shank if you hold on too long.

Ben Crenshaw sometimes exemplifies the problem I am discussing. He has a lovely, flowing backswing, but then his hips snap to the left side and he leaves the club well behind. From this position he can react by holding on and leaving the club open, thereby blocking the shot. Or in compensation he might turn his hands sharply to square up the clubface; the pull hook results. That's why Ben has always played his best when his tempo is very slow. He can then control his hand movement. But if he gets too quick early in the downswing, as his teacher Harvey Penick always told him not to do, then he hits a variety of bad shots.

Step Two: Rotate and Release

You have now initiated the downswing with the left hip, and the left shoulder should be following. It's important to be aware of the position your shoulders were in at address, because they will have to pass through that position on your way through impact. But the question is, when do the shoulders pass through?

The motion of the left hip continues the chain reaction of the swing. Your hands drop to a position just below your right shoulder, while your hips will soon be almost in the square position; but they are not rotating now as you achieve the squat look in your lower body by sitting on your right knee. The shoulders are still in a closed position relative to your target, but at the same time you have pulled the club in front of your right shoulder to the position where your elbow is above your right hip. This is important.

It is very common for fine, strong ball-strikers to have their hands in front of them. By "in front" I mean that their hands are within the width of their shoulders. Should the club get behind you (this is where the hands are now behind your right shoulder) it is because your shoulders have rotated too quickly, thereby leaving your hands in a weak position and decreasing their ability to deliver the punch you require through impact.

Think about a boxer throwing a punch. He does not punch from behind him but from in front of his right or left shoulder. Or consider a tennis player on his forehand; he certainly does not hit the ball with his arm behind his shoulder. No, you want your arms in front of you as you approach impact and unleash the stored-up power through the ball.

So it is that the club continues to move down until the right elbow is above the right hip. Your shoulders have started to get close to their address position. The shoulders should still be slightly shut and pointing to the right of your target. It is at this point that you must think about rotating your left hip in tandem with your left shoulder through their address positions, allowing the right side—that is, the shoulder, hip, and arm— to release the club with a tremendous amount of speed through impact. The harder and faster you can do this from this point, the more efficient a golfer you will be. Hogan explained in his book how he wished he had three right hands to apply more power at the ball. This was because once he reached this position he knew he could move as hard and fast as he wanted to and would still hit the ball squarely. In fact, the harder and faster he went through here the straighter and farther the ball went.

Here is a superb feeling to strive for as you are pouring the power on through the ball. While your left side is opening up and clearing as you come into impact, feel that you can now hit the ball as hard as you can with your right arm and shoulders, and that you are now covering the ball with your right shoulder and are chasing the ball down the target line with it. This is an exciting sensation that I am always striving for and that I hope I can create to the end of my golfing days. And I wish the same for you.

Let that right shoulder go, then, and chase the ball down the line. You have created the set you need at the top of your backswing, and you have maintained it by pulling down and waiting as your left side opens up to impact. You have kept your feet firmly on the ground through the first part of the downswing, and then as you rotate and release the club in the second part your right heel will come up off the ground and you will finish with all the weight on the left foot. This is because the momentum of your body rotation has led your right side to this classic finish position. You may feel that you want to take a step forward with your right foot toward the target as a result of this momentum. This is a good feeling to have, as it means you have transferred your weight correctly. The angle of your shaft at impact as you release the set in the wrists is the same as it was at address, and your head at impact remains behind the ball, where you had it at address. You have rotated your upper body around your lower, and now you are being carried along by the forces that you created and that have increased during your swing. Let yourself go; feel free to do so, because you have been in the correct positions so there is no need to hold back. At the end you will feel that you have expended all of your energy through the clubhead, and you will finish solidly on your left foot with your right foot up on its toes.

Left Shoulder and Left Side Opening Through Impact

Notice that my left shoulder is still almost square to the target, and that my right side is now unloading.

Look how quickly my left side has rotated from the position at left, allowing my right side to completely unload.

Here my right side has released through to the target and is chasing after the ball.

You will also feel that you have been the source of a controlled explosion through the ball. All the forces have come together at the exact appropriate moment—through the ball, that is. You will have done everything possible to produce a perfectly synchronized swing. Robert Baker, a talented young teacher who worked with David Leadbetter and who helps me, has a nice way of defining the synchronized swing. The great secret in golf, Robert says, is when you have synchronized your moves so that the left hip finishes at the same time as the left shoulder, the right shoulder, the grip end of the club, the shaft, and the head. All of these forces coalesce at the ball. It's a fantastic feeling that I am always striving for. It is an ideal state. This is the feeling that brings us back to the golf course day after day. Of course, we cannot reach this level of excellence—of perfection, really—time after time. But the idea is to work toward it over time. That's the way to improvement. That's the way to get to the point where you will finish your swing and observe the ball flying on a penetrating trajectory, streaking toward the target.

Downswing Drills

Right Arm Drill

This drill will help to teach you the feeling of how the right side works in the downswing, and will also help to create more width in the backswing. Remember that we want to add width to the swing by allowing the right arm and elbow to move away from the body on the way back, but they will come in close on the way down. This drill also promotes the proper use of the right shoulder and by doing so helps inhibit sliding forward or overrotating with the left hip. It also helps you make a better turn away from the ball and then through impact, simply because it frees you up; the right arm begins to travel on its own track and provides a wonderful feeling of freedom and release.

I love this drill, which is why you will often see me on the course taking practice swings with my right arm only. I think most of us are stronger in our right side, and therefore it is only natural that when you are under pressure and tighten up slightly, swinging the club with the right arm may help you to a freer and unencumbered movement.

Here's how to do the drill. Assume your normal address position, then place your left hand in your left pocket or on your left hip. Swing the club back to the top of the backswing position with your right arm only, allowing the wrist to set or cock at the top, then let it swing through the ball without trying to hit the ball hard. This drill should be done as smoothly as possible and with very little force. You will feel yourself carried through by the momentum of the club past the ball. Feel the weight of the clubhead as it falls and let that weight flow through the ball; the club swings and you go along for the ride. You should feel that your right shoulder is now loaded, and you will also feel a slight stretching sensation under the shoulder blade. By turning your shoulder fully you take the strain out of the right arm and wrist, thereby allowing the club to swing on an easier and freer path. You will be amazed at the feelings that you will get when you're not holding or swinging the club with both hands. Again, please do not try to hit the ball too hard; this drill is strictly to develop timing and feel. Remember that with only one hand on the club, you may injure your wrist or shoulder if you try to swing too hard. Try to be sensible at first and then build up to a stronger swing with one hand later, when you feel comfortable with the increased velocity.

At first you will probably want to *hit* the ball with your right arm and hand, and you will very likely hit the first few shots fat or heavy. Most of the time this is because you are jumping off your right side or trying to turn your hips too quickly from the top. This is what we call "hitting from the top." But after a few swings you should feel that you can just let the clubhead fall, and as a result of not forcing you will make solid contact with the ball. You will also feel a sense of timing or waiting for the club to be in a position before you turn your body and hips. Move the hips or body too fast and you'll have a tough time getting the club back squarely to the ball. When you get it just right, you will be surprised how far you can hit the ball with such little effort.

As you continue to do this drill, you will strengthen the muscles in your right shoulder and begin to feel a little of what "covering the ball" feels like. You will feel more balanced, because you will be using your right side and shoulder as well as your left. You will derive the added benefit of slowing your swing down, particularly in the transition area from backswing to downswing. I have always had a tendency to swing the club quickly and sometimes I lose the feel of the clubhead, and this drill or practice often helps me regain some feel.

Incorporate this drill in your practice sessions as often as you can. I like to use a seven-iron and to place the ball on a tee. I strongly suggest putting the ball on a tee, as this encourages you to swing through and not at the ball; you won't feel the need to try to pick or scoop the ball up off the turf.

I have always had a very strong left side, and this drill helped me be aware of my right side more, something I think would benefit most golfers. But then I went to work on my right side and essentially retrained it. After having done this drill for a while—probably no more than a month—I began to feel that my left side was guiding or steering until the exact moment when it would get out of the way and clear so that the right side could pour on the power through the ball. I can assure you that when done properly this drill will really accelerate your feel. This is precisely what a good drill should do.

Closed Stance Drill
Here is another fantastic drill for helping you feel the correct move through the ball. It does wonders in helping you learn the feeling of "chasing down the line," or sweeping through the ball with your right side. I have always hit the ball best when I have the feeling of the right side firing very hard through impact as the left gets out of the way. In a sense, I want to feel that my right side is overpowering my left as I come through the ball. This drill has probably helped me more than any other that I have tried over the years. I have seen the results of this drill over time and have probably spent more hours working on it than any of the others. If I had to choose one drill that could cure a multitude of faults in the swing, this one would be it. In fact, just about every day when I warm up on the practice tee, or in the hotel room in the morning, I try to swing as many times as possible with this drill. It helps me create the right feelings and keeps my lower body really soft and passive. My good friend Mark McNulty has been playing with a slightly closed stance on all his clubs because he feels it keeps him from moving his hip out too quickly.

Take your normal setup. Now move your left foot a little closer to the ball and slightly behind it. Now you want to pull your right foot back and point the toe out to the two o'clock position. Try to keep your feet about twelve to fifteen inches apart and make sure that you are aimed at least 60 degrees right of your target with your feet. Your hips will be slightly shut, but you must make sure that your shoulders are square to your intended target. Do not try to hit the ball too hard, just swing the club and try to feel what is happening. I do this drill with a seven-iron and even then I'm only trying to hit the ball at 60 percent of my normal strength.

Now swing to the top and let instinct take over. Your objective is to swing through the ball, not at it. Because the ball is slightly outside your left foot, you will need to go after it with your right shoulder. Keep the left side quiet and feel yourself swinging the right shoulder out and over the ball. And be sure to keep as level as possible; keep your right side high. Try not to let your left shoulder dip in the backswing, and keep your shoulders swinging freely through the ball. If your hips are working too hard you will not be able to bring the club back squarely to the ball. This drill is particularly effective for slicers. I have seen dramatic improvements when people who slice the ball do this drill.

Again, use a tee and do this drill twenty times or so before you try to hit with a normal stance. Every so often as you get used to the drill, try a longer club. The ball flight will be straighter than normal, not curving much one way or the other. And also observe the way your chest opens up to the target through the ball. You will come to sense how little restriction you require in your swing. You ought to feel a free-wheeling sensation as you sweep through the ball in a sort of controlled and balanced abandon.

Hitting Balls with Feet Together for Balance
This is another very good practice method that many players use. It helps to promote stability and balance and is very simple.

Place your feet together and hit balls with an eight-iron to start, again not swinging too hard. As you become more confident, progress through the bag up to your woods. I am sure you will be pleasantly surprised at how little force your legs need apply. Your legs do create power in the swing, but not through force and aggression, rather through support, stability, and then speed at the right moment. Note that though your feet are together, you still come off your right side as you come through the ball.

Baseball Bat Drill

I have mentioned the baseball bat before, and suggested a drill with it to practice your takeaway and swing plane. It is also useful here, and I prefer it to swinging a heavy club, which I think places an enormous amount of strain on the wrists. A baseball bat is heavier but more evenly weighted. I feel that it is a good idea when making changes to swing something heavier than a golf club. This will accelerate your feel and build new habits more quickly.

To do this drill, take your normal setup and swing the baseball bat as you would a golf club. Picture the shaft plane on the way back and rotate your arms and shoulders to keep the two halves of the baseball bat on plane. Then try to see if you can match the plane on the way down, squaring the line at impact, then match the plane on the follow-through so you create a mirror image of the backswing and downswing. In effect, the line down the middle is where your clubhead should be. In this way you are making yourself aware not only of the plane but also of the clubhead.

Towel Under Left Arm for Connection

I am sure you have heard the word "connection" used in analyses of the swing. It's a useful word to describe the marrying of the arms and hands to the body throughout the swing. The goal is to have them work together as a unit rather than independently or against one another.

A good way to help feel this is to hit half-shots with a nine-iron or wedge while keeping a towel under your left arm. If at any stage your left arm works away from your body, the towel will fall, thereby indicating that you have lost connection.

Remember this is just a drill to create feel, and you don't want to hit the ball too hard. Just swing the club.

Take a small hand towel or facecloth and place it under your left biceps close to your armpit. Now before you hit any balls, just swing back and forth with a half swing and you will feel the arms swinging in unison with the body. When you feel that the towel will not fall, place a ball on a tee and try to repeat the motion. You will probably find that on your first effort with the ball in front of you, the towel will fall. You are trying to hit the ball too hard. If you normally hit your nine-iron 110 yards, then the distance you are looking for with this drill is about 50 yards maximum. I suggest that at first you try to hit it only 30 yards, then build up from there.

As you progress with this drill, start each practice session with the short irons and then go up slowly to the middle irons. But you don't want to do this drill with more than a seven-iron, because the momentum in the longer clubs will take your arms away from the body after impact. Again you can see this drill is meant to create a feel for what you should be conscious of in the swing.

Hitting Balls Out of the Bunker for Stability

Use a long iron off a good lie in a fairway bunker. The reason for this drill is that it helps you learn to avoid using your legs too violently from the top of your swing. If you are too active with your legs, you will lose your footing before impact. You won't be able to get back to the ball if you lose your footing early.

chapter eight

THE SHORT GAME

If you have a good short game you have a powerful ally. Feeling confident that you can save strokes around the green is a wonderful asset, a tremendous mental boost hole after hole and one that builds as you go along in your development as a complete golfer. Time and time again I have seen golfers save their rounds with their short games when they weren't hitting the ball well. It's a great feeling to be confident that you can get the ball up and down when you miss a green. I've had that feeling fairly regularly during my career, but like all golfers I want it more. A strong short game keeps a round going, and can definitely mean the difference between winning and losing.

For instance, I would not have won the 1994 British Open without getting up and down for par on the thirteenth and fourteenth holes in the last round. On the thirteenth I hit my approach over the back of the green and had to hit a high lob shot with my 60-degree wedge because I didn't have much green to work with. And on the fourteenth, where I went over the green by ten yards, I had to play a low, running shot up a bank with a seven-iron. In both cases I employed the same principles, although I was required to hit two totally different shots.

The Basic Chip Shot

To me the basic principle of chipping, and of the short game as a whole, is to get the ball on the green. This might seem obvious, but many golfers try to get too fancy with a chip shot and often leave the ball short or run it through the green, particularly on difficult shots. You don't want to have to hit two chip shots. There are exceptions, as I will point out. But in just about all cases, remember: Chip the ball so that it stays on the green. You want your next shot to be a putt, not another chip shot, or worse, a bunker shot.

Given this strategy, the idea is to get the ball on the green as soon as possible and use as much of the green as possible. Obviously there are times when not much green is available because of an intervening bunker or a pin cut near an edge. In such a case make sure you hit the ball far enough so that it won't have any chance of finding any intervening hazard; it is far better to be long and past the hole than to get too cute with the shot.

But with the exception of when you need to use a lob shot to carry a hazard, the rule is to get the ball on the green as quickly as possible so that it can roll; this sort of shot will require the least amount of movement. The general rule—and I stress "general"—is to carry the ball one-third of the way and run it two-thirds of the way. Work on this bread-and-butter shot and you will be able to take care of quite a lot in the short game.

Why would I prefer you to use more of the green instead of hitting the ball deeper into the green and having it run less? I like to use an analogy of throwing a ball here. Is it easier to stand on the edge of a green and throw a ball three feet and let it run twenty feet, or to throw it twenty feet and let it run three feet? I think it's easier to throw it the three feet and let it run the longer distance. Less force is required, and less motion. And the less motion you need, the more margin for error you will build in. The less movement you need to propel the ball a certain distance the better. It's more efficient to use a five-iron to chip the ball a lengthy distance than to use a sand wedge, which requires you to hit the ball hard and take a fairly long backswing.

Strategy and planning mean so much when you are chipping. For instance, there are times you actually may want to chip twice. A good example is the fifteenth hole at the Augusta National Golf Club. If I have hit my second shot over the green at this par-five, when the pin is cut in the bottom left corner of the green, I am now faced with a very touchy shot back up a slope to a green that runs swiftly away from me, with the pond in front of the green on the other side. If I hit my chip just a little too hard, it will run that extra amount and go down into the water. So if I chip the ball onto the green, I must ensure that it will land there ever so softly.

But maybe it's smarter not even to hit the chip onto the green. What's wrong with keeping it a foot or two short of the green? Now I'll probably be putting, or if I am chipping, I will certainly have an easier second chip. I like to call this "stalking the hole." If I chip the ball down to the water with my first shot, now I must go to the other side of the water. If I hit my wedge thin, I'm back in the same position behind the green. And then I wouldn't chip it in the water a second time, would I?

This may be an unusual situation, but it's worth keeping in mind and no doubt occurs from time to time when you play. Ask yourself if you ever chip the ball into trouble. I'll wager you do. We all do, unfortunately, and, I think, inexcusably. My point is always to try to make your next shot easier. If you're in a difficult spot, don't go from bad to worse.

Method for the Basic Chip Shot

In the accompanying illustrations I am using an eight-iron, but no matter what club I'm using, I employ the same basic setup. I am standing close to the ball, with my legs and feet close together. My knees are bent while my hands are near my kneecaps, especially my lower hand. The feeling I have is of

Stance open; weight forward; ball just inside back foot

being over the ball. My weight is forward, which helps me strike the ball with a crisp, descending blow. Always try to keep tension out of your left shoulder and arm. This will allow you to swing the club through freely.

Tempo is crucial in chipping. The basic principle is to ensure your clubhead is accelerating onto the ball. If your backswing is five miles an hour, I don't care if your follow-through is five-and-a-half miles an hour—at least you are accelerating the clubhead. It should always accelerate through the ball so that you put a positive hit on the ball. The softer you want to hit the ball, the slower you make your backswing.

Too often, golfers will take the club back at twenty-five miles an hour and bring it forward at ten. That's a big deceleration, and it results in a weak mishit. If there is an equation here, it would be to go back at one and return to the ball at one and a half—that is, ten on the backswing and fifteen on the throughswing. This provides a little margin. I tend to be too quick going back. You want to make sure that you take the club back low and slow with any kind of chip shot.

Variations on the Basic Chip Shot

There is no end to the variety of shots around the green. And some golfers are capable of playing many shots. Seve Ballesteros has the best all-round short game I have ever seen. He can hit four different shots around the green with the same club, whereas most of us are limited to one or two shots. I think Seve has a unique combination of flair, technique, confidence, and courage. He always seems to feel he can pull the shot off, no matter how delicate a shot it is, or how little the margin of error. There can't be anything worse, I think, than trying to hit a shot that you're not certain you can pull off. That doesn't exactly inspire confidence.

There aren't many golfers around with Ballesteros's touch and confidence. Tom Watson is another talented player who has won many tournaments with his creativity around the greens. He's able to commit to a shot and to go ahead and attempt it. It's as if he and Ballesteros enjoy chipping because it offers them the opportunity to be creative. I myself have found that chipping is more fun than putting, because it opens up the possibilities for creative shotmaking. You can hit these little bump-and-runs into the fringe, flop shots; there's even a hook chip shot that I like to use and that I'd like to describe.

The "Hooked" Chip Shot

I call this a "hook" chip because I hit it with what feels like a mini hook swing. It's a useful shot when you have to chip over rough ground or even into a soft spot; the topspin will take the ball right through the soft ground even if the first bounce is into it. You can also use the shot when you have some debris in front of you—like pine straw or a bit of sand or any uneven surface—that will kill the momentum of an ordinary chip that pitches into it. If you take an eight- or nine-iron, play the ball off your back foot and hood the blade so that you take loft off the club while aiming it slightly to the left. Take the club back on an inside path, following through to the right of your target. Because the clubface is pointing slightly to the left, the inside to outside swing path will set the ball off on line. The overspin or "hook" spin you impart to the ball will help it run right through the questionable terrain.

The Three-Wood Chip from Rough Off the Green

This shot has become popular during the last few years because of the way the grass is cut around greens. Often there is a collar of fairly thick rough just off the edge of the green, or perhaps in a second cut of fringe. There is hardly any margin for error if you take a lofted club, because the ball is usually sitting down and you will have to slide the blade of that club right under the ball. This is very difficult to do when the ball is down into the grass and when the grass is so thick that it could intercept the blade of the iron and stop its momentum or turn it.

A three-wood, however, has just enough loft to slide through the grass and carry the ball the three or four inches through the rough and onto the first cut of closely mown fringe or onto the green. You don't want to use this shot, though, when you are more than three or four inches from the short fringe or green; the ball won't have popped up far enough to carry through more rough than these few inches, and will be trapped by the thick grass once again.

I like to grip well down the shaft on this shot, perhaps three or four inches, while using a reverse overlap grip, as you can see in the accompanying illustrations. Again my weight is forward to encourage a descending blow, while I have placed my hands ahead of the ball at address to take a little loft off the three-wood. Hit the ball with your normal putting stroke and you will be amazed at how easily and cleanly it pops over the rough.

The Flop Shot over a Greenside Bunker
Here you must build in a reasonable margin of error. It can be dangerous to land the ball just over the bunker because you are trying to hit the ball near the flag when the hole is cut near the bunker. Remember that you want your next shot to be a putt and not a bunker shot. Ballesteros or Phil Mickelson might be looking to hole the shot, but most of us want to get the ball on the green and let it run a few feet past the hole.

Use a lofted club, probably a lob wedge, and hit the ball with enough force to carry the hazard easily. Stand to the ball with the blade wide open, your feet open to your target, and your knees quite bent. Try to keep the clubhead as shallow as possible through impact while cutting across the ball, almost as if you were just trimming the top of the grass under the ball. The steeper you are, the more inconsistent the result. When you play this shot properly, the ball will come out high and land softly. And remember, as always: Accelerate through the ball.

The Longer, Running Pitch Shot

Here you want to carry the ball some distance, but keep it low and get it running. Use this shot when you have some green to work with; it's really a long chip shot that will run up to the hole.

More and more, golf course architects are returning to the idea at the heart of links golf that a golfer should be able to run the ball onto the green along the ground, or, sometimes, to land the ball on the green with a low-flying shot and let it skip back to the hole. That's what the ground is there for—to put some bounce back into golf.

I can't think of a better example than the eighteenth at the Old Course in St. Andrews, Scotland. There are so many little humps and hollows around the green and on the green, including, of course, the deep Valley of Sin at the front of the green. If you have to chip through it, this is where your imagination comes in, where you can use your senses. The key is to ascertain where the flattest spot is along your line, because the first bounce is critical. An upslope will kill the speed of the ball, while a downslope will cause the ball to pitch too fast off it, so you need to ensure that the club you choose will pitch the ball on the flattest spot you see.

Don't get too fancy with this shot. The idea is always to pick the flattest spot, even if you have to land the ball short of an upslope that leads to the green. I may be using a nine-iron where there's a lot of apron and the hole is cut only fifteen feet on the green, but if I'm chipping up the hill I will always try to ensure that my first bounce is on the flat spot before it goes up, so that it maintains its speed going up the hill. If you pitch the ball straight into the face of the slope, the ball is going to pop up and might not even get over the top and onto the green.

Pick your spot, but don't become engrossed in chipping to an exact spot. If you focus too intensely on a single spot you will invariably hit the shot so that the ball will finish there rather than land there. I see that so many times. I advise you to pick your spot and then without focusing sharply on it, pick the club that you know will pitch the ball there; then trust your feel, go ahead, and make the shot to the hole. Look at the hole once you have selected the club you feel will pitch the ball on that flat spot.

My stance is open because there is little turn and body action involved. This is a hands, arms, and shoulder stroke, with the hands kept fairly low at address, and also back and through the ball. Keep everything compact here and you will give yourself the best chance of hitting a clean, positive shot that will run up to the hole. It's very important, as always, to keep your head as steady as possible.

The Basic Bunker Shot

The most important thing to understand about greenside bunker play is that there is so much margin for error in bunker play. The bunker shot is one of the most forgiving shots in golf.

If you hit the ball a little heavy—that is, if you take too much sand—it will come out with less spin and roll forward. If you hit the ball a little thin—that is, if you take too little sand—it will come out with more spin and stop more quickly. Both shots will go about the same distance. In general, if your method is right in the sand, then you will get away with more here than with any other type of shot.

The same principle applies here as in chipping. Your primary objective is to get the ball onto the green so that your next shot is a putt and not another bunker shot or chip shot. There are times when you will need to play away from the pin to ensure that your next shot is a putt. If you have a marginal lie—for instance, a plugged lie—and you know the ball is going to run quite a distance, then aim to land the ball where it will not run through the green. It's far more advisable to have a thirty-five-foot putt after intentionally hitting a bunker shot away from the hole than to have a twenty-foot shot from deep rough just off the green. There are times in match play or when you are close to the lead in a tournament when you will want to take a chance, and that's fine. High risk, high reward. But then don't knock yourself if the shot doesn't come off, especially when there may have been only a one in ten chance that it would.

Many amateurs feel a sharp increase in anxiety when they face a bunker shot. But you can reduce your anxiety and actually look forward to bunker shots if you understand a few principles and the common technique for sand play. As with all shots around the green, approach a bunker shot with an understanding of method and a positive thought to make an accelerating swing. Always be 100 percent committed to the shot.

Method for the Standard Greenside Bunker Shot
Stand open to the ball, while ensuring that the ball is just inside your left foot. Weaken your grip slightly to encourage the clubface being open at address and also set it open. Let your knees bend so that you feel on top of the ball. Take the club

back along the line of your feet, with the clubface facing your target, and swing through the ball along the line of your feet as well. The shape of the swing will feel more upright than your normal swing, but don't allow it to get too steep, which happens when you abruptly pick the club up. Use your arms and shoulders to initiate the backswing.

You want to hit slightly down into the sand two to three inches behind the ball. Ensure that the clubhead continues to accelerate through the sand all the time. Anytime you decelerate in a bunker shot, the ball will not come out as positively as it should.

Many amateurs worry themselves over how far to hit behind the ball. The principle is that the length of the shot, or how much you open the clubface, determines how far behind the ball you should contact the sand; on the basic shot of thirty feet that I am describing, I advocate your hitting about two to three inches behind the ball. When you open the clubface of a sand wedge you increase the amount of bounce on the bottom of the club. This is why you need a slightly descending blow; and remember that because of this bounce the club will not dig into the sand. Let the clubface glide through the sand—you will feel you are thumping the sand—and keep it open until impact, as you see in these illustrations. The ball will pop out of the bunker smoothly and gently, and then run itself out along the green.

Practice the basic bunker shot and you will soon feel confident. You will feel much more assured in your approach to the green as well, because you will be confident that if you do find a greenside bunker you will be able to get the ball up and down. Do that once a round, then twice, and a few more times as you mature in your sand play, and you will be a changed golfer. That's what sound bunker play can do for you: It's an indisputable energy boost.

chapter nine

EFFICIENT PUTTING

You don't need a hot putter to win golf tournaments. Now, that may sound radical. But I believe that winning does not depend on holing putt after putt but upon being a very solid putter and knowing that you are going to two-putt from thirty feet every time. That's not always easy to do, but a reliable method will go a long way toward giving you the confidence that you can do it.

Of course, you also need to make the four-to-six-footers to save pars and make birdies when you hit the ball close to the hole. But that still is not fantastic putting. Fantastic putting is when you have eight or ten fifteen-footers a round and you make the majority of them. The putt I holed at the British Open only happens once in a blue moon. The only way you can increase your odds of making that sort of putt, or any putt, is by building a sound putting stroke and developing touch while also learning to read greens.

Think about all the best putters over the years: Bobby Jones, Bobby Locke, Jack Nicklaus, Ben Crenshaw. They putted with great feel from distance, and if the putt didn't go in they were left with only a tap-in. They rarely missed putts inside ten feet. The golfer who gets nearer this standard will find that he has taken the pressure off his long game.

There is also a bonus from becoming an effective putter. If you build a sound stroke, you will from time to time have a great putting streak. You can't win as many tournaments as I did, of course, without having a hot streak in which you are holing the longer putts and missing very few of the short ones. But at the same time, you can't make this happen. Hot putting streaks seem to just happen when they are going to happen. Nevertheless, if you examine them I think you'll agree that they occur because you feel so good over the ball. And you can only feel good over the ball once you have found a method that works for you.

Putting is so individual—so personal—that you must be quite vigilant about the elements that hinder you from being effective and also the elements that help you. Everybody has a different way to putt, and I don't believe there is one golden rule. If you examine the way Bobby Locke putted from a closed stance, the way Bobby Jones putted from a slightly open stance, the variety of methods Jack Nicklaus has used (and he has been a marvelous putter for most of his career), the way Ben Crenshaw putts with his long, flowing stroke, you find a blatant contradiction of methods. Putting is therefore the hardest subject in golf to write about. A golfer can stand with his or her legs twisted and be a good putter, or can use one arm and be a good putter.

At the same time, all sound putters have a few things in common. I have tried to incorporate these into my setup and stroke and will share them with you and explain why I think they are critical. They certainly have helped me over the years. If you take one or two ideas out of this chapter that help you on the greens, then I will feel my effort here has been worthwhile.

Don't be afraid to add your personal touches. Add them, however, only after you have constructed a solid foundation. I have putted exceptionally well at times because the first two or three floors of this part of my game were sound. At other times my putting has been only average, and sometimes less than average, because I did not pay enough attention to my basics.

I don't mind admitting that I have not always paid as much attention to detail in putting as I have to the full swing. The simple truth is that I was not as interested in that part of the game. I felt it was more important to work on building an efficient swing. And I still believe that the swing is the most important aspect of golf, even more so with amateur golfers. The higher one's handicap, in fact, the more important it is to work on one's swing. I don't care if you are taking twenty-six putts every round. If you are taking four shots to reach every green, on average, you will still be barely breaking 100. The swing is definitely the thing in any higher-handicap player's program to improve.

But this doesn't mean you should ignore your putting. When I became a better putter it did wonders for my confidence, because I knew I did not have to hit each green to make par or hit perfect shots to have chances for birdies. My point is that putting is more difficult to understand than other parts of the game. I firmly believe some people are naturally gifted putters while others are destined to struggle. Golfers who are frustrated on the greens often don't spend enough time practicing putting. That is true for me and I suspect it is for you as well. (If you are a naturally good putter, then you are indeed fortunate.) I feel I have something to say about putting because I too have struggled with this tricky part of golf but have turned the corner to where I feel I am a better than average putter on the PGA Tour. And isn't that what we all want—to be better than average, to be able to pick up some shots on our opponents with our putting?

Guard against laziness, then. I didn't do that, and in 1995 in particular I suffered from having taken my putting for granted. Instead of paying attention to my stance I went out to the putting green and told myself, "Well, this is sort of how I was standing last year when I was putting so well." I wasn't disciplined enough to go out on the putting green and stand there for six or seven weeks in a row, twenty minutes a day, and tell myself, "Right, there's the posture, there's the position of my shoulders, there's the weight on my left side where I want it, okay, now I'll consider the pace of the green." I did not spend the time on these basic elements, so I missed more putts. I lost the posture I had had when I had putted well; I was standing too far from the ball and crouching over it. Bad posture, bad putting.

The Decision to Change

Until the 1988 British Open I had not given enough thought to putting because I was refining the changes to my swing. But then Seve Ballesteros beat me in the championship by putting better than I did the last round. I didn't have the effectiveness with the putter that he had; he beat me on the greens pure and simple. But the good news was that I now saw the road I had to take—I had to work on my putting. That was the last step in my becoming a golfer who could compete week in and week out.

That was when I started to become inventive in analyzing and criticizing my putting. That was when I told myself, "Look, what you're doing is not going to work under pressure. Let's simplify things and get down to basics."

I asked myself how I would teach somebody to become an efficient putter and came up with the same answer I had when I was thinking about the swing. I didn't want anything in my putting game that did not serve a purpose. I wanted no extra motion, and I wanted everything working to bring the face of the putter through the ball square to where I was aiming, while the blade was accelerating. I was trying to get as logical as I could about putting while still allowing for creativity and flair. But these latter ingredients would come later, as with the swing. First I would have to change my mechanics. And I think my putting has changed even more than my swing. It's totally different from what it was years ago.

The first thing I looked at was my stance. I was standing very open to the ball during the 1988 British Open. There was no reason for that except that I had been doing so for some time. It did not add up logically, so I decided to square up my

stance. Many superb putters, such as Jones and Nicklaus, have
stood open to the ball. That's a personal preference that you
may want to try as well. But if you feel cockeyed over the ball,
then it could be that an open stance does not work for you.

Squaring up my stance helped me immensely. I had always
been particularly weak on left-to-right putts, which made
sense when I thought about how I was standing to the ball.
Standing open invariably leads to the shoulders being too
open, which in turn encourages a stroke that cuts across the
ball. And so I would take the putter outside my intended line
on the backstroke and cut across the ball at impact. (It's fine for
your shoulders to be *slightly* open, as I will explain in the section on posture on page 147.)

Standing open also made it more likely that I would sneak
a peek at the hole at impact, or as we say, I would "come out"
of the putt. When you stand open, it is all too easy to look up;
your eyes are already forward. But if you stand square, you are
less apt to look up. That's one less moving part during the
stroke, which promotes stability.

New: square stance   **Old: open feet and shoulders**

A square stance also helps you build trust in your stroke so that you don't have to look up. You look up because you are anxious about where the ball is going, how it's come off the putter face. But if you are confident and aware that your mechanics are better, you won't feel the need to look up—the impulse to look up will dissipate over time. Putting is a matter of picturing your distance to the hole, then looking down at the ball while retaining a mental image of that distance. You trust that image and then make your stroke. You see the hole in your mind's eye when you are over the ball.

Prior to the 1988 British Open, I was not good at retaining the image of the hole. And that led to inconsistency. I either putted with good feel and no direction one day, or good direction and no feel the next day. It became clear to me that I needed to feel confident of my direction before I could even concern myself with the feel, because it would not matter how good my feel was if I was unable to start the ball on the line I had picked. I determined that I was going to make the transition from exclusively a feel putter to a putter who had better mechanics in all aspects.

It's odd to me now that I did not appreciate that if I stood more squarely to the target I would keep the putter on line longer. That meant I could mishit a putt and it could still go in or finish close. Adopting a square stance simplified matters, even though it felt uncomfortable for some time. It represented a crucial first step in my assembling a putting stroke that depended on principles rather than feel alone. Every time you do something such as standing open you have to make a counteraction, a compensatory movement somewhere along the way. My tendency was to stand open, a habit I still fight to this day. I have to stay on top of this because it is a source of error.

Weight Forward

As I squared up my stance and focused on a more rational approach to putting, I asked myself why I had always kept the majority of my weight on my back foot. I had read that to put topspin on the ball and get it rolling you have to hit up on it. I reasoned that it would be easier to do this if I kept my weight back. But upon further consideration it became obvious that this led to my mishitting a lot of putts. I would hit the ball on the bottom half of the putter because the blade was working up, away from the sweet spot. And a mishit putt is just like a mishit shot. It will be more deflected by spike marks, for instance. The solidly hit putt will not be as influenced.

I had to change habits that I had ingrained from ten years of hitting up on the ball to feeling as if I were now hitting down on the ball. I watched video footage of Jones, Locke, and other great putters, and saw that they made a slightly descending stroke; it wasn't an ascending stroke at all. It's difficult to discern exactly how much of a descending blow a fine putter such as Crenshaw, for example, makes, but I was still certain that when he was putting his best his stroke was ever so slightly downward, and sometimes on the flat spot where the blade is exactly parallel to the ground, looking neither up nor down. I took that information in hand and tried to make a more descending blow. I now putt my best when I keep the putter down and low through the ball. I like to feel I am making contact with the ball just prior to when the arc of the putter head flattens out. The golfer who hits up on the ball, I think, either has the ball too far forward in his stance or is allowing his left wrist to break down. In either case it's not likely that a solidly struck putt will result.

An experiment helped me determine that the proper way to putt was with a slightly descending stroke. We measured the distance it takes a putted ball to start rolling, and, on longer putts, the distance the ball is airborne. We discovered that these distances are dependent on the kind of stroke made. If you hit down on the ball, it goes into a roll within six inches. It gets airborne for about a yard on a forty-foot putt when you use an ascending stroke, while with a flat or level stroke it gets airborne for only a couple of feet.

When your ball gets airborne, its subsequent roll is determined by what kind of turf it hits when it comes down. If it strikes an area where the grain is running against you, it will bounce. Conversely, it will take off if the grain is with you. This is why a descending stroke is preferable to an ascending stroke—the ball starts rolling sooner. You want the ball to get rolling off the head of the putter as soon as possible.

A Shoulder Adjustment

I used to putt with my left shoulder noticeably higher than my right, to encourage my hitting up on the ball. But after I decided to make my stroke more level it made sense to do the same with my shoulders. I dropped my left shoulder to nearer the same height as my right shoulder, allowing for the natural difference in inclination because the right hand is lower on the club. This adjustment helped tremendously in producing a flatter stroke.

Old: Putter is too high through the finish.

**New: Stance with weight forward and shoulders
more level promotes descending stroke and
lower path through ball.**

A Grip Change

There are many ways to grip the putter, and I have tried a number of them. For years I used a double reverse overlap grip, with the index and middle fingers of the left hand on top of the last two fingers of the right hand. Then in 1989 I changed to the standard Vardon grip that I use with my swing. I used that until the 1995 PGA Championship, which means that was my grip of choice when I won the 1992 and 1994 British Opens and the 1994 PGA Championship.

But putting is so much feel, and the smallest feeling of discomfort can lead to mistakes. There isn't much room for error on the putting green, especially as you get closer to the hole. I felt that over time my left hand was breaking down through the

Single finger reverse overlap grip

stroke, and so at the 1995 PGA Championship I changed to the single reverse overlap, where the index finger of the left hand overlaps the pinkie and ring fingers of the right hand. This helped keep my left hand more solid, and I began to putt more consistently. But I would not be afraid to change again. I don't think that the grip is as important in putting as it is in the full swing. This is because the putting stroke is not nearly as long, of course, as the swing; it's easier, at least in theory, to keep the blade on line no matter how you grip the putter.

Posture

Posture on the green is again more or less a matter of how you feel. The ideal posture for putting is dead square to the target line, I think, so that there is less need for compensations. And you will also want a solid base, almost rigid. I don't mean that you should not feel some springiness in your legs, but you want to have the sensation of being rooted to the ground. The less movement down below the better, because the slightest motion from the hips down will throw your stroke out of kilter.

As much as I advocate a square stance, it is also acceptable to be slightly open or slightly closed. Find the square position, then modify it by small increments according to what you need to do to feel comfortable. In saying this, however, I am referring only to the placement of your feet. Your shoulders are another matter.

I have found that keeping your shoulders slightly—and I emphasize slightly—open while setting up to a putt is acceptable, because it allows your shoulders to move freely through the ball. In fact, slightly open shoulders in putting are preferable in my opinion to absolutely dead-square shoulders; keeping my shoulders square makes me feel restricted at impact, and can increase tension in my upper body. As for closed shoulders while putting, I don't advocate this at all. Always try to keep tension out of the left side—shoulder, arm, and wrist—so as to maintain free movement through impact.

A Reminder

As you read my advice on putting, remember that these are the elements I have found that promote efficiency of motion and repetition. These are important, because you can almost manufacture the fluidity once you have the basics down. It is always interesting to watch golfers become smoother in their strokes as they are more confident in their mechanics.

Ensure that the basics are in order before you build in mannerisms. Sometimes people will say to me that they like to slice their putts. I always wonder why they like to do this, because I think it adds a complication. Golf is difficult enough; why would you want to make it more complicated?

Today's Stroke

The condition of greens has improved so much in the last twenty years that you don't see many slow, grainy greens anymore. Maintenance procedures have advanced to where greens are smoother and often much faster than in years past. This is becoming more the case not only on the courses for tournament play, but on most courses. Bobby Jones used to putt on much slower greens, and so did golfers of the 1960s.

Improved greens have led to a different stroke: Golfers today putt more with their shoulders and arms than with their wrists. Golfers on the slower and less consistent greens of some years ago were much wristier putters. When you had to hit a putt hard from thirty feet you had to put a certain amount of wrist into the stroke; you had to *hit* the putt. Today's golfers do not give the ball so much of a hit with the hands as a stroke with the arms and shoulders; because the ball rolls so well on today's greens, they need only get it in motion.

I think that the arms-and-shoulders stroke, with just a hint of hit at the ball, is the most efficient way to putt. I also know that the reason I am not as consistent a putter as I would like to be is that I grew up on slower greens in Rhodesia. I sometimes have too much hit, too much hand action, in my putting stroke. We are who we are, products of our early environment.

Think about the courses you usually play, then decide to what degree you want to be an arms-and-shoulders putter as opposed to a hands-and-wrists putter. There's a combination that works for each of us in there somewhere. And also be aware of which is your dominant tendency, because you will need to adjust when you go from one type of green to the other. The first thing you should do when you get to a new course is hit your first ten putts from twenty-five or thirty feet so that you can assess the speed. Don't worry about the short putts; get the speed first and then go to the short ones.

I have always putted my best when I'm not thinking about the speed because I have it down; I'm confident enough of my feel for the pace of the greens that I can concentrate on line.

We all putt better when we are not frightened of the speed, but if we are unsure of this component we will be unsure of the break. Speed awareness triggers line awareness.

Rarely is a golfer off line by more than a few inches, even on longer putts. But we all hit putts far too short or too long. That suggests we need to emphasize speed. It's why I always include this entry at the back of my diary every year: "*Speed is 90 percent of putting.*" It sure is.

Placement of the Putter

The most noticeable aspect of the way I putt is that I set my putter in front of the ball, then set it behind the ball. This accomplishes four things. I made all of these changes consciously after thinking about what I wanted to accomplish with my putting stroke.

First, setting the putter in front of the ball helps ensure that I am aiming the face where I want it. By placing the blade ahead of the ball I get an uninterrupted view of the line I have chosen; the ball does not intrude between the blade and the hole. This was the first reason I started placing the putter ahead of the ball, which was early in 1992 when I began to use a mallet putter. I never set the putter in front of the ball until I used a mallet putter.

Second, the movement makes me take the same amount of time over each putt, from the first hole to the last. I tend to walk fast, think fast, swing fast, and putt fast. Placing the putter in front of the ball slows me down just enough so that I don't rush my stroke. It's a small action that helps me discipline myself. I take the same amount of time over a putt for the British Open now as I do over a putt on the first hole of a tournament. In fact, I take about the same amount of time for a drive as I do for a four-foot putt. The idea is to stay within your comfort zone and not rush or get too slow. You don't want to rush in the heat of pressure at a major championship, nor do you want to be so slow that you think about the mechanics of your stroke.

Third, it helps me get more weight on my front side and thereby promotes the slightly descending stroke I want.

The fourth thing that placing the putter in front of the ball accomplishes is that it helps keep the ball a little farther back in my stance. I tended to get the ball too far forward, again thinking that I wanted to sweep upward on the ball. But that got the ball off my left toe and sometimes off my left shoulder. That meant I had to make a forced move to keep the putter low through the ball, once I started thinking about that. Now I like to feel that the ball is just left of my sternum, almost opposite my heart. This placement encourages a slightly downward stroke.

If you follow the suggestions I have made here, I am confident that you will become a more reliable putter. Don't forget to allow for personal mannerisms, because flair is definitely an important part of putting. But also don't be afraid to rid yourself of mannerisms that accomplish nothing. The idea in putting, as in the swing, is to keep things as simple and logical as possible, because simple things are easier to reproduce day in and day out.

chapter ten

SWING SEQUENCES

Early Swing Sequences, "Face-on" and "Behind"

Overview

These swing sequences were taken in 1981, when I was playing the European Tour, and in the spring of 1993, after I won the Players Championship, where I probably hit the ball as well as I ever have for 72 holes. I was swinging at about an eight out of ten then, and I like to think there is even room for improvement from this swing. I often refer to this second sequence because I like many of the things I was doing and had worked on to achieve since 1981. To look at my swing then and to examine my swing now is to notice again that tendencies from early on in one's life remain. But just as bad habits will stay with you so will good habits if you develop them. It's a question of training good habits and being disciplined to fulfill your commitment to change for the better.

My tendency has always been to take the club back with the face too square to the line. This creates a very steep backswing plane, as is most apparent in frames three through five of the "behind" (1981) sequence. The result is that the shoulders, hips, and legs don't rotate around the correct axis, and I get a steep tilt at the top of my backswing.

You can see in frame two of the "behind" sequence that my clubface is too square to the line, and actually shut when compared to my turning body. I used to believe that the idea is to take the club back with the face as square to the line as it can be. Frame four of the "behind" photos shows what happens when you take the club back square to the line and not square to your body—the result is that the club goes back to the outside and reaches the steep position at the top of frame four. This is simply the continuation of a poor takeaway; the backswing at the top is contrived and very weak. There is very little torquing or winding up of the body, so I now have to try to create this winding in the downswing. I've done that well, as is apparent in frame five; however, in this frame, the club is now coming into the pre-impact area on too flat a plane because of the steep plane in the backswing. This is a golf demonstration of the physical law that for every action there is an equal and opposite reaction. To compare frames three and five in the "behind" sequence is to see just how much difference there is in the shaft planes at the respective stages of my swing.

Throughout my career I have fought getting too steep on the downswing, which comes from getting too flat or shallow, or allowing the club to get too far behind me at the start of my downswing. This is a direct result of getting too steep on the backswing, which I then instinctively counter by shallowing the shaft out to start the downswing. My response to that now is to get steep again as I come into the ball. If I were to continue without getting steep into the ball, the club would come in from much too far inside, and the result would be a big hook that starts well right of the target.

The way I compensated around this move was to slide my body laterally toward the target too much. This gave me time to allow my arms and clubhead to catch up as I was coming into the impact area and to square up at impact. Obviously, all these extra moves took a lot of my power away, sometimes as much as 40 percent, and led to day-to-day inconsistencies. One day I would hit a five-iron 170 yards and the next day I would struggle to hit it 150 yards. It was impossible for me to play consistent golf.

The steepness in the backswing also leads to a reverse pivot, which is evident in frame four of the "face-on" (1981) sequence. If you look at the more recent swing sequence you will see that there are still similarities to the 1981 sequences, which confirms my point that our old tendencies stay with us. Still, if I were to grade myself on zero to ten, with ten being perfect and zero poor, I would give myself only a three for the 1981 sequence and probably an eight for the more recent sequence. However, I continue to work diligently on all the keys that have helped me over the past fifteen years since I made changes. I am also more confident now as a result of knowing my tendencies and continuing to improve.

Even through all the poor mechanics that are apparent in my backswing during the early sequences, and due to hard practice and, I suppose, a certain amount of talent, I still recover well to a very good impact position. This is evident in frame six of the "face-on" sequence. Also note that my grip was extremely weak then and that you can barely see one knuckle of my left hand in frame one of the "face-on" sequence.

Analysis of 1981 Sequences

The majority of my comments relating to these 1981 sequences apply to the frames taken from behind. You learn more about the swing from this angle. However, please note the associated positions in the "face-on" sequence as well. I learned—and continue to learn—a great deal from examining these sequences.

Frame one: Poor posture, not enough flex in my knees, causing me to get too much weight over my toes. Back too rounded.

Frame two: Club outside the line and closed relative to body. Hips and legs are turning too early.

Frame three: Club has gone vertical, and left shoulder is dropping down toward the ball. Note also that the left knee has shot out and my right knee has straightened. The shaft is on far too steep a plane.

Frame four: This, believe it or not, is the top of my backswing. The club is not fully set at the desired 90-degree angle and is already starting to flatten out.

Frame five: I've recovered and there is a certain amount of tension or coil, but for all intents and purposes, I may as well have started my swing here because everything else was inefficient.

Frame six: Because the downswing's too flat, I've compensated by sliding my body toward the target. This is "correcting" one bad move with another. I'm coming from the outside just before impact and over the top of the ball, so the club has now released left of where it should be.

Frame seven: I have held off my release as a result of trying to recover in the backswing, and I have lost a lot of clubhead speed. My shoulders are on a very steep plane, my right foot is sliding backward in an attempt to prevent my coming over the top and hooking the ball, and my left foot is twisting badly.

Frame eight: I am in fact rotating my shoulders on a plane nearer the shaft plane. My lower half is unstable, my right foot is sliding, and I have rolled well onto my left ankle. It's a wonder I could even walk after hitting so many balls this way.

Frame nine: It is obvious in this frame and in the two previous frames that I am trying to hold on and retain my balance. My left foot has slipped to a 45-degree angle in this frame. I'm trying to maintain my balance, but given what has come before, this is difficult.

Analysis of 1993 Sequences

Frame one: I have turned my toes out at address and by increasing the gap between my knees, I have created a very solid look of stability. I've assumed a relaxed posture with good knee flex and a straight lower back.

Frame two: The club has moved back and around with no lower body movement. The toe of the club is now square to my turning upper body, although in the "face-on" frame it still could be a little more rotated.

Frame three: My shoulders have now reached the position where they are pulling my lower body around. So I am using my lower half only as it is needed, not prematurely. However, the clubface is still a little closed. Ideally, the toe of the club should be pointing at the sky.

Frame four: This shows an ideal position at the top, a nice rounded coil with the hips and the upper body behind the ball. I have maintained the flex in my right knee and am poised to explode at the ball.

Frame five: However, it is apparent, especially in the "face-on" sequence, that my hips have slid too far toward the target. I have started to release the club too early. The angle between my left forearm and the shaft is diminishing, which results in a loss of power. Since the clubface was a little too closed on the backswing, I'm trying to prevent it from getting too far behind me on the way down. I'm constantly working on this problem, and I know that when I get it right my swing will become more efficient.

Frame six: This is a very good impact position. But I do feel that the upper half of my body is hanging back slightly because of the earlier hip slide.

Frame seven: It's evident that I have released the club too far to the left. This is because of the early release that was visible in frame five. I am also holding onto the release a little—not letting the club freely swing through the ball, that is—and am therefore sacrificing some distance.

Frames eight and nine: I have swung through to a balanced finish with my shoulders rotating through the ball on a flatter plane than during the 1981 sequence; at the same time, there is still evidence of some tilt—especially in frame eight. In frame nine my shoulders are more level than in the final frame of the 1981 sequence, especially as seen in the "face-on" sequence. All in all, I have made a more stable and simple swing that is much more consistent than in 1981. However, the same idiosyncrasies remain, and I'm constantly working on them.

What You Can Learn

If you have a very good setup and address position then your chances of making a good start to the backswing are enhanced dramatically. The position at the top of my swing in frame four of the 1993 sequence is one that every golfer should strive to emulate; I try to emulate it myself. Although you may not be as supple as I am—and I am far less supple than many others—you can still create a similar position given your own limitations. The sequences also show the importance of being supple—it is always a good idea to work on your flexibility. I encourage you to do so if you can.

Practice helps your swing. There can be no doubt about that. But practice does not make your swing perfect. Study what the top touring professionals have in common and work on these elements. You are bound to improve by simple observation, understanding, and sound practice.

I refer to photos and swing sequences often. Images of my swing when I am playing well and when I am playing poorly are always in my mind's eye. Once you understand what you are trying to do, and once you can picture what you hope to accomplish in your swing, then thinking about your swing off the course as well as on it can help immeasurably. Pictures allied with words help build understanding and an appreciation of the efficient golf swing. The combination has certainly helped me, and I am confident it will also help you.

You can also learn a lot by seeing the differences in the comparative sequences that follow.

chapter eleven

SWING JOURNAL

During the course of my career I have kept a journal of my thoughts, primarily about my swing as I was working on it. I did not do this on a regular basis, but simply jotted notes down as they occurred to me, to reinforce ideas in my mind. Often after working with David Leadbetter I wanted to think about what we had discussed and to work things out in my own mind. Then I could go over these ideas with David when next I saw him, and also learn to trust my own judgment. As my swing became more dependable during the early 1990s the frequency of my entries decreased, but I still make a notation from time to time. Writing thoughts down helps me focus on what I want to do, and why.

When I look back through the journal now, I am struck by how I was obviously struggling toward the clear understanding of the swing that I sought. It's a never-ending effort that I enjoy—most of the time, because it's never easy when things are not going well—and keeping these notes helped me clarify matters. I include them here to give you an understanding of what I have been thinking about over the years. This is a record of my own attempts to improve over the long term and demonstrates, I think, just how difficult but also how satisfying the struggle can be. Of course, there are contradictions in the journal, because my thinking here reflects a work in progress—my golf swing and game, that is. That's the way it will always be. I might add that a lot of these notes were based on my feelings at the time. In some cases I have exaggerated my observations to emphasize certain things for myself. Please keep this in mind, since a lot of what I state in here I would never teach anyone.

I encourage you to keep a journal of your own. It's a useful way to measure progress and to remind yourself what you were working on the last time you were on the practice tee. At the end of a session, just write down in a notebook what you were working on so that you can refer to it when next you practice. Golfers often have a week or more between practice sessions, and without such an aid you won't remember what you were thinking about the last time. A journal will help you keep the thoughts and the feel from one session to the next.

SEPTEMBER 30, 1982

1. Stand taller to the ball.
2. Try to swing club on a more upright plane.
3. Low and slow takeaway with about 75 degrees wrist cock at top of swing. Maintain cupping of left wrist throughout.
4. Turn hips in more barrel-like fashion. Ensure that the left hip does not drop lower than its position at address throughout the swing. That is, feel as though the hips face opposite the target at the top of the swing. The hips must move or revolve around or with the body instead of tilting.

The body at the top of the swing should be well over the right foot with stored or torqued-up energy staying on the inside of the right foot. If the left heel comes off the ground, this will *encourage* the weight to go out at the initial stage of the swing, and then at the top the hips will tilt instead of turning! This will result in an improper turn and encourage a steep descent on the downswing. By keeping the left heel down during the backswing, the backswing will automatically be shortened so the tempo must be slowed down! If anything the left foot should roll onto its instep and then during the downswing the *feeling* of the knees separating should become apparent. Ninety percent of the weight must be on the right side of the body, which will result in the head staying behind the ball through impact and thus achieving a good release and extension through the ball. The body must be arched at the finish into a reverse "C" or bowed position.

At address the head and chin are slightly raised. The shoulders are slightly tilted; this is natural because the right hand is reaching lower than the left. There is a slight cup in the left wrist. The feet are turned out, the left foot about 10 degrees to the left from a 90-degree angle to the target, the right foot 5 to 10 degrees.

Waggle the arms and wrists only, taking the club back on the line of the intended backswing.

Chipping

The less wrist used, the softer the strike, because the angle of attack is shallower. However, there is a certain amount of wrist required in chipping, but you must use more arms and shoulders than wrists. The head must remain dead still throughout all short game shots, that is, chipping, sand play, and putting. It is so important in putting that the head and body remain dead still. When the head moves, so does the body. With all short game play the hands must always lead the clubhead and the clubhead must remain as square to the target as long as possible.

With sand play the grip may be changed to suit the required shot. There must always be more acceleration through impact than any other stroke. For really consistent sand play the divot or amount of sand taken must be the same depth, not too deep and not too shallow. The coarser the sand the harder you have to hit down and through. Finer sand requires caution so as not to get too deep!

Putting

Keep the putter face as square to the target as possible at all times. The hands, arms, and shoulders must work together as a unit. The hands at address must be slightly ahead of the ball and remain ahead throughout the stroke. Keep the putter head as low to the ground as possible at all times. Remember: Low, slow, and accelerate through. No jabbing. If you hit the ball when the putter head is accelerating you will be able to keep the ball on line longer. This will make you a more consistent putter.

Game Strategy

Always aim at the biggest part of the fairway, unless you are hitting the ball like a machine. This also applies to approach play to the greens. However, you must apply percentages here and weigh each situation according to what you feel you can do. Only you know how *you feel*.

OCTOBER 30, 1982

Pre-setup

Stand behind ball and pick line and type of shot required. Move in, keeping the line in mind, from the left while placing the right foot into position first. Then bring the left foot into the desired position.

Checkpoint: Ensure that you are not getting too open with your feet, hips, and shoulders.

Grip

Left hand showing one and a half knuckles to two knuckles, the V formed pointing to the right shoulder. The right hand must be pushed down the grip so that the lifeline of the right hand fits in snugly over the left thumb.

Grip pressure: The left hand holds the club firmly, using about 70 to 75 percent of my strength, with the pressure getting weaker going down through the right hand. The right hand still holds the club firmly but not as firmly as the left.

The ball must be addressed in the middle of the clubface, as any other position will encourage faults.

Feet: The left foot is positioned at 75 to 80 degrees (varying through the driver to the wedge) and the right foot remains a static 80 degrees throughout all clubs (except chipping and sand play).

Hips, shoulders, and knees: These should be square to the target with all the long clubs (driver through five-iron) and then start opening for the short irons. This is because a less forceful shot is needed with shorter clubs. Direction is the all-important factor with the shorter clubs.

Checkpoints: Ensure that you do not stand too far away from the ball as this will encourage crouching (loss of height) and improper weight transfer during the swing. Also ensure that you do not stand too narrow. The width of your stance should be the width of the shoulders with a driver, tapering or getting narrower as you get to the shorter irons.

Takeaway

The plane of the swing is the first thought before the club is taken back. The plane gets more upright as the club gets shorter. You cannot swing the nine-iron on the same plane as the driver.

Keep the club low to the ground for the first eighteen inches to two feet of your backswing. You take the club back with your shoulders, arms, and wrists, all together. This is then the trigger for the rest of the body, which *will* follow if the shoulders, arms, and wrists have taken the club back together.

At the top of the swing there should be approximately 70 to 75 degrees of wrist cock. On the downswing the club must be pulled down, keeping the triangle formed at the top intact. The feeling then is to retain this until it feels as though the hands are about three to four inches in front of the ball. The club is then released on the intended line of flight of the ball.

If the shot is to be a draw, the club must be released to the line intended. Conversely on a cut shot the club must not be released until late, and then down the left side of the target.

The hips must not tilt at all through the swing. The left hip must remain at the same height throughout the swing, at the position you set the hip at address. Retain that height. You must also try to keep the left shoulder at the same height as you set it at address. Adhere to these two pointers and you will never tilt!

If the left heel comes off the ground at all, it must roll off the ball or instep of the left foot. The heel must stay on the ground as long as possible with the longer clubs. It must stay on throughout the swing from the four-iron through the pitching wedge.

Feel your knees separating for a split second at the start of your downswing. This will encourage a good lateral move at the start.

At impact you should have 90 percent of your weight on your right side. You will encourage this to happen if you hold the triangle of your shoulders, arms, and wrists as long as possible. This will also delay your release and keep you from hitting the ball too high. You will reach a good, high finish, held only momentarily in the reverse "C" position.

The swing plane is the most important thing in my golf swing.

Supination

This is created when the left hand remains bowed through impact. The forearm rotates after impact, releasing the clubhead down the line of the target, still in the plane of the swing. This is undoubtedly the secret to consistent ball-striking, especially with the irons. Best examples: Ben Hogan, Byron Nelson, Ken Venturi, Hale Irwin, Tom Weiskopf.

When the left wrist is bowed incorrectly through impact, errant shots will result, the most frequent type being a hook. To ensure against this happening, the thumb of the left hand must remain on top of the shaft, with the clubhead coming in low and after impact released. The normal result when this is done correctly is a very piercing flight of the ball, which is essential for consistent and extremely accurate iron play!

The things to remember while trying or using this move are:

1. Make sure the club is taken away low from the ball.
2. Make sure the backswing is completed.
3. Make sure the weight is transferred.
4. Make sure a full turn is achieved.

When Beginning to Hit the Ball Well

A common fault of mine when I start hitting the ball well is that I try to hit it too far. I should remember to always swing smoothly and ensure there are absolutely no snatching or jerky moves throughout the swing. The most common such move in my case is when my legs and knees become too violent at the top of the backswing. This comes from trying to hit the ball too hard. I need to remember that long tee shots come from trying to swing the club smoothly.

Hands

The right hand during the grip should be stretched a little, down the grip of the club. The lifeline in the right hand will probably fit a little more snugly over the left thumb if this is done properly.

During the downswing the back of the right hand should be arched as much as possible. Trying to keep the back of the hand moving toward the target laterally as long as possible will help you achieve this.

After impact—delay this action as long as possible—the left hand then supinates. When I encounter trouble with the strike, I try to swing the club with firmer wrists and with less wrist cock or set at the top of the backswing. This helps my feel and also helps to coordinate my arm swing with my body rotation. I like to use this as a drill.

Downswing or Initial Movement on the Downswing
As the downswing starts, try to feel the distance from the left knee to the hands on the club is increasing. Feel the separation of the knees for a split second.

Keep the right heel on the ground for as long as possible. This will help to get a really good extension after impact.

MAY 20, 1983

The single most important thing in my swing is the setup. The clubface *must* be square (almost to feel closed) in relation to the body alignment at setup.

At this stage it feels like I am aiming or aligning my body and feet to the right of the target with the clubface aiming straight or even slightly left of the target. This is just the feeling. In actual fact both clubface and feet/body are aiming straight at the target when another person checks from behind.

I've also had the feeling of turning the ball over, and this has helped me to get my swing path on the correct line again. I also have the tendency to kick too hard with the legs on the downswing. What results is the right knee causes the rest of the body to move out and over the ball. The correct feeling is to *feel* as though the right knee stays static throughout the downswing until the ball has been struck and is on its way.

My grip feels very strong at the moment with my usual tendency to hold the clubface open. However, when I return the clubface to square the grip is perfect!

I am sure that this is the most important key to my consistent ball–striking. I have had this feeling on only two other occasions. The first was during the South African Circuit in 1979 when I won the Asseng and hit the ball really fantastically the whole season. The other was the Swiss Open in 1980 when I won, and I have never hit the ball that way again—unbelievable.

I must practice turning the ball over occasionally, keeping the swing path in mind.

SEPTEMBER 5, 1983

During the week of the World Series I realized something that may change the approach to my thinking on the golf course.

In the previous six months on tour I had extreme difficulty in believing I had the ability to hit the ball perfectly in seventy-two holes and win a golf tournament.

The big problem was that I was attacking the flag too aggressively, and during the World Series I tried only to hit the greens. Invariably you will find the longest putt you will have is between thirty and thirty-five feet.

This approach takes a lot of pressure off you as on most occasions you'll hit a straight shot into the middle of the green, thereby avoiding the hazards surrounding the green. This results in more birdie putts (even though thirty-footers) and more greens hit in regulation.

NOVEMBER 20, 1983, *Kingston Heath, Melbourne*

I must stand a little wider.

There is too early a break of my wrists going back and therefore not enough extension.

My left foot is pointed too much toward the target. This causes an improper turn; the left knee goes out toward the ball and not toward the right knee.

I can see noticeable head movement. I am not staying behind the ball enough through impact. This was probably due to a strong wind during the week.

I am too flat-footed at impact.

Practice
1. Left foot position at address.
2. Minimize leg movement going back to create a tighter turn.
3. Feel knee separation before impact.
4. Stay behind the ball and release down target line.
5. Swing easier with *less* leg force.

OCTOBER 16, 1986, *Lancome Trophy, Paris*

Width

During the two weeks of my playing in the World Match Play Championship and now just having completed the first round in the Lancome, I have noticed that with the change of climate from America to Europe there seems to be a distinct lack of width in my golf swing. I think it is probably due to a few factors:

1. Colder climate; therefore body is not as supple as normal.
2. Never having been aware that I actually did lose width.
3. Not turning wide enough on backswing and not getting weight on right side in backswing.
4. Adverse weather making me more conscious of keeping the ball in play—rather than playing good, solid, pure and open golf.

Make sure that the tempo at address (the waggle) is not too violent and forceful. A good tip is to ground the club behind the ball and not waggle at all. This will make for a smoother takeaway and prevent me from snatching the club into the backswing too quickly.

Key thoughts at the moment: Ensure stance is wide enough. Ensure clubface and body are aligned correctly.

It is very important for me to allow enough room under my chin at address so that the left shoulder can pass underneath during backswing. The idea is to make a free backswing—the fewer things that hinder this the better. I think this is one of the habits I have always had, and has been the cause of many noncompletions of turns. The result has been short and fast swings.

Backswing

Club, hands, arms, and shoulder—one piece to eight o'clock. Clubface must be at least 45 degrees to target line. Rotate club with left forearm to ten o'clock. The clubface must now be square to the plane/path. The farther the butt of the club is from the ball the greater the width; this distance is the determining factor for width. I must try to maintain this feeling throughout the swing.

Downswing

Picture the plane triangle throughout the backswing. Pull the club down from the top, keeping the right foot firmly planted on the ground until the club is well past impact. The right knee must remain very passive throughout the downswing. The more violent the right knee is on the way down, the deeper the divot and the harder and more inconsistent the strike.

The legs *control* the pace of the swing; that is, the more violent and quicker the legs the more violent and quicker the swing.

1. Keep legs as passive as possible, ensuring they support the swing properly by being in the correct positions.
2. For knockdown shots, grip down one inch and keep the legs as passive as possible. This will result in a very controlled flight of the ball, which should go ten to fifteen yards shorter than you normally hit the club.
3. *Putting:* The head and body should be kept as absolutely still as possible. Only the shoulders and arms move. The head must stay down until the ball has been hit.
4. *Chipping and sand play:* The head must stay dead still and remain down until well after the ball has been struck. The legs must keep dead still on all short game shots; they are there for power, not accuracy!

Notes after Reading Sam Snead's Article in *Golf Digest,* February 1984:

Walter Hagen: Was like a general on a battlefield. He was in total *control* and there was nothing that could happen out there that could shake him.

Ben Hogan: Had the ability to concentrate totally during the round. He never got too high when things were going well and never got too low when they were going badly. He always had *composure* (control of himself) and never got down.

Bobby Jones: Had a fine rhythm. He *coordinated* his arms with his lower body, as though they worked as one unit. People who swing too fast have a tough time coordinating their arms and legs.

Jack Nicklaus: I don't think it ever occurred to Jack that he might not *succeed.* People like Jack find a way to win.

Arnold Palmer: Didn't just think he'd make every putt—he honestly expected to make them all. All good putters have one thing in common: They get themselves in a position that's comfortable.

Tom Watson: Is a *fearless* scrambler. He spends a lot of time working on short putts (six to ten feet). He figured out a long time ago that those long approach putts are a lot easier if you have confidence in your ability to make the short ones coming back.

All good sportsmen and -women always have plenty of time to do things. Think well in advance of what's coming up and ensure you have enough time to do it. People tend to make mistakes when hurried or pushed into things. Always have enough time.

Successful people are always in *control* of themselves. They always keep their *composure.*

Resolve never to give up, no matter what the situation. Many of the tournaments won today have resulted from simply hanging in as others faltered. A golf tournament is never over until you or your opponents have holed the last putt. (Jack Nicklaus)

The secret to a bad shot or bad break is putting it behind you as quickly as possible. (Bobby Locke)

Study the line of the putt and the slope for speed. The three-foot area around the hole should be given extra attention, as this is where the ball is most prone to the slope of the green because of the slow speed as it approaches.

The secret to long-lasting play is to play golf for the love of the game. If one adopts this attitude all the game's benefits will be enjoyed. At times this may be difficult, but if adopted, success will prevail. Never ever denounce the game. No single person alive or dead is bigger or better than the wonderful game of golf.

Dedication is thinking about the swing and the game even when you're on holiday.

During the final stages of a golf tournament/championship, particularly the majors, the nature of the competition changes. Instead of being a test of golf it becomes an ordeal of character and experience. For most this is unknown territory. A Watson or a Nicklaus, veterans of this situation, knows how to handle it. They become icily analytical, cautious, and patient because they know that the novices will destroy themselves in their excitement. Once you've been there you can do it (win) again and again.

Wide and Wide: Exercises to Improve the Use of the Right Arm in the Golf Swing.

1. Take an imaginary address position with both arms extended, but not gripping or together. Keep the arms relaxed and in front of you. Now swing the right arm back simulating the position it would assume in the backswing. Make sure it reaches the full position of the backswing with the right elbow in the natural, comfortable position. Imagine the club in the right hand pointing at the target at the top of the swing. Now pull the right arm down, retaining the cock in the hand for as long as possible—then by returning the elbow and arm to the correct address position (the arm should nearly straighten) the wrist must now be unhinged as it approaches

impact. These two movements when coupled will create the necessary power the right side should achieve in the downswing. Keep as wide as possible on the way down, as this will help achieve the shallow descent of the club on the downswing and create the consistent strike. The wrist cock must simultaneously be maintained for as long as possible.

2. If the right elbow comes into contact with the body at any stage during the downswing it will cause untold problems. The arms, particularly the right arm, must be allowed to swing freely throughout the swing.

3. To achieve the maximum power at impact, the left shoulder must not pass the position it was in at address. This is a must, because otherwise you will lose the tension and/or torque you have created in the backswing. This will then *force* you to go harder at the ball and make you lose the control you so badly desire.

4. Another good exercise to help regain lost feel is to practice swinging in the dark. This helps you feel what your body is doing and also where all the pressures of your strength are being directed. One exercise I'm going to try, to build confidence and muscle/body awareness, is to hit balls blindfolded. One needs someone to place the ball in the correct position after you've taken your address and to line the clubface up. This I think should not only help your balance but give you confidence in your brain-to-muscle communication.

My Golfing Checklist

1. Correct Address

1. Feet, hips, and shoulders aligned.
2. Clubface square to intended target line.
3. Grip: one and a half to two knuckles visible on left hand; right-hand lifeline fits snugly over left thumb; make sure right thumb and forefinger not gripping the club too tightly because this will promote an early release.

2. Takeaway

1. Picture the plane with each swing.
2. Take the club back smoothly and low to the ground.
3. Let the clubface open naturally, maintaining the right-wrist angle at address and letting the left forearm rotate until the left arm reaches parallel. The clubface at this stage must be square to the plane of that particular club. For instance, the driver face will be more open than the nine-iron because of the flatter swing plane. The wrists should be in the same cocked position as at address. If the left arm is kept straight, the shoulder will follow throughout the backswing. And if the right-wrist angle is maintained, then the right elbow will fold automatically.

3. Backswing

From the parallel position three things occur until the backswing is completed. The shoulders turn fully 90 degrees while the wrists fold and then set (cock fully). If this has been adhered to and the address position is correct, then the hips will be in the correct position. The right knee will be coiled with the pressure or tension trying to rip the spikes under the ball of the right foot out of the ground. The left knee follows the rest of the body and should point to or behind the ball at the top of the swing.

OCTOBER 8, 1987

Today I had the feeling of turning the hips out of the way on the downswing. I have to wait for the backswing to complete before really working on turning the hips hard out of the way.

The backswing is still a little laid off, so I have to work on getting it back on line at the top.

I also had the feeling of right elbow straightening on the downswing, therefore getting a little shallower through impact.

I worked on posture—keeping the back straighter—and got the ball farther up in the stance.

MARCH 1988, *Doral*

From the top of the backswing make sure the first move down is the hips turning or turning out of the way. Clear the hips completely when the hands and arms get to hip height on the way down. As soon as they start turning out of the way, hit the ball with the right hip, and let the weight go through at the same time. If the hips move laterally at all from the top, the club will come way too much from the inside, creating a severe hook.

As the hips turn out from the top, it's much easier to clear and move onto the left side.

Turn out of the way, and then hit it.

Do not slide the hips.

MARCH 1988, *Greater Greensboro Open*

Do not try to do too many things perfectly.

Groove the fundamentals: There aren't too many of them. Once you have the fundamentals well in grasp, the quality of your bad shots will enable you to still play solid golf.

My Fundamentals Are:

1. Stance and posture.
2. Grip.
3. Slow and smooth takeaway.
4. Turn the hips and shoulders together ensuring good brace into the right knee and that the left knee points behind the ball.
5. On the downswing, turn the hips smoothly to initiate the downswing and make sure the left hip turns out of

the way briskly and does not slide toward the target. If this is done correctly the right hip remains high on the downswing and the club returns on a great return plane. Groove these fundamentals.

Hit lots of balls with right arm only.

Not too strong with right-hand grip.

Alignment and ball position: A good drill is hitting balls with ball outside left foot.

Distance from ball: comfortable—not too far away from it; weight evenly distributed through feet.

Flex and slight bow in knees at address.

Maintain flex in right knee throughout the backswing.

Right shoulder must pass through the ball with all the weight finishing on left foot at finish.

Left shoulder and shoulders: Ensure full shoulder turn on backswing with right knee flex, then on downswing they must move a little laterally and get parallel to ground when hands are just past hip height—then release with chest and torso quadrant. The right arm must straighten just after impact.

Right knee must wait for hands to get hip high (or lower) before firing down the line and finishing behind the left knee at finish.

Putting: Try to keep the shoulders level to the ground at address. Make sure the putter stays low and slow on the way back. It should go back slightly on the inside toward the right toe. On through stroke, keep the putter low and stay down as long as possible. Try to get more weight on the left foot at address.

1. Grip.
2. Ball position, stance, and straight back.
3. Smooth and slow takeaway (rotate the clubhead).
4. Good wide, full turn into right knee, left knee behind ball at the top.
5. Turn the hips back and then turn them out smoothly—no slide.

MARCH 30, 1988, *Greater Greensboro Open*

On page 102 of the Hogan book there is a diagram that illustrates supination. The mistake I'd been making was that my left wrist wasn't arching up high enough at impact. That is, at impact I must try to create as straight a line from the ball through my left shoulder; that is, from either looking from behind the target line or back from the target line.

The left shoulder goes around, the right hip stays high, and the club stays on line a long way through impact. Bingo—perfect shot.

Hit hard with right arm/shoulder/hand.

Hit hard with right side—but do not let it pass the left until way past impact.

APRIL 22, 1988

1. Make sure on the downswing that the right heel starts to come off the ground. This coupled with the hips turning (not sliding) out of the way on the downswing will result in the weight transferring through the impact zone.

2. At impact the right heel must be off the ground and you should be on the ball of the right foot. The right hip must remain as high as possible with the whole, repeat whole, right side releasing—no holding back.

3. The shoulders should be rotating through the ball on a flatter plane if both the above are adhered to. The left shoulder through impact should be more around than up. A good feeling is to feel the left elbow staying as close to the body as possible through impact.

Further Thoughts

1. Off right heel onto ball of right foot.
2. Left heel remains in same place throughout downswing/follow-through. Roll over on it—don't spin out of the way.

3. Right hip remains high on downswing and follow-through.
4. Hips turn/snap left when club is halfway down! No sliding toward target.
5. Left shoulder goes around and not up. Keep left elbow close to body through impact to help this feel.
6. Hit *hard* with right side.

MAY 4, 1988, *Las Vegas*

The Right-Hand Grip

The right hand, particularly the thumb and forefinger, is of immense importance in the gripping of the golf club, for me.

During the past twenty years I have undoubtedly used these incorrectly. I've made them pinch the grip of the golf club—and the results have been disastrous. As Ben Hogan explains in his book, these two fingers can be total swing wreckers. This done correctly will have positive effects on the following:

1. Take the tension out of the right hand.
2. Enable me to take the club back smoother and slower, and also lower.
3. Rotate the clubhead more with the forearms and not the hands.
4. Will allow the right hand to set more at the top of the backswing and get the club on parallel.
5. The left hand will be in control more, and allow a pull, more than a throw, from the top.
6. The club will set in the V (formed by thumb and forefinger of right hand) and will eliminate the casting move.

The results of this change, which occurred yesterday, have been very rewarding. It has lengthened my backswing by a foot or more. The driver gets past parallel, for the first time ever.

Also ensure when practicing to remember to practice all the other moves over the years. Particularly, keeping a lot of flex and tension in the right knee at the top of the backswing. The left knee goes behind the ball. Get off right heel on downswing, keeping the right hip high at the finish with all the weight on left foot.

JUNE 12, 1988, *Atlanta*

While on the practice tee, I realized that during my career I have managed to virtually neglect my right side on the downswing. I feel like I always pull *too* much with my left side. This causes a few problems on the way down, as follows.

1. Makes me slide toward the target too much.
2. By doing that, it makes me come down too steep, and too narrow.
3. Makes the club lay off on the way down.
4. Gets me ahead of the ball.
5. Because the body is ahead at impact it's very hard to flight the ball correctly, as the club is on too steep a descent.
6. It's very, very difficult to release the club correctly.

The feelings and moves to generate are:
1. Make sure of full turn.
2. On downswing feel as if throwing the club with right arm, shoulder, and hand.
3. Chase after the ball with right shoulder.
4. Feel back of right shoulder aiming at the target on follow-through, with all the weight finishing on left foot.
5. Make sure the right side works hard on the downswing.
6. The right thumb and forefinger are potential swing wreckers if used incorrectly. Make sure they grip the club correctly or they will release the club too early.

In a nutshell, use the right side, particularly the arm and shoulder, and hit hard with these.

Do not let the left side overpull the club down.

P.S.: The right shoulder (from the top of a good full back-swing) must work down and then through the ball, staying low and maintaining the same height as it then knocks the chin up into the finish.

JUNE 29, 1988

A really true and correct feeling to promote the correct down-swing to impact is:

1. Make sure the club gets to the correct position throughout the backswing to the top.
2. Picture the plane of the shoulders on the backswing and follow-through.
3. To initiate the downswing, pull the club with hips, shoulders, and arms (with all three connecting) to where the arms are parallel to ground, and then hit through the ball as hard as possible with right side. Right heel starts coming off the ground at this halfway-down stage. Right hip stays high as left hip clears totally.
4. Right shoulder stays low and chases the ball through impact, and the club feels like it releases left. Do not try to get to impact from the top of the swing; there is this intermediate state of pulling that occurs first.

JULY 3, 1988

1. Make sure of the full turn, rotating the clubhead, keeping the right knee flexed but supple so the weight can transfer, and allow the right thumb and forefinger to be in the correct place so at the top of the swing there is more set of the wrists.
2. Turn the left hip out of the way quickly only after you have got the arms and hands to hip high.
3. Turn the left hip high and come off the right heel on the downswing (only when hands get to parallel). Hip

high on downswing. Make sure left foot—especially the toes—does not spin out through impact and follow-through. It must roll.

4. Picture shoulder plane with each club on practice tee (90 degrees to ground from breast–chest plate).

AUGUST 28, 1988

Make sure that the weight goes onto the right side at the top of the backswing (no reverse pivot). The hips must turn fully and keep a shallow plane to them. Turning the left knee behind the ball will help to achieve this. Also keep the knee at the same height; do not let it lose height and work down toward the ball, which is bad. This will cause a very steep plane in the hips.

Once this is achieved properly the correct motion from the top is to move the left hip back to the left, and when the arms/hands get to hip height on the downswing, snap the hips to the left and keep the left forearm rotating through impact. Make sure that the top of the arm stays close to the armpit (no gap at any time through impact/follow-through, and the left shoulder goes around and not up).

Once you have achieved this feeling, hit the ball as hard as possible with the entire right side, particularly the shoulder.

If the right shoulder comes up through impact, then turn more and get more weight onto the right side during the backswing.

DECEMBER 12, 1988

1. Good grip, stance, and posture; 20 balls
2. Turn left knee behind ball and make sure it maintains same height, i.e., let it fold behind the ball.
3. Make sure that you do not try to get hips through to finish of swing from top. From the top, pull down, and when the hands are hip high, turn left hip out of the way and come up off the right heel. Also feel right arm straightening and increasing the angle on the way down.

Clubface on plane, wrist cupped, and shaft on plane.
Very easy to let club come from outside (at this stage).

Get weight back and ensure clubface rotates on takeaway—done with forearms and not hands.

Picture shoulder plane throughout swing and through impact.

JANUARY 1990

1. Wait for the hands to get to hip height and begin turning the hips through on the way down.
2. Slow the hips down and make sure of a full turn on the way back.
3. If the swing gets too choppy and short, it's because the hips are turning out too rapidly from the top of the backswing.
4. Keep flex in right knee.

OCTOBER 31, 1990

Important: Quiet legs on backswing. Make sure the torso turning back turns the hips and the legs. Legs must not move first (i.e., left knee must not shoot out toward ball on takeaway).

Putting

1. Right thumb to go off or just on right edge of grip; to feel as though shoving putt with right hand.
2. Shoulders should be relaxed, with left shoulder at same height as right, so they are both parallel to ground.
3. Must hit down and through putt, with putter staying low to ground after ball has been hit.

Chipping and Sand Play

1. On short shots and out of the sand and deep rough the clubhead must go through the ball low and stay

low (unless a high shot is required), and keep clubface open, aiming at direction of intended shot through impact and follow-through.

2. Relax shoulders.

Important: During the full swing, if the right arm has unloaded correctly through impact (that is, fully extended through impact), at the three-quarters follow-through position it will be straight and extended.

1. Closed drill.
2. Pause at the top drill; flex in right knee.
3. Cross the line at the top.
4. Right-arm-only drill.
5. Cupping left wrist.
6. Left shoulder down and through impact.
7. Left shoulder down through impact and around.

JULY 9, 1993, *Flying from Orlando to Gander*

Make sure the posture is good and no round shoulders and that the lower back is flat and flexed. The hip exercise that Chris [Verna] gave me should increase the awareness.

Rotate the club from the eight o'clock to the ten o'clock position, making sure there is a good cup in the left wrist (exaggerate it) and the right elbow is not getting tight (stick it out). The clubshaft should also be on plane at the ten o'clock position.

Make sure that there is a full set (feel the wrists ache from stretching) at the top with the clubface on plane as well. The right elbow must be free and away from the body (lots of right arm swings).

From this position at the top I must feel the left arm tracking down the right side of my chest and the clubhead being thrown at the ball from the top (early release). The butt of the club (halfway down) must point behind right hip with the back of the left hand facing the ball. Feel as though the toe of the club is squaring up to the ball early.

Hit lots of balls with the closed-stance drill, making sure you're getting behind the ball and that shoulders are square to the target. Left toe must be pointed behind the ball and good flex maintained in the right knee throughout the backswing and downswing.

Wait for the hands to get hip high on the way down before rapidly rotating the shoulders (keeping the clubhead in line with the sternum) and make sure the hips rotate to the left simultaneously, and that they do not slide to the target too much.

In the wind, always make sure that the left shoulder stays high during the backswing and that you feel the left shoulder blade pointing at the ball at the top of the backswing.

Putting

Make sure you stand absolutely square (no open left foot) to your intended line. Feet shoulder width apart (outside of shoulders/outside of feet). And make sure lower half does not move during the follow-through.

chapter twelve

THOUGHTS FOR EFFICIENT GOLF

1. Play from tees according to your ability. Too many amateurs play from tees that are out of their range and soon lose their confidence. On the other hand, you will gain confidence while playing the proper tees because you will be hitting shots that are within your ability and will put less pressure on your swing. As you progress, play a few holes farther back, then perhaps nine holes. In this way you can gauge your progress. But if you play from tees that make the course too difficult for you, you will lose confidence and go backward. This is what is so hard about golf: There are contradictions. I've said, after all, that as a kid I liked to play the course as difficult as possible. The best way to play this game is to do what your feelings and instincts tell you. Generally, however, work from easy to difficult. Don't start with difficult, and don't reach difficult until you are comfortable with your progress.

2. Play at a pace within your comfort zone, but always tend toward the fast rather than the slow. Your golfing mind works better when you get on with the game. As you walk to your ball, figure out whose shot is next. Then prepare yourself by getting your yardage, and putting your glove back on if you

like to take it off between shots. Don't rush, but be ready to play when it's your turn.

3. Keep in mind that an effective shot is rarely the most glamorous shot. You will feel awfully good if after missing a drive out there to a less than favorable position from which you cannot go for the pin, you then hit your approach in forty feet from the hole. Nobody else may appreciate that you have hit a fine shot in, but you can enjoy the satisfaction of having played intelligently. Then, bolstered by knowing you played the smart shot in, you may well hole the putt. You didn't play the first part of the hole very well but you could walk away with a birdie. This, to me, is efficient golf.

4. Remember that there is a difference between confidence and cockiness. Playing the Memphis Open a few years ago, I was thinking that I had never driven the ball as well. It seemed I had not missed a fairway in weeks. Just after I had that thought, I drove the ball out of bounds. There was nothing the matter with reminding myself how well I had been driving the ball, but I forgot to regroup and then hit the drive with just that little bit of excessive pride—and carelessness. I didn't regroup and get into my routine, but simply went ahead and hit the shot as if there were no need of my doing the things that had been responsible for my accurate driving.

The shot was a wakeup call for me. From then on I didn't allow myself to cross the line from confidence to cockiness. And I went on to win the tournament.

5. We all take golf personally. I don't care what level a player you are, the game will still get to you from time to time. If you're hurting on the course, try to leave the bad feeling there and not take it home with you. It's hard sometimes to do this, but you have to. You will last longer in the game if you leave it behind as quickly as you can.

6. Keep things in perspective. I didn't win on the PGA Tour in 1995 or 1996 after winning frequently the four previous seasons. Many times I was asked why I was not doing better, and from time to time I wondered about the same thing. But then I realized that due to the overwhelming demands on my time I didn't practice as much. Nobody could have prepared me for the change in my daily routine that my success had created.

7. Golf offers so much time for introspection. This can be good or bad, depending on how you approach the hours you spend on the course. Use the time wisely and you will find you get more out of a round, even a bad round. Don't brood. Find a way to enjoy the walk, the fresh air, and remember—you could be in the office working.

8. I would advise younger players to find a mentor, an older adult they trust and whose company they enjoy. George Blumberg played that role for me for many years; he was quite an influential person in my life. He also helped Gary Player in his early days as a professional. We used to call him Uncle George in South Africa. I got very close to him and his wife, Brenda, and would stay with them in their home. He knew so much about golf around the world, and also the game's history. If I had a question I would ask Uncle George. "What was golf like in the United States? What was it like in the 1960s?"

I trusted Uncle George when he told me to start my professional career in Europe. That was the right place for me to gain experience.

9. Youngsters would do well to play without taking any drops anywhere. Forget about winter rules; they don't exist. This will help the young player to be more creative, especially given the excellent conditioning of so many courses today. When you do get a bad lie, play it from there even if it was caused by somebody else's neglect and even if you are playing the most casual golf.

Golf was not designed to be played on a perfect surface; you have to learn to hood a little seven-iron from an ugly lie or a divot in the fairway.

10. Simple strategies breed victories. Cover all your bases as best you can, leaving very little to chance, though you must realize that you cannot control everything that happens to you on the course and you certainly cannot control what other players are doing. As the tournament unfolds, develop an idea of what the winning score will be and play around that. Keep a rudder on your game and try to ensure it's heading in the right direction.

Here's an illustration of this point. Suppose you tell a golfer that he has to play for his life and that he has to shoot an even-par round. You'll see him hitting three-woods and one-irons off the tee and longer irons to the green, because he knows he can put those clubs together to get the ball on the green and have a good chance for pars. He's not going to have a real good putt for birdie unless he hits a brilliant shot, but he'll get the ball on the greens somehow. What he'll be trying to do is to take double-bogey, out-of-bounds, and water-hazards out of the picture, because he's got a better chance of making par from the fairway than from the rough. The only chance he is taking is that he might bogey a hole, but he won't make double-bogey and have to make two birdies to make up for it. You can recover from a bogey the next hole, but you need two birdies to make up for a double bogey.

I hit quite a number of three-irons off the tee during qualifying rounds at the Old Course for the 1975 British Open at Carnoustie, when I was an amateur. I shot 150 there to make the field. That was one of the proudest moments of my life, since I was an eighteen-year-old amateur and I beat many pros to get in. But I used my head there. I knew 150 would probably qualify, and I just played smart golf to get there.

Invariably when you employ a strategy like this you become so confident that suddenly your good shots are the rule and count much more than your bad shots. And that's how you play for your life.

11. Never aim for a hazard, even if you are trying to work the ball left or right off it. I often make this mistake, because I never believe a ball's going to go dead straight or that the wind won't affect the flight. I did it on the ninth hole in the first round of the 1995 Tour Championship at Southern Hills in Tulsa, where I had won the 1994 PGA Championship. I tried to turn my drive just off the left edge of a deep bunker on the right side of the fairway. The ball went straight and finished in an awkward spot in the bunker. That mistake led to a couple of others, and I walked away with a triple bogey. You should not make a triple bogey after hitting a tee shot that missed your target by only a foot. Give yourself more margin of error than that—much more.

12. We can all play smarter golf. When I'm playing and thinking my best, I get on the back nine the last day of a tournament and set a target for myself that I think nobody will beat. Then there's another, secondary target when you give the other guys a slight chance. Then there's a further target that will keep you in the tournament.

The back nine at Augusta National is one of the most interesting places to think about strategy. I like to think that if I'm leading by one going into the back nine at the Masters and shoot 32, four under, I'll blow everyone out of the water by three shots. But I probably don't have to shoot 32; what I have to do is shoot 34 or 35. If I go out and play a smart nine holes, take all the trouble out of play, and just go along and shoot 34, then I should win. If I shoot 35, I might let another two guys have a chance, because another guy who needs to shoot 34 and is in the same frame of mind as I am will have to take one more chance than I do. If he takes that chance and it pays off, he could win. Okay, fair enough. Let's see if he has the ability to do it.

The bottom line is that it's a calculated, put-your-game-on-the-line thing. It's not a straight-out gamble or flier; you don't pull the blackjack card on the nineteen count. But it's a matter of playing with some savvy, of sticking within reason with your plan. You plug along and stick with what you are doing and have the confidence that things will come right in the end.

13. Don't ever think that you can understand the golf swing 100 percent. There are so many intricate moves in the swing that nobody can say exactly why he hit a shot this way or that. But maybe you can get to 80 percent correct in your understanding. And that's enough to keep you playing well and recovering from the errors you tend to make.

14. There is no doubt that the short game is critical to scoring. But you will wear yourself down eventually if you have to chip and putt to play well all the time. It's just too hard on a golfer to go through the highs and lows of hitting the ball in the cabbage and trying to recover. To me the highest pleasure in the game is in learning a swing that will keep the ball in play.

The Principles of Efficient Golf

It's never a simple matter to condense one's thoughts on the game into very few words. But I think this is a superb exercise, and quite often thinking of one simple catchphrase will spark off other ideas that are key for you. One of my golden rules has always been to keep my left shoulder high and make sure that my left shoulder blade is behind the ball at the top of the back-swing. This allows many good things to happen during my swing.

Trying to condense my thoughts is sort of a test for myself. How well do I understand what I am trying to do in this intriguing game? And so here are my closing thoughts on the principles of the swing, followed by my core beliefs about the strategy of the game. You may want to go through the same exercise of condensing your thoughts. It can only help to try to distill your ideas down to the basic principles.

Swing

- Set up in a tall posture and maintain height and spine angle throughout the swing.
- Use a stronger rather than a weaker grip.
- Keep your lower half quiet and soft back and through.
- Maintain flex in right knee.
- Turn the shoulders back and through.
- Set the club at the top.
- Initiate the downswing by turning the left hip.
- Squat on the right knee.
- Make sure the hips don't overpower the rest of the body.
- Maintain spine angle.
- Cover the ball with the right side.
- Width, width, width.
- Balance, balance, balance.

Strategy

- Be yourself.
- When in doubt, play the shot that is easiest for you.
- With putting, be more into speed than line or stroke.
- Patience, patience, patience.
- Never try to force things.
- Take a long-term approach to improvement.
- Persevere, Persevere, Persevere.

READERS' NOTES

A NOTE ABOUT THE AUTHORS

Nick Price was born in 1957 in South Africa but moved at an early age to Rhodesia (now Zimbabwe). In 1974 he won the World Junior title in California, and since then thirty-two tournaments in Africa, Europe, Asia, and America. In addition to the PGA Championship (1992 and 1994) and the British Open (1994), his victories include the World Series of Golf, the Players Championship, and, in all, tournaments in ten countries. He lives with his wife, Sue, and their three children in Florida.

Lorne Rubenstein is the author of *Links: An Insider's Tour Through the World of Golf* and *Touring Prose*. Widely published in golf and general-interest magazines, he has won the Golf Writers Association of America Award three times and, in Canada, the National Magazine Award. His column in the Toronto *Globe and Mail* has run for eighteen years. He lives in Toronto with his wife, Nell.

A NOTE ON THE TYPE

This book was set in a version of the well-known Monotype face
Bembo. This letter was cut for the celebrated Venetian printer Aldus
Manutius by Francesco Griffo, and first used in Pietro Cardinal
Bembo's *De Aetna* of 1495.

The companion italic is an adaptation of the chancery script type
designed by the calligrapher and printer Lodovico degli Arrighi.

Composition and art program by North Market Street Graphics,
Lancaster, Pennsylvania
Printed and bound by Quebecor Printing,
Kingsport, Tennessee
Designed by Judith Henry

Good Housekeeping

PASTA!

**OUR BEST RECIPES FROM FETTUCCINE ALFREDO &
PASTA PRIMAVERA TO SESAME NOODLES & BAKED ZITI**

HEARST BOOKS

A division of Sterling Publishing Co., Inc.

New York / London
www.sterlingpublishing.com

GOOD HOUSEKEEPING

Rosemary Ellis
EDITOR IN CHIEF

Sara Lyle
LIFESTYLE EDITOR

Susan Westmoreland
FOOD DIRECTOR

Samantha B. Cassetty, M.S., R.D.
NUTRITION DIRECTOR

Sharon Franke
FOOD APPLIANCES DIRECTOR

BOOK DESIGN by Memo Productions
EDITED by Sarah Scheffel
Photography Credits on page 158

Library of Congress
Cataloging-in-Publication Data
Good Housekeeping pasta! : our best recipes from fettuccine alfredo & pasta primavera to sesame noodles & baked ziti / Rosemary Ellis, editor in chief ; Susan Westmoreland, food director.
      p. cm.
   Includes index.
   ISBN 978-1-58816-875-7
1. Cooking (Pasta) I. Westmoreland, Susan. II. Good Housekeeping Institute (New York, N.Y.) III. Title: Pasta!
   TX809.M17G66 2011
   641.8'22--dc22
               2010028166

10 9 8 7 6 5 4 3 2 1

The Good Housekeeping Cookbook Seal guarantees that the recipes in this cookbook meet the strict standards of the Good Housekeeping Research Institute. The Institute has been a source of reliable information and a consumer advocate since 1900, and established its seal of approval in 1909. Every recipe has been triple-tested for ease, reliability, and great taste.

Published by Hearst Books
A division of Sterling Publishing Co., Inc.
387 Park Avenue South, New York, NY 10016

Good Housekeeping is a registered trademark of Hearst Communications, Inc.

www.goodhousekeeping.com

For information about custom editions, special sales, premium and corporate purchases, please contact Sterling Special Sales Department at 800-805-5489 or specialsales@sterlingpublishing.com.

Distributed in Canada by Sterling Publishing c/o Canadian Manda Group, 165 Dufferin Street Toronto, Ontario, Canada M6K 3H6

Distributed in Australia by Capricorn Link (Australia) Pty. Ltd.
P.O. Box 704, Windsor, NSW 2756 Australia

Manufactured in China

Sterling ISBN 978-1-58816-875-7

Good Housekeeping

PASTA!

OUR BEST RECIPES FROM FETTUCCINE ALFREDO & PASTA PRIMAVERA TO SESAME NOODLES & BAKED ZITI

Lasagna Toss Bolognese (page 70)

CONTENTS

Penne with Yellow Peppers and Sweet Onion (page 28)

FOREWORD

Welcome to *Good Housekeeping*'s collection of favorite pasta recipes. We've gathered the tried-and-true recipes that our editors and readers tell us they make again and again. You'll find dozens of sauces that can be prepared while the pasta water boils—just right for those who, like many cooks, rely on serving pasta a few nights a week. Whether you're shopping the express lane of the grocery store or finding inspiration at your local farmers' market, there are recipes to suit.

If you like to keep dinner in the freezer, whip up our Big-Batch Tomato Sauce—you can stir in everything from store-bought meatballs to fresh shrimp or clams and deliver dinner in a flash. Having a crowd over? No problem. Check out our baked pasta chapter, where you'll find Sunday Baked Ziti and Meatball Casserole, Spaghetti Carbonara Pie, Butternut-Squash Lasagna, and more great crowd-pleasers.

Another pasta plus is versatility. You toss it with greens and tuna to make a sublime Provençal Pasta Salad—perfect for a picnic supper or light dinner. Combined with cheese, pasta makes a delicious, protein-rich meatless meal. Even meat eaters will love our Butternut-Squash Lasagna, with its cheesy layers of roasted squash.

For special occasions you'll find an array of impressive dishes to choose from, like our luscious Seafood-Stuffed Shells and Ruffled Pasta with Lamb and Mint. For everyday family meals, we offer our creamiest ever Macaroni and Cheese Deluxe, Linguine with White Clam Sauce, and Spaghetti and Meatballs, plus lots of quick and easy stovetop pastas starring fresh seasonal vegetables.

Each and every one of the recipes has been triple tested in the Good Housekeeping kitchens to ensure superb results. Many of the recipes are classic Italian, while others are inspired by the cuisines of China, Vietnam, Greece, and France. Just be assured that one common thread runs throughout all of our very best pasta recipes—great taste.

SUSAN WESTMORELAND
Food Director, *Good Housekeeping*

PERFECT PASTA EVERY TIME!

Perfectly cooked pasta is firm yet tender to the bite, or *al dente* as Italians say, with sauce coating each delicious mouthful. Some of the most common mistakes—mushy (or sticky) spaghetti, watery lasagna, sauce that pools in the bottom of the bowl instead of clinging to the noodles as it should—can easily be avoided by following a few simple guidelines:

- **For best taste and texture,** look for pasta, either Italian or American, made from durum wheat or semolina flour. Choose pasta packaged in cardboard boxes and resist the urge to transfer it from the original box to a clear decorative container. The cardboard keeps out light, which can destroy riboflavin, an important nutrient that is found in pasta.

- **Store dried pasta in a cool, dark place.** Regular durum wheat pasta should last for up to a year. Whole-wheat pasta has a shorter shelf life: no longer than six months and sometimes less. Read package instructions to be sure. Fresh pasta should be refrigerated according to package directions, usually for up to a week. It can also be frozen for as long as a month. It's best not to thaw frozen pasta before cooking.

- **Use plenty of boiling water.** A good rule of thumb is 4 quarts for each pound of pasta. Bring it to a rolling boil (covering the pot hastens the process), then add about 2 teaspoons of salt per pound of pasta. Salted water takes longer to boil, so be sure to add the salt just before adding the pasta. Don't be tempted to omit the salt—it's essential for proper seasoning.

- **Stir frequently to prevent sticking.** Once you've salted the water and it's at a full boil, stir in the pasta. Cover the pot, if necessary, to return the water quickly to a boil. Uncover and continue cooking, stirring often, until the strands separate. There's no need to add oil to pasta cooking water. In fact, the oil might keep the sauce from adhering to the pasta. Stirring is all you need to prevent sticking.

- **Cook according to package directions.** There's no set rule for how long each pasta shape should cook. Spaghetti from one manufacturer may take longer than the same size spaghetti from another, depending on the type of wheat used and how it was processed. So always read the box—it will give you the correct cooking time.

- **Check for doneness often** before the suggested cooking time has elapsed. The goal is pasta that's tender yet still slightly firm, or al dente. The only way to test it is by tasting. Remove a piece from the pot and rinse it briefly under warm water, then bite into it. There should be no hard white center. Remember that the pasta will continue cooking from the residual heat even after you drain it. If the cooked pasta will be baked later, undercook it slightly.
- **Drain well in a colander,** shaking to make sure all excess water has been removed. Don't rinse pasta unless the recipe specifies to do so. Rinsing can remove starch that helps the sauce cling and provides important nutrients.

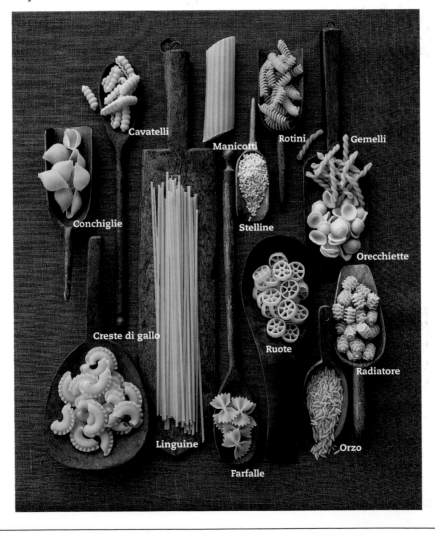

Cavatelli

Manicotti

Rotini

Gemelli

Conchiglie

Stelline

Orecchiette

Creste di gallo

Ruote

Radiatore

Linguine

Orzo

Farfalle

THE SHAPE OF PASTAS TO COME

The recipes in this book use a wide variety of Italian pastas and Asian noodles, ranging from the familiar macaroni and spaghetti to the more exotic creste di gallo and rice noodles. In most cases, particularly if a shape is not common, the ingredients list will suggest an easily found substitution. If you don't recognize the particular pasta called for, this glossary tells you what to look for. It may also be pictured in the photograph on page 9.

LONG STRANDS

Capellini: Extremely thin spaghetti—sometimes called "angel hair"
Fusilli: Wavy strands, "corkscrew pasta"
Spaghetti: Thin, round strands
Spaghettini: Thin spaghetti
Speghettoni: Thick spaghetti
Vermicelli: Very thin spaghetti—between capellini and spaghettini in thickness

FLAT RIBBONS

Egg noodles: Short, flat, and slightly curled when dry—no-yolk versions are widely available
Fettuccine: Flat noodles about ¼ inch wide
Lasagna: Very wide, flat pasta—also available in "no-cook" form
Linguine: Thin noodles about ⅛ inch wide
Mafalda: Wide and with a ruffled edge
Tagliatelle: A little wider than fettuccine

TUBULAR PASTAS

Bucatini: Long, thin tubes
Elbow macaroni: Small, curved tubular pasta
Manicotti: Large tubes of pasta for stuffing
Penne: Pasta tubes with diagonally cut ends
Rigatoni: Large, ribbed tubes
Ziti: Medium tubes

SMALL PASTAS

Campanelle: Tiny bell- or flower-shaped pasta
Cavatappi: Small corkscrews
Ditalini: Short tubular pasta—very similar to tubettini
Orecchini: Pasta "earrings"
Orzo: Rice-shaped pasta
Stelline: Tiny star-shaped pasta

ONE-OF-A-KIND PASTAS

Cavatelli: Short ridged pasta
Conchiglie: Medium shells
Creste di gallo: Curved pasta with ridged edge
Farfalle: Literal translation is "butterflies"—known in America as bow ties
Gemelli: Two short strands of pasta that have been twisted together
Orecchiette: Small rounded pasta disks—literal translation is "little ears"
Radiatore: Shaped like small radiators
Rotini: Corkscrew shape
Ruote: Wagon-wheel-shaped pasta—also called rotelle

STUFFED PASTAS

Pierogi: Round Polish pasta dumplings filled with meat, potatoes, or cheese
Ravioli: Plump pasta pillows filled with cheese or meat
Tortellini: Small pasta rings filled with cheese or meat

ASIAN NOODLES

Cellophane noodles: Also called bean threads or mai fun
Chinese-style egg noodles: Wheat-flour noodles similar to egg linguine used in the dishes lo mein and chow mein
Rice sticks: Very thin noodles that are cooked by soaking or deep frying
Soba: Thin brownish noodles made from buckwheat flour
Udon noodles: Long, thick, chewy Japanese wheat-flour noodles

MATCHING PASTA TO SAUCE

Choosing the right pasta to enhance a particular sauce is a bit of an art. Shells, for example, are just right for capturing tiny bits of meat and vegetables, while delicate Asian dishes require slender noodles. The Good Housekeeping Test Kitchens have carefully chosen the pasta shapes for all the recipes that follow. If you're devising a recipe on your own, here are some simple suggestions to help you get it right.

- **Capellini, vermicelli, and other thin pastas** are best with light, delicate sauces. Heavier meat sauces can slip off the strands and sink to the bottom of the bowl.
- **Flat ribbons, such as fettuccine and linguine,** work well with cheese and cream sauces, as well as lighter meat, vegetable, or seafood sauces.
- **Tubular pastas like ziti, penne, and rigatoni** are strong enough to stand up to heartier meat sauces and chunky vegetable sauces. They are also ideal in baked dishes.
- **Most tiny pastas, such as ditalini and tubetti,** are best suited for soups. The exception is orzo, which is good in soups but is also often combined with meat or vegetables and served as a main or side dish.

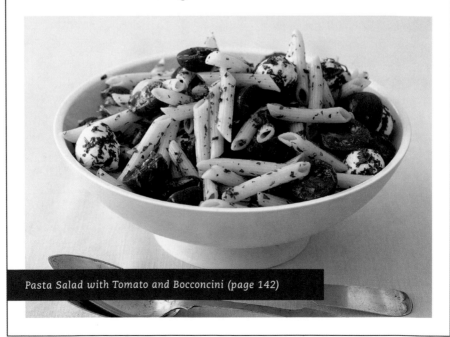

Pasta Salad with Tomato and Bocconcini (page 142)

BASIC PASTA SAUCES

Here is a simple recipe for pesto plus four more basic pasta sauces that you can turn to again and again. Serve them on their own, tossed with your favorite type of pasta, or use them in recipes specified throughout this book.

HOMEMADE PESTO

Pesto is the perfect use for all that fresh summer basil. To serve it with pasta, save ¼ cup pasta cooking water and stir it, along with the pesto, into 1 pound cooked pasta. To store the pesto, spoon it into half-pint containers and drizzle a few tablespoons of olive oil on top. Cover and refrigerate for up to one week.

TOTAL TIME: 10 MINUTES

MAKES: ABOUT ¾ CUP

2 CUPS FIRMLY PACKED FRESH BASIL LEAVES	¼ CUP OLIVE OIL
1 GARLIC CLOVE, CRUSHED WITH GARLIC PRESS	1 TEASPOON SALT
	¼ TEASPOON COARSELY GROUND BLACK PEPPER
2 TABLESPOONS PINE NUTS (PIGNOLI) OR WALNUTS	½ CUP FRESHLY GRATED PARMESAN CHEESE

In blender or a food processor with knife blade attached, puree basil, garlic, pine nuts, oil, salt, and pepper until smooth. Add Parmesan and blend until combined.

EACH TABLESPOON: ABOUT 65 CALORIES | 2G PROTEIN | 1G CARBOHYDRATE
6G TOTAL FAT (1G SATURATED) | 0G FIBER | 3MG CHOLESTEROL | 256MG SODIUM

SPAGHETTI WITH OIL AND GARLIC SAUCE

Cooking mellows the garlic, creating a light yet flavorful sauce. Serve with freshly grated Parmesan cheese.

ACTIVE TIME: 5 MINUTES · **TOTAL TIME:** 25 MINUTES
MAKES: 6 MAIN-DISH SERVINGS

1 PACKAGE (16 OUNCES) SPAGHETTI OR LINGUINE

¼ CUP OLIVE OIL

1 LARGE GARLIC CLOVE, FINELY CHOPPED

⅛ TEASPOON CRUSHED RED PEPPER (OPTIONAL)

¾ TEASPOON SALT

¼ TEASPOON COARSELY GROUND BLACK PEPPER

2 TABLESPOONS CHOPPED FRESH PARSLEY

1 In large saucepot, cook pasta as label directs. Drain.

2 Meanwhile, in 1-quart saucepan, heat oil over medium heat. Add garlic and cook just until golden, about 1 minute; add crushed red pepper, if using, and cook 30 seconds longer. Remove saucepan from heat; stir in salt and black pepper. In warm serving bowl, toss pasta with garlic-oil mixture and parsley.

EACH SERVING: ABOUT 360 CALORIES | 10G PROTEIN | 57G CARBOHYDRATE
10G TOTAL FAT (1G SATURATED) | 1G FIBER | 0MG CHOLESTEROL | 361MG SODIUM

EASY ADD-INS FOR OLIVE OIL AND GARLIC PASTA

Spaghetti with Oil and Garlic Sauce is just the starting point for many delicious possibilities.

- Add 4 to 6 coarsely chopped anchovy fillets in oil, drained (or 1 to 1½ teaspoons anchovy paste), and 2 tablespoons capers, drained, to cooked garlic-oil mixture; reduce heat and stir until anchovies break up, about 30 seconds.

- Add ½ cup Gaeta, Kalamata, or green Sicilian olives, pitted and chopped, to cooked garlic-oil mixture; reduce heat and stir until olives are heated through, about 1 minute.

- Add 2 to 3 ounces crumbled firm goat cheese to tossed pasta; toss again.

- Add ⅓ cup chopped dried tomatoes to pasta with garlic-oil mixture and parsley; toss.

- Substitute 2 to 4 tablespoons chopped fresh basil, oregano, chives, or tarragon for parsley.

- Add 1 bag (10 ounces) cleaned spinach, 1 can garbanzo beans, drained and rinsed, and ½ cup golden raisins; toss until the beans are heated through and the spinach is slightly wilted.

MARINARA SAUCE

We use this versatile herbed tomato sauce in several recipes throughout the book, but it's also a delicious pasta sauce in its own right. For a superquick meal, serve it over cheese ravioli from the refrigerator case.

ACTIVE TIME: 10 MINUTES · **TOTAL TIME:** 30 MINUTES

MAKES: 3½ CUPS, ENOUGH FOR 4 MAIN-DISH SERVINGS

2	TABLESPOONS OLIVE OIL	2	TABLESPOONS TOMATO PASTE
1	SMALL ONION (4 TO 6 OUNCES), CHOPPED	2	TABLESPOONS CHOPPED FRESH BASIL OR PARSLEY (OPTIONAL)
1	GARLIC CLOVE, FINELY CHOPPED	½	TEASPOON SALT
1	CAN (28 OUNCES) PLUM TOMATOES		

1 In nonreactive 3-quart saucepan, heat oil over medium heat; add onion and garlic and cook, stirring, until onion is tender, about 5 minutes.

2 Stir in tomatoes with their juice, tomato paste, basil, if using, and salt. Heat to boiling, breaking up tomatoes with side of spoon. Reduce heat; partially cover and simmer, stirring occasionally, until sauce has thickened slightly, about 20 minutes.

EACH ½ CUP: ABOUT 65 CALORIES | 1G PROTEIN | 7G CARBOHYDRATE | 4G TOTAL FAT (1G SATURATED) | 1G FIBER | 0MG CHOLESTEROL | 388MG SODIUM

BIG-BATCH TOMATO SAUCE

Perfect for baked ziti and lasagna, this recipe makes a mildly seasoned sauce. Heat 2½ cups of it for each pound of pasta.

ACTIVE TIME: 15 MINUTES · **TOTAL TIME:** 1 HOUR 15 MINUTES
MAKES: ABOUT 10 CUPS

3	TABLESPOONS OLIVE OIL	3	CANS (28 OUNCES EACH) PLUM TOMATOES IN PUREE
3	CARROTS, PEELED AND FINELY CHOPPED	1	BAY LEAF
1	LARGE ONION (12 OUNCES), CHOPPED	¾	TEASPOON SALT
2	GARLIC CLOVES, FINELY CHOPPED	¼	TEASPOON COARSELY GROUND BLACK PEPPER

1 In nonreactive 5-quart Dutch oven, heat oil over medium heat. Add carrots and onion and cook, stirring occasionally, until vegetables are very tender, about 20 minutes. Add garlic; cook, stirring, 2 minutes.

2 Add tomatoes with their puree, bay leaf, salt, and pepper to Dutch oven; heat to boiling over high heat, breaking up tomatoes with side of spoon. Reduce heat; cover and simmer 15 minutes. Remove lid and simmer until sauce has thickened slightly, about 20 minutes longer. Discard bay leaf.

EACH ½ CUP: ABOUT 60 CALORIES | 2G PROTEIN | 10G CARBOHYDRATE | 2G TOTAL FAT (0G SATURATED) | 2G FIBER | 0MG CHOLESTEROL | 280MG SODIUM

CLASSIC BOLOGNESE SAUCE

A staple in Bologna, Italy, this tomato-based meat sauce, enriched with cream and mellowed by long simmering, is well worth the time. Use 2½ cups sauce to coat 1 pound pasta. Freeze leftovers in small batches.

ACTIVE TIME: 10 MINUTES · **TOTAL TIME:** 1 HOUR 35 MINUTES
MAKES: 5 CUPS, ENOUGH FOR 12 MAIN-DISH SERVINGS

2	TABLESPOONS OLIVE OIL	½	CUP DRY RED WINE
1	MEDIUM ONION, CHOPPED	1	CAN (28 OUNCES) PLUM TOMATOES, CHOPPED
1	CARROT, PEELED AND FINELY CHOPPED	2	TEASPOONS SALT
1	STALK CELERY, FINELY CHOPPED	¼	TEASPOON GROUND BLACK PEPPER
1½	POUNDS GROUND MEAT FOR MEAT LOAF (BEEF, PORK, AND/OR VEAL) OR GROUND BEEF CHUCK	⅛	TEASPOON GROUND NUTMEG
		¼	CUP HEAVY OR WHIPPING CREAM

1 In nonreactive 5-quart Dutch oven, heat oil over medium heat. Add onion, carrot, and celery; cook, stirring occasionally, until tender, about 10 minutes.

2 Add ground meat and cook, breaking up meat with side of spoon, until no longer pink. Stir in wine and heat to boiling. Stir in tomatoes with their juice, salt, pepper, and nutmeg. Heat to boiling over high heat. Reduce heat and simmer, stirring occasionally, 1 hour.

3 Stir in cream and heat through, stirring constantly.

EACH ½ CUP: ABOUT 210 CALORIES | 13G PROTEIN | 6G CARBOHYDRATE
15G TOTAL FAT (6G SATURATED) | 1G FIBER | 58MG CHOLESTEROL | 696MG SODIUM

SAY CHEESE

Look beyond Parmesan and mozzarella—the pasta-topping staples—to these flavorful alternatives. For best flavor and texture, prepare cheese as you go—whether recipes call for it grated, shredded, crumbled, or sliced.

- **Grana padano:** A cow's-milk cheese similar in flavor and texture to Parmesan.

- **Fontina:** Rich and nutty cow's-milk cheese, a good substitute for mozzarella (it melts like a dream).

- **Pecorino-Romano:** Piquant and full-flavored cheese made of sheep's milk; grate some instead of Parmesan.

- **Feta:** Tangy, salty, and crumbly, this cheese made of sheep's or goat's milk is a good way to add extra zest to citrus-tinged seafood pasta.

- **Ricotta salata:** A sheep's-milk cheese similar to feta, but drier, with a milder, milky flavor; a wonderful addition to dishes accented with fresh tomatoes.

  TIP Semihard and hard cheeses last several weeks in the fridge. Cover them with waxed paper, then with plastic wrap or foil. Change the wrapping every few days.

VEGGIE PASTAS

Whole-Wheat Penne Genovese (page 32)

ROTELLE WITH RATATOUILLE

For this scrumptious variation on the classic Provençal dish, eggplant, peppers, and onions are oven-roasted for extra flavor, then tossed with pasta. Garnish with curls of Parmesan cheese for a handsome and tasty finishing touch.

ACTIVE TIME: 20 MINUTES · **TOTAL TIME:** 55 MINUTES
MAKES: 4 MAIN-DISH SERVINGS

1   MEDIUM EGGPLANT (ABOUT 1½ POUNDS), CUT INTO 1-INCH CUBES

1   MEDIUM RED PEPPER, CUT INTO 1-INCH PIECES

1   LARGE RED ONION, CUT INTO 1-INCH CHUNKS

2   GARLIC CLOVES, CRUSHED WITH GARLIC PRESS

3   TABLESPOONS OLIVE OIL

1½ TEASPOONS SALT

½   TEASPOON GROUND BLACK PEPPER

1   PINT RED AND/OR YELLOW CHERRY TOMATOES, EACH CUT IN HALF

1   CUP LOOSELY PACKED FRESH BASIL LEAVES, COARSELY CHOPPED, PLUS WHOLE LEAVES FOR GARNISH

1   TABLESPOON RED WINE VINEGAR

1   PACKAGE (16 OUNCES) ROTELLE OR FUSILLI

1   Preheat oven to 450°F. In large roasting pan (17" by 11½") or 15½" by 10½" jelly-roll pan, toss eggplant, red pepper, onion, garlic, oil, salt, and pepper until vegetables are well coated.

2   Roast the vegetables 35 to 40 minutes or until they are tender and lightly browned, stirring occasionally.

3   In large bowl, toss tomatoes with chopped basil and vinegar; set aside to allow flavors to develop.

4   Meanwhile, in large saucepot, cook pasta as label directs.

5   When pasta has reached desired doneness, remove ¼ *cup pasta cooking water* and reserve. Drain pasta. Add pasta, roasted vegetables, and reserved cooking water to tomatoes in bowl; toss well to distribute vegetables. Garnish each serving with basil leaves.

EACH SERVING: ABOUT 595 CALORIES | 18G PROTEIN | 104G CARBOHYDRATE | 13G TOTAL FAT (2G SATURATED) | 9G FIBER | 0MG CHOLESTEROL | 1,040MG SODIUM

PASTA PRIMAVERA

This dish is traditionally made in spring, when the first tender young vegetables appear—thus the name *primavera*, which means "spring" in Italian. We used fresh asparagus and sugar snaps and cooked them along with the pasta to save time.

ACTIVE TIME: 15 MINUTES · **TOTAL TIME:** 36 MINUTES

MAKES: 6 MAIN-DISH SERVINGS

½ CUP HEAVY OR WHIPPING CREAM

3 TABLESPOONS BUTTER OR MARGARINE

4 OUNCES SHIITAKE MUSHROOMS, STEMS REMOVED AND CAPS THINLY SLICED

2 VERY SMALL YELLOW SQUASH OR ZUCCHINI (4 OUNCES EACH), CUT INTO 2"-BY-¼" MATCHSTICK STRIPS

4 GREEN ONIONS, THINLY SLICED

1 TABLESPOON CHOPPED FRESH PARSLEY

1 PACKAGE (16 OUNCES) FETTUCCINE

1 POUND ASPARAGUS, TRIMMED AND CUT ON DIAGONAL INTO 1½-INCH PIECES

4 OUNCES SUGAR SNAP PEAS, STRINGS REMOVED

¾ CUP FRESHLY GRATED PARMESAN CHEESE

¼ TEASPOON SALT

1 In 1-quart saucepan, heat cream to boiling and boil 1 minute. Remove saucepan from burner and set aside.

2 In nonstick 10-inch skillet, melt butter over medium heat. Add mushrooms and cook, stirring, 1 minute. Add squash and cook, stirring, until vegetables are tender, about 3 minutes. Remove from heat; stir in green onions and parsley. Keep warm.

3 Meanwhile, in large saucepot, begin cooking pasta as label directs. After pasta has cooked 7 minutes, add asparagus and sugar snap peas to pasta water. Cook until pasta and vegetables are tender, 3 to 5 minutes longer. Drain pasta and vegetables, reserving ½ *cup pasta cooking water.*

4 In warm serving bowl, toss pasta and vegetables with reserved pasta water, Parmesan, and salt. Stir in cream and mushroom mixture.

EACH SERVING: ABOUT 490 CALORIES | 18G PROTEIN | 64G CARBOHYDRATE | 18G TOTAL FAT (11G SATURATED) | 4G FIBER | 52MG CHOLESTEROL | 462MG SODIUM

PORTOBELLO PASTA

A delicious sauté of mushrooms, sweet red pepper, and onion tossed with bow ties and baby spinach.

TOTAL TIME: 35 MINUTES

MAKES: 4 MAIN-DISH SERVINGS

1 TABLESPOON OLIVE OIL

1 LARGE ONION (12 OUNCES), CUT IN HALF AND THINLY SLICED

1 LARGE RED PEPPER, THINLY SLICED

2 GARLIC CLOVES, CRUSHED WITH GARLIC PRESS

2 PACKAGES (6 OUNCES EACH) SLICED PORTOBELLO MUSHROOMS, EACH HALVED

1 TABLESPOON BALSAMIC VINEGAR

1¼ TEASPOONS SALT

¼ TEASPOON GROUND BLACK PEPPER

1 PACKAGE (16 OUNCES) BOW TIES (FARFALLE)

1 BAG (6 OUNCES) BABY SPINACH

1 In 12-inch skillet, heat oil over medium heat until hot. Add onion and red pepper, and cook 10 to 12 minutes or until vegetables are tender and golden, stirring often. Add garlic and cook 30 seconds, stirring.

2 To onion mixture in skillet, add mushrooms, vinegar, salt, and black pepper, and cook over medium-high heat about 10 minutes or until mushrooms are tender, stirring often.

3 Meanwhile, in large saucepot, cook pasta as label directs.

4 When pasta has reached desired doneness, remove ½ cup pasta *cooking water* and reserve. Drain pasta. Return pasta to saucepot; stir in mushroom mixture, spinach, and reserved cooking water.

EACH SERVING: ABOUT 515 CALORIES | 20G PROTEIN | 96G CARBOHYDRATE | 5G TOTAL FAT (1 SATURATED) | 7G FIBER | 0MG CHOLESTEROL | 1,000MG SODIUM

LINGUINE WITH MUSHROOM SAUCE

This sauce combines dried and fresh mushrooms for rich, earthy flavor. Serve with a salad of baby greens tossed with a lemon vinaigrette.

ACTIVE TIME: 20 MINUTES · **TOTAL TIME:** 40 MINUTES PLUS STANDING

MAKES: 6 MAIN-DISH SERVINGS

½ CUP BOILING WATER

1 PACKAGE (ABOUT ⅓ OUNCE) DRIED PORCINI MUSHROOMS

2 TABLESPOONS OLIVE OIL

1 MEDIUM ONION (6 TO 8 OUNCES), CHOPPED

2 GARLIC CLOVES, FINELY CHOPPED

8 OUNCES SHIITAKE MUSHROOMS, STEMS REMOVED AND CAPS THINLY SLICED

12 OUNCES WHITE MUSHROOMS, TRIMMED AND THINLY SLICED

½ TEASPOON SALT

¼ TEASPOON GROUND BLACK PEPPER

1¼ CUPS CHICKEN BROTH

1 PACKAGE (16 OUNCES) LINGUINE

2 TABLESPOONS BUTTER, CUT INTO PIECES (OPTIONAL)

¼ CUP CHOPPED FRESH PARSLEY

1 In small bowl, pour boiling water over porcini mushrooms; let stand about 30 minutes. With slotted spoon, remove porcini, then strain mushroom liquid through sieve lined with paper towels; set aside. Rinse mushrooms to remove any grit, then chop.

2 In 12-inch skillet, heat 1 tablespoon oil over low heat. Add onion and garlic and cook, stirring frequently, until onion is tender. Add shiitake mushrooms and cook, stirring, 5 minutes. Add remaining 1 tablespoon oil, white and porcini mushrooms, salt, and pepper; cook until mushrooms are tender, about 7 minutes. Add reserved mushroom liquid and cook, stirring frequently, until liquid has evaporated, about 2 minutes. Add broth and heat to boiling; cook until broth has reduced by one-third.

3 Meanwhile, in large saucepot, cook pasta as label directs. Drain. In warm serving bowl, toss pasta with sauce, butter, if using, and parsley.

EACH SERVING: ABOUT 365 CALORIES | 13G PROTEIN | 64G CARBOHYDRATE | 6G TOTAL FAT (1G SATURATED) | 4G FIBER | 0MG CHOLESTEROL | 475MG SODIUM

PENNE WITH YELLOW PEPPERS AND SWEET ONION

Long, slow cooking makes sweet onion and yellow peppers even sweeter and more flavorful. Be sure to stir often to prevent scorching. For photo, see page 6.

TOTAL TIME: 20 MINUTES

MAKES: 4 MAIN-DISH SERVINGS

2 TABLESPOONS OLIVE OIL	¼ TEASPOON COARSELY GROUND BLACK PEPPER
2 MEDIUM YELLOW PEPPERS, THINLY SLICED	1 TABLESPOON BALSAMIC VINEGAR
1 JUMBO SWEET ONION (12 OUNCES) SUCH AS WALLA WALLA OR VIDALIA, THINLY SLICED	½ CUP CHOPPED FRESH BASIL
	1 PACKAGE (16 OUNCES) PENNE RIGATE OR ELBOW TWIST PASTA
½ TEASPOON SALT	

1 In 12-inch skillet heat olive oil over medium heat until hot. Add yellow peppers, onion, salt, and black pepper, and cook until vegetables are tender and golden, about 15 minutes, stirring frequently. Remove skillet from heat; stir in balsamic vinegar and chopped basil.

2 Meanwhile, in large saucepot, cook pasta as label directs.

3 When pasta has cooked to desired doneness, remove ½ cup pasta *cooking water*. Drain pasta and return to saucepot. Add yellow-pepper mixture and reserved pasta cooking water; toss well.

EACH SERVING: ABOUT 525 CALORIES | 16G PROTEIN | 95G CARBOHYDRATE | 9G TOTAL FAT (1G SATURATED) | 5G FIBER | 0MG CHOLESTEROL | 455MG SODIUM

PASTA WITH ROASTED VEGETABLES AND ARUGULA

Sweet roasted squash, red peppers, and onions contrast nicely with peppery arugula. If you prefer, substitute regular pasta for the whole-wheat.

ACTIVE TIME: 25 MINUTES · **TOTAL TIME:** 55 MINUTES

MAKES: 4 MAIN-DISH SERVINGS

- 1 PACKAGE (ABOUT 20 OUNCES) BUTTERNUT SQUASH CHUNKS, CUT INTO 1-INCH PIECES
- 4 GARLIC CLOVES, EACH CUT IN HALF
- 2 MEDIUM RED ONIONS, EACH CUT INTO 8 WEDGES
- 2 MEDIUM RED PEPPERS, CUT INTO ½-INCH-WIDE STRIPS
- 2 TABLESPOONS OLIVE OIL
- ¼ TEASPOON COARSELY GROUND BLACK PEPPER
- 1 TEASPOON SALT
- 1 POUND WHOLE-WHEAT FUSILLI OR CORKSCREW PASTA
- 2 BUNCHES ARUGULA (ABOUT 4 OUNCES EACH), TOUGH STEMS TRIMMED, LEAVES COARSELY CHOPPED
- 2 TABLESPOONS WHITE OR DARK BALSAMIC VINEGAR

GRATED PARMESAN CHEESE (OPTIONAL)

1 Preheat oven to 450°F. Toss squash, garlic, onions, red peppers, oil, black pepper, and salt in 15½" by 10½" jelly-roll pan until evenly mixed. Roast 50 minutes or until the vegetables are tender and lightly golden, stirring occasionally.

2 Meanwhile, in large saucepot, cook fusilli as label directs.

3 When pasta has reached desired doneness, remove ½ *cup pasta cooking water*; reserve. Drain pasta and return to saucepot. Add roasted vegetables, arugula, vinegar, and reserved cooking water; toss until well mixed. Serve sprinkled with Parmesan, if you like.

EACH SERVING: ABOUT 610 CALORIES | 19G PROTEIN | 115G CARBOHYDRATE | 9G TOTAL FAT (1G SATURATED) | 16G FIBER | 0MG CHOLESTEROL | 610MG SODIUM

PASTA WITH ASPARAGUS PESTO

If you love traditional pesto made from basil, try this fresh twist made with steamed asparagus, pine nuts, garlic, and Pecorino-Romano.

ACTIVE TIME: 20 MINUTES · **TOTAL TIME:** 30 MINUTES
MAKES: 4 MAIN-DISH SERVINGS

1½ POUNDS ASPARAGUS, TRIMMED

¼ CUP OLIVE OIL

2 TABLESPOONS PINE NUTS (PIGNOLI), TOASTED

¼ TEASPOON GROUND BLACK PEPPER

1 GARLIC CLOVE, CRUSHED WITH GARLIC PRESS

¾ CUP PACKED FRESH BASIL LEAVES

1 TEASPOON SALT

⅓ CUP GRATED PECORINO ROMANO CHEESE, PLUS ADDITIONAL FOR SERVING

1 POUND ORECCHIETTE OR MEDIUM SHELL PASTA (CONCHIGLIE)

1 If using thin asparagus, cut each stalk crosswise in half; if using medium asparagus, cut stalks into 1½-inch pieces. In 12-inch skillet, heat 1 *inch water* to boiling over high heat. Add asparagus and cook 5 minutes or until tender. Remove and reserve ½ cup of the asparagus cooking water; drain the asparagus.

2 Set aside 1 cup thin asparagus stalks or ½ cup medium asparagus tips. In blender at low speed, with center part of cover removed to allow steam to escape, blend remaining asparagus with oil, pine nuts, pepper, garlic, ½ cup basil, salt, and reserved asparagus cooking water until almost smooth. Add Romano cheese and blend until well mixed.

3 Meanwhile, in large saucepot, cook pasta as label directs.

4 Slice remaining ¼ cup basil leaves. Drain pasta and return to saucepot. Add asparagus sauce, sliced basil, and reserved asparagus, and toss until evenly mixed. Serve with additional Romano cheese on the side.

EACH SERVING: ABOUT 620 CALORIES | 21G PROTEIN | 88G CARBOHYDRATE | 20G TOTAL FAT (4G SATURATED) | 16G FIBER | 7MG CHOLESTEROL | 830MG SODIUM

WHOLE-WHEAT PENNE GENOVESE

An onion-flecked white bean sauté adds heft to this fresh and healthy pesto pasta dish, making it light yet satisfying. For photo, see page 18.

ACTIVE TIME: 15 MINUTES · **TOTAL TIME:** 30 MINUTES
MAKES: 6 MAIN-DISH SERVINGS

12 OUNCES WHOLE-WHEAT PENNE OR ROTINI

1½ CUPS PACKED FRESH BASIL LEAVES

1 GARLIC CLOVE

3 TABLESPOONS WATER

3 TABLESPOONS EXTRA-VIRGIN OLIVE OIL

¼ TEASPOON SALT

¼ TEASPOON GROUND BLACK PEPPER

½ CUP GRATED PARMESAN CHEESE

1 SMALL ONION (4 TO 6 OUNCES), CHOPPED

1 CAN (15 TO 19 OUNCES) WHITE KIDNEY BEANS (CANNELLINI), RINSED AND DRAINED

1 PINT GRAPE TOMATOES (RED, YELLOW, AND ORANGE MIX IF AVAILABLE), EACH CUT INTO QUARTERS

1 In large saucepot, cook pasta as label directs.

2 Meanwhile, make pesto: In food processor with knife blade attached, blend basil, garlic, water, 2 tablespoons oil, salt, and pepper until pureed, stopping processor occasionally and scraping bowl with rubber spatula. Add Parmesan; pulse to combine. Set aside.

3 In 12-inch skillet, heat remaining 1 tablespoon oil on medium until very hot; add onion and cook 5 to 7 minutes or until beginning to soften. Stir in white beans, and cook 5 minutes longer, stirring occasionally.

4 Reserve ¼ cup pasta cooking water. Drain pasta and return to saucepot; stir in white bean mixture, pesto, cut-up tomatoes, and reserved cooking water. Toss to coat.

EACH SERVING: ABOUT 375 CALORIES | 15G PROTEIN | 59G CARBOHYDRATE | 10G TOTAL FAT (2G SATURATED) | 9G FIBER | 5MG CHOLESTEROL | 435MG SODIUM

PASTA WITH FARM-STAND VEGGIES

Gather summer's star veggies at the farmers' market—corn, tomatoes, and zucchini—and combine them with campanelle, a ruffled pasta that resembles a flower.

ACTIVE TIME: 25 MINUTES · **TOTAL TIME:** 40 MINUTES

MAKES: 4 MAIN-DISH SERVINGS

1   PACKAGE (16 OUNCES) CAMPANELLE OR CORKSCREW PASTA

2   TABLESPOONS OLIVE OIL

2   GARLIC CLOVES, CRUSHED WITH GARLIC PRESS

1   TEASPOON GROUND CUMIN

PINCH GROUND CINNAMON

3   CUPS FRESH CORN KERNELS (FROM 5 TO 6 EARS)

2   SMALL ZUCCHINI (6 OUNCES EACH), EACH CUT LENGTHWISE INTO QUARTERS, THEN CROSSWISE INTO ¼-INCH-THICK PIECES

1½ TEASPOONS SALT

½   TEASPOON GROUND BLACK PEPPER

1   PINT CHERRY TOMATOES, HALVED

1 In large saucepot, prepare pasta as label directs.

2 Meanwhile, in 12-inch skillet, heat oil over medium-high heat until hot. Add garlic, cumin, and cinnamon, and cook until fragrant, 30 seconds, stirring. Add corn and cook 4 minutes, stirring occasionally. Add zucchini, salt, and pepper, and cook 6 minutes, stirring occasionally. Add tomatoes and cook until tomatoes are heated through and zucchini is tender, about 2 minutes more.

3 When pasta has reached desired doneness, drain, reserving ¼ cup *pasta cooking water*. In large serving bowl, toss pasta, corn mixture, and reserved cooking water until combined.

EACH SERVING: ABOUT 620 CALORIES | 20G PROTEIN | 115G CARBOHYDRATE | 11G TOTAL FAT (2G SATURATED) | 8G FIBER | 0MG CHOLESTEROL | 1,055MG SODIUM

BOW TIES WITH TOMATOES, HERBS, AND LEMON

A quick toss with hot pasta is the only "cooking" this sauce needs. Make it in summer when ripe tomatoes and basil are at their best.

ACTIVE TIME: 15 MINUTES · **TOTAL TIME:** 20 MINUTES PLUS STANDING
MAKES: 4 MAIN-DISH SERVINGS

2 POUNDS RIPE TOMATOES (6 MEDIUM), CHOPPED	1 TEASPOON FRESHLY GRATED LEMON PEEL
¼ CUP LOOSELY PACKED FRESH MINT LEAVES, CHOPPED	2 TABLESPOONS OLIVE OIL
¼ CUP LOOSELY PACKED FRESH BASIL LEAVES, CHOPPED	1 TEASPOON SALT
1 GARLIC CLOVE, CRUSHED WITH GARLIC PRESS	¼ TEASPOON GROUND BLACK PEPPER
	1 PACKAGE (16 OUNCES) BOW TIES (FARFALLE) OR ZITI

1 In warm serving bowl, combine tomatoes, mint, basil, garlic, lemon peel, oil, salt, and pepper. Let stand at room temperature at least 15 minutes or up to 1 hour to allow flavors to develop.

2 Meanwhile, in large saucepot, cook pasta as label directs. Drain. Add pasta to tomato mixture and toss well.

EACH SERVING: ABOUT 535 CALORIES | 17G PROTEIN | 97G CARBOHYDRATE | 9G TOTAL FAT (1G SATURATED) | 6G FIBER | 0MG CHOLESTEROL | 711MG SODIUM

MIDDLE EASTERN GARBANZO BEANS AND MACARONI

A flavorful stew of pantry staples—canned beans, crushed tomatoes, and dried spices—tossed with pasta makes a satisfying vegetarian entrée.

ACTIVE TIME: 10 MINUTES · **TOTAL TIME:** 30 MINUTES

MAKES: 6 MAIN-DISH SERVINGS

1 TABLESPOON OLIVE OIL

1 TABLESPOON BUTTER OR MARGARINE

1 LARGE ONION (12 OUNCES), CUT INTO ¼-INCH DICE

2 GARLIC CLOVES, CRUSHED WITH GARLIC PRESS

1 TEASPOON SALT

1 TEASPOON GROUND CUMIN

¾ TEASPOON GROUND CORIANDER

¼ TEASPOON GROUND ALLSPICE

¼ TEASPOON COARSELY GROUND BLACK PEPPER

1 CAN (28 OUNCES) CRUSHED TOMATOES

1 CAN (15 TO 19 OUNCES) GARBANZO BEANS, RINSED AND DRAINED

12 OUNCES MACARONI TWISTS, SUCH AS GEMELLI, OR ELBOW MACARONI

¼ CUP LOOSELY PACKED FRESH PARSLEY LEAVES, CHOPPED, PLUS SPRIGS FOR GARNISH

1 In nonstick 12-inch skillet, heat olive oil with butter over medium heat until hot and melted. Add onion and cook 20 minutes or until tender and golden, stirring occasionally. Stir in garlic, salt, cumin, coriander, allspice, and pepper; cook 1 minute.

2 Add tomatoes with their juice and garbanzo beans to skillet; heat to boiling over medium-high heat. Reduce heat to medium-low; simmer 5 minutes, stirring occasionally.

3 Meanwhile, in large saucepot, cook pasta as label directs.

4 Drain pasta; return to saucepot. Toss bean mixture with pasta; heat through. Toss with chopped parsley just before serving. Garnish each serving with a parsley sprig.

EACH SERVING: ABOUT 400 CALORIES | 14G PROTEIN | 73G CARBOHYDRATE | 6G TOTAL FAT (1G SATURATED) | 8G FIBER | 0MG CHOLESTEROL | 1,045MG SODIUM

PASTA WITH BROCCOLI RABE AND GARBANZOS

Bitter greens are paired with sweet golden raisins and tossed with pasta and beans. High in protein, this is a great meatless meal.

ACTIVE TIME: 20 MINUTES · **TOTAL TIME:** 30 MINUTES
MAKES: 4 MAIN-DISH SERVINGS

2 BUNCHES BROCCOLI RABE (ABOUT 12 OUNCES EACH), TOUGH STEMS TRIMMED

2 TABLESPOONS OLIVE OIL

3 GARLIC CLOVES, CRUSHED WITH SIDE OF CHEF'S KNIFE

¼ TEASPOON CRUSHED RED PEPPER

1 CAN (15 TO 19 OUNCES) GARBANZO BEANS, RINSED AND DRAINED

¼ CUP GOLDEN RAISINS

1 PACKAGE (16 OUNCES) PENNE OR ZITI

1¼ TEASPOONS SALT

GRATED PARMESAN CHEESE (OPTIONAL)

1 In large saucepot, heat 4 *quarts water* to boiling. Add broccoli rabe and cook 3 to 5 minutes or until thickest parts of stems are tender. Drain broccoli rabe and cool slightly. Cut into 2-inch pieces.

2 Wipe saucepot dry. Add oil, and heat over medium-high heat until hot. Add garlic and crushed red pepper, and cook 1 minute, stirring. Add broccoli rabe, garbanzo beans, and raisins, and cook about 3 minutes to heat through, stirring often. Remove saucepot from heat.

3 Meanwhile, in another large saucepot, cook pasta as label directs.

4 When pasta has reached desired doneness, remove ⅔ *cup pasta cooking water* and reserve. Drain pasta. Add pasta, reserved cooking water, and salt to broccoli rabe mixture; toss well. Serve with Parmesan, if you like.

EACH SERVING: ABOUT 665 CALORIES | 25G PROTEIN | 119G CARBOHYDRATE | 11G TOTAL FAT (1G SATURATED) | 9G FIBER | 0MG CHOLESTEROL | 1,160MG SODIUM

VEGETABLE LASAGNA TOSS

Loaded with fresh vegetables and beans, this easy pasta dinner is perfect for a weeknight family dinner.

ACTIVE TIME: 10 MINUTES · **TOTAL TIME:** 20 MINUTES

MAKES: 4 MAIN-DISH SERVINGS

8   OUNCES LASAGNA NOODLES

1   TABLESPOON EXTRA-VIRGIN OLIVE OIL

2   GARLIC CLOVES, CRUSHED WITH PRESS

1   BAG (12 OUNCES) BROCCOLI FLORETS

1   CUP LOW-SODIUM CHICKEN BROTH

1   CAN (15 TO 19 OUNCES) WHITE KIDNEY BEANS (CANNELLINI), DRAINED AND RINSED

3   LARGE TOMATOES, COARSELY CHOPPED

⅓   CUP FRESHLY GRATED PECORINO-ROMANO CHEESE, PLUS ADDITIONAL FOR SERVING

1 In large saucepot, cook noodles as label directs but increase cooking time by about 2 minutes so that noodles are al dente.

2 Meanwhile, in nonstick 12-inch skillet, heat oil over medium heat; add garlic and broccoli and cook 1 minute, stirring frequently. Add broth; cover and cook 8 minutes. Stir in beans; cover and cook 2 to 3 minutes longer or until broccoli is very tender. Stir in tomatoes; remove from heat.

3 Drain lasagna noodles; add to broccoli mixture in skillet and sprinkle with Romano cheese. Toss to coat noodles. Serve with additional Pecorino-Romano on the side.

EACH SERVING: 425 CALORIES | 19G PROTEIN | 71G CARBOHYDRATE | 8G TOTAL FAT (2G SATURATED) | 11G FIBER | 8MG CHOLESTEROL | 380MG SODIUM

GARLICKY BROCCOLI PASTA

Pasta with garlic and broccoli is a time-honored tradition, and with good reason: The combination is absolutely delicious.

ACTIVE TIME: 15 MINUTES · **TOTAL TIME:** 25 MINUTES
MAKES: 6 MAIN-DISH SERVINGS

---

1 PACKAGE (16 OUNCES) ORECCHIETTE OR FUSILLI

1 BUNCH BROCCOLI (ABOUT 1 POUND)

2 TABLESPOONS EXTRA-VIRGIN OLIVE OIL

3 GARLIC CLOVES, THINLY SLICED

¼ CUP WATER

½ TEASPOON SALT

½ CUP FRESHLY GRATED PECORINO-ROMANO CHEESE

1 In large saucepan, cook pasta as label directs.

2 Meanwhile, trim broccoli. Coarsely chop stems and florets. You should have about 5 cups broccoli.

3 In nonstick 12-inch skillet, heat oil over medium heat until hot. Add garlic and cook, stirring, until golden, 2 to 3 minutes. Stir in broccoli, water, and salt. Cover and cook, stirring occasionally, until broccoli is tender, 8 to 10 minutes.

4 Drain pasta, reserving ½ *cup pasta cooking water*. Return pasta to sauce-pot. Add Pecorino-Romano, broccoli mixture, and reserved cooking water to pasta; toss until well combined.

EACH SERVING: ABOUT 370 CALORIES | 146G PROTEIN | 61G CARBOHYDRATE | 8G TOTAL FAT (2G SATURATED) | 4G FIBER | 7MG CHOLESTEROL | 395MG SODIUM

SPAGHETTI WITH BEETS AND GREENS

In this innovative dish, garlicky beet greens are tossed with spaghetti, tinting the pasta a beautiful pinkish-red! If you're not going to use beets immediately, trim the tops ahead of time, since they leach moisture and color from the beets. Refrigerate the greens and the beets in separate plastic bags and use them within two days.

ACTIVE TIME: 20 MINUTES · **TOTAL TIME:** 35 MINUTES

MAKES: 4 MAIN-DISH SERVINGS

2	BUNCHES BEETS WITH TOPS (ABOUT 3 POUNDS TOTAL)	2	GARLIC CLOVES, CRUSHED WITH GARLIC PRESS
1	PACKAGE (16 OUNCES) SPAGHETTI	⅛	TEASPOON CRUSHED RED PEPPER
3	TABLESPOONS OLIVE OIL	1	TEASPOON SALT

1 Cut tops from beets; reserve. If beets are not uniform in size, cut larger beets in half. Place beets and ½ *cup water* in deep 3-quart microwave-safe baking dish; cover and cook in microwave oven on High 15 to 20 minutes, or until beets are tender when pierced with tip of knife. Rinse beets under cold running water until cool enough to handle. Peel beets; cut into ½-inch pieces.

2 Meanwhile, in large saucepot, cook spaghetti as label directs. Trim and discard stems from beet greens. Coarsely chop beet greens; set aside.

3 In 12-inch skillet, heat oil, garlic, and crushed red pepper over medium heat 5 minutes or until garlic is lightly golden. Increase heat to medium-high; add beet greens to skillet, and cook 3 minutes, stirring. Add cooked beets and salt, and cook 1 to 2 minutes or until mixture is heated through.

4 When spaghetti has reached desired doneness, remove ¾ *cup pasta cooking water*; reserve. Drain spaghetti and return to saucepot. Add beet mixture and reserved cooking water; toss well.

EACH SERVING: ABOUT 560 CALORIES | 17G PROTEIN | 96G CARBOHYDRATE | 12G TOTAL FAT (2G SATURATED) | 8G FIBER | 0MG CHOLESTEROL | 855MG SODIUM

VEGETABLE LO MEIN

By using precut vegetables, we've eliminated much of the work in this Asian favorite. If you cannot find Chinese lo mein noodles in your grocery store and do not have access to an Asian market, substitute linguine for the lo mein.

TOTAL TIME: 20 MINUTES

MAKES: 4 MAIN-DISH SERVINGS

1   PACKAGE (16 OUNCES) CHINESE LO MEIN NOODLES OR LINGUINE

⅓   CUP HOISIN SAUCE (SEE TIP)

2   TABLESPOONS REDUCED-SODIUM SOY SAUCE

½   TEASPOON CORNSTARCH

3   TEASPOONS VEGETABLE OIL

1   PACKAGE (10 OUNCES) SLICED MUSHROOMS

1   TABLESPOON GRATED, PEELED FRESH GINGER (SEE TIP, PAGE 99)

1   PACKAGE (10 OUNCES) SHREDDED CARROTS

3   SMALL ZUCCHINI (ABOUT 6 OUNCES EACH), EACH CUT LENGTHWISE IN HALF, THEN CUT CROSSWISE INTO ¼-INCH-THICK SLICES

3   GREEN ONIONS, CUT INTO 1-INCH PIECES

1   CUP REDUCED-SODIUM CHICKEN BROTH

2   TABLESPOONS SEASONED RICE VINEGAR

1   In large saucepot, cook lo mein noodles as label directs but do not use salt.

2   Meanwhile, in cup, stir together hoisin sauce, soy sauce, and cornstarch until smooth; set aside.

3   In 12-inch skillet, heat 2 teaspoons vegetable oil over medium-high heat until hot. Add mushrooms and cook, stirring frequently, about 5 minutes or until mushrooms are golden and liquid has evaporated. Stir in ginger; cook 30 seconds. Remove mushroom mixture to bowl.

4   In same skillet, heat remaining 1 teaspoon vegetable oil; cook carrots 2 minutes, stirring frequently. Stir in zucchini and green onions and cook about 10 minutes longer or until vegetables are tender-crisp. Stir in chicken broth, cornstarch mixture, and mushroom mixture. Heat to boiling; cook 1 minute.

5   To serve, toss noodles, vegetable mixture, and rice vinegar in large serving bowl.

TIP Hoisin sauce, used in many Chinese dishes, is made from sugar, soybeans, sesame seeds, and spices and has a sweet, smoky taste. Once opened, it will keep in the refrigerator for several months.

EACH SERVING: ABOUT 570 CALORIES | 20G PROTEIN | 111G CARBOHYDRATE | 7G TOTAL FAT (1G SATURATED) | 9G FIBER | 0MG CHOLESTEROL | 970MG SODIUM

SESAME NOODLES WITH CARROTS AND CUCUMBER

Kids and grown-ups alike will take to this Chinese-restaurant favorite made with a peanut butter and sesame dressing spiked with orange juice.

TOTAL TIME: 15 MINUTES

MAKES: 6 MAIN-DISH SERVINGS

1 PACKAGE (16 OUNCES) SPAGHETTI

1 CUP FRESH ORANGE JUICE

¼ CUP SEASONED RICE VINEGAR

¼ CUP SOY SAUCE

¼ CUP CREAMY PEANUT BUTTER

1 TABLESPOON ASIAN SESAME OIL

1 TABLESPOON GRATED, PEELED FRESH GINGER (SEE TIP, PAGE 99)

2 TEASPOONS SUGAR

¼ TEASPOON CRUSHED RED PEPPER

1 BAG (10 OUNCES) SHREDDED CARROTS (ABOUT 3½ CUPS)

3 KIRBY CUCUMBERS (ABOUT 4 OUNCES EACH), UNPEELED AND CUT INTO MATCHSTICK-THIN STRIPS

2 GREEN ONIONS, THINLY SLICED, PLUS 6 WHOLE GREEN ONIONS FOR GARNISH

2 TABLESPOONS SESAME SEEDS, TOASTED (OPTIONAL)

1 In large saucepot, cook pasta as label directs.

2 Meanwhile, in medium bowl, with wire whisk or fork, mix orange juice, vinegar, soy sauce, peanut butter, oil, ginger, sugar, and crushed red pepper until blended; set the sauce aside.

3 Place carrots in colander; drain pasta over carrots. Put pasta and carrots in large serving bowl and add cucumbers, sliced green onions, and sauce; toss. If you like, sprinkle the pasta with sesame seeds. Garnish with whole green onions.

EACH SERVING: ABOUT 445 CALORIES | 15G PROTEIN | 76G CARBOHYDRATE | 9G TOTAL FAT (2G SATURATED) | 5G FIBER | 0MG CHOLESTEROL | 1,135MG SODIUM

CHEESY PASTA

Spaghetti with Pesto and Tomato-Mozzarella Salad (page 50)

FETTUCCINE ALFREDO

This luscious classic takes its name from Roman restaurateur Alfredo di Lello, who created it in the early 1900s. Be sure to use only freshly grated Parmesan cheese and, for a delicious splurge, make it authentic Italian Parmigiano-Reggiano.

ACTIVE TIME: 10 MINUTES · **TOTAL TIME:** 25 MINUTES
MAKES: 6 MAIN-DISH SERVINGS

1   PACKAGE (16 OUNCES) FETTUCCINE (SEE TIP)

1½ CUPS HEAVY OR WHIPPING CREAM

1   TABLESPOON BUTTER OR MARGARINE

½   TEASPOON SALT

¼   TEASPOON COARSELY GROUND BLACK PEPPER

¾   CUP FRESHLY GRATED PARMESAN CHEESE

CHOPPED FRESH PARSLEY

1   In large saucepot, cook pasta as label directs. Drain.
2   Meanwhile, in 2-quart saucepan, heat cream, butter, salt, and pepper to boiling over medium-high heat. Boil until sauce has thickened slightly, 2 to 3 minutes. In warm serving bowl, toss pasta with sauce and Parmesan. Sprinkle with parsley.

TIP For a more delicate rendition of this dish, seek out fresh fettuccine in the refrigerated section of your supermarket.

EACH SERVING: ABOUT 560 CALORIES | 16G PROTEIN | 59G CARBOHYDRATE | 29G TOTAL FAT (17G SATURATED) | 2G FIBER | 96MG CHOLESTEROL | 532MG SODIUM

LIGHT FETTUCCINE ALFREDO

For a weeknight family supper, you might prefer this low-fat version of the classic Alfredo sauce. We shaved off calories—and added sautéed garlic, onion, and broccoli flowerets—while keeping the sauce smooth and cheesy.

ACTIVE TIME: 15 MINUTES · **TOTAL TIME:** 30 MINUTES
MAKES: 6 MAIN-DISH SERVINGS

2	TEASPOONS VEGETABLE OIL	½	TEASPOON SALT
1	SMALL ONION (4 TO 6 OUNCES), FINELY CHOPPED	¼	TEASPOON COARSELY GROUND BLACK PEPPER
1	LARGE GARLIC CLOVE, CRUSHED WITH GARLIC PRESS	½	CUP FRESHLY GRATED PARMESAN CHEESE
2	CUPS SKIM MILK	1	PACKAGE (16 OUNCES) FETTUCCINE
1	CUP CHICKEN BROTH	1	PACKAGE (16 OUNCES) BROCCOLI FLOWERETS
3	TABLESPOONS ALL-PURPOSE FLOUR		

1 In nonstick 12-inch skillet, heat oil over medium heat. Add onion and garlic and cook until onion is golden, about 8 minutes. In bowl, with wire whisk, whisk milk, broth, flour, salt, and pepper until smooth. Add to onion mixture and cook, stirring, until sauce has thickened and boils; boil 1 minute. Stir in Parmesan.

2 Meanwhile, in large saucepot, cook pasta as label directs. After pasta has cooked 7 minutes, add broccoli to pasta water. Cook until pasta and broccoli are done, 3 to 5 minutes longer. Drain pasta and broccoli.

3 In warm serving bowl, toss pasta and broccoli with sauce.

EACH SERVING: ABOUT 410 CALORIES | 19G PROTEIN | 69G CARBOHYDRATE | 6G TOTAL FAT (2G SATURATED) | 4G FIBER | 8MG CHOLESTEROL | 654MG SODIUM

FUSILLI WITH BLUE CHEESE AND TOASTED WALNUTS

It takes just five main ingredients and a few minutes to create this irresistible combination—pasta curls tossed with a rich blue-cheese sauce, sweet green peas, and toasted walnuts.

ACTIVE TIME: 10 MINUTES · **TOTAL TIME:** 15 MINUTES
MAKES: 4 MAIN-DISH SERVINGS

1 PACKAGE (16 OUNCES) FUSILLI OR CORKSCREW PASTA

⅔ CUP HALF-AND-HALF OR LIGHT CREAM

⅓ CUP WATER

¼ TEASPOON SALT

¾ CUP CRUMBLED BLUE CHEESE (3 OUNCES), PLUS ADDITIONAL ¼ CUP (1 OUNCE) FOR GARNISH

1 PACKAGE (10 OUNCES) FROZEN PEAS, THAWED

¾ CUP WALNUTS, TOASTED (SEE TIP, PAGE 113) AND CHOPPED

FRESH PARSLEY SPRIGS FOR GARNISH

1 In large saucepot, cook pasta as label directs.

2 Meanwhile, in 1-quart saucepan, heat half-and-half, water, and salt to simmering over medium heat. Stir in ¾ cup crumbled blue cheese and heat through.

3 Place peas in a colander; drain fusilli over peas.

4 In large serving bowl, toss pasta mixture with blue-cheese sauce and walnuts. Garnish with remaining ¼ cup crumbled blue cheese and parsley sprigs.

EACH SERVING: ABOUT 765 CALORIES | 28G PROTEIN | 101G CARBOHYDRATE | 28G TOTAL FAT (9G SATURATED) | 8G FIBER | 34MG CHOLESTEROL | 730MG SODIUM

SPAGHETTI WITH PESTO AND TOMATO-MOZZARELLA SALAD

Pesto doesn't take that long to make from scratch and your reward is big flavor. Combined with sweet cherry tomatoes and mozzarella, you've got a pasta version of a Caprese salad. For photo, see page 44.

ACTIVE TIME: 20 MINUTES · **TOTAL TIME:** 35 MINUTES
MAKES: 6 MAIN-DISH SERVINGS

1	PACKAGE (16 OUNCES) THIN SPAGHETTI OR LINGUINE	1½	PINTS RED AND/OR YELLOW CHERRY TOMATOES, EACH CUT IN HALF
1	LARGE BUNCH FRESH BASIL	1	TABLESPOON RED WINE VINEGAR
1	SMALL GARLIC CLOVE, PEELED	¼	TEASPOON GROUND BLACK PEPPER
5	TABLESPOONS OLIVE OIL	8	OUNCES FRESH MOZZARELLA CHEESE, CUT INTO ¾-INCH CUBES
¾	TEASPOON SALT		
½	CUP FRESHLY GRATED PARMESAN CHEESE		

1 In large saucepot, prepare pasta as label directs.

2 Meanwhile, reserve 12 small basil leaves for garnish. From remaining basil, remove enough leaves to equal 2 cups firmly packed. Wash basil well; pat dry with paper towels. In food processor with knife blade attached, blend basil leaves, garlic, 4 tablespoons oil, and ½ teaspoon salt until smooth, stopping processor and scraping down bowl occasionally. Add Parmesan; pulse to combine. Set aside.

3 In medium bowl, mix tomatoes, vinegar, and pepper with remaining 1 tablespoon oil and remaining ¼ teaspoon salt. Gently stir in mozzarella.

4 Drain spaghetti, reserving ½ *cup cooking water*. Return spaghetti and reserved pasta cooking water to saucepot; add pesto and toss well to coat pasta. Spoon spaghetti mixture into large shallow bowl; top with tomato-mozzarella salad. Garnish with reserved basil leaves.

EACH SERVING: ABOUT 540 CALORIES | 20G PROTEIN | 63G CARBOHYDRATE | 23G TOTAL FAT (8G SATURATED) | 3G FIBER | 35MG CHOLESTEROL | 550MG SODIUM

SPAGHETTI WITH RICOTTA AND PEAS

Smoky bacon gives crunch, and sweet peas add color to this cheesy sauce. To minimize cleanup, the peas are cooked in the pot along with the pasta.

ACTIVE TIME: 15 MINUTES · **TOTAL TIME:** 20 MINUTES
MAKES: 4 MAIN-DISH SERVINGS

4   SLICES BACON

1   MEDIUM ONION (6 TO 8 OUNCES), FINELY CHOPPED

1   PACKAGE (16 OUNCES) SPAGHETTI (SPAGHETTINI) OR VERMICELLI

1   PACKAGE (10 OUNCES) FROZEN PEAS

1   CONTAINER (15 OUNCES) PART-SKIM RICOTTA CHEESE

½   CUP GRATED PECORINO-ROMANO OR PARMESAN CHEESE

½   TEASPOON SALT

¼   TEASPOON COARSELY GROUND BLACK PEPPER

1 In 12-inch skillet, cook bacon over medium heat until browned. Transfer to paper towels. Pour off all but 1 tablespoon bacon fat from skillet. Add onion and cook until tender and golden, 8 to 10 minutes.

2 Meanwhile, in large saucepot, cook pasta as label directs.

3 During last 2 minutes of pasta cooking time, add frozen peas. When pasta has reached desired doneness, remove 1 *cup pasta cooking water*. Drain pasta and peas. Return to saucepot and toss with onion, ricotta, Romano, salt, pepper, and reserved cooking water. Crumble in bacon and toss again.

EACH SERVING: ABOUT 745 CALORIES | 37G PROTEIN | 103G CARBOHYDRATE | 20G TOTAL FAT (10G SATURATED) | 7G FIBER | 54MG CHOLESTEROL | 880MG SODIUM

FUSILLI WITH HERBED RICOTTA AND GRAPE TOMATOES

Add a little bit of the pasta cooking water to ricotta, and you've got an instant sauce.

ACTIVE TIME: 10 MINUTES · **TOTAL TIME:** 20 MINUTES
MAKES: 4 MAIN-DISH SERVINGS

12 OUNCES FUSILLI OR CORKSCREW PASTA

1 CUP PART-SKIM RICOTTA CHEESE

1 TABLESPOON FRESH OREGANO LEAVES, CHOPPED

¼ CUP FRESHLY GRATED PECORINO-ROMANO CHEESE, PLUS MORE FOR SERVING

¼ CUP PACKED FRESH BASIL LEAVES, CHOPPED

1 PINT GRAPE TOMATOES

1 In large saucepot begin cooking pasta as label directs.

2 Meanwhile, in small bowl, combine ricotta, oregano, Pecorino, and half of basil.

3 When 3 minutes of cooking time remain for pasta, add tomatoes to the pot.

4 Drain pasta and tomatoes, reserving ¼ cup *pasta cooking water*. Return pasta and tomatoes to pot. Add reserved cooking water to ricotta mixture; stir into pasta and tomatoes. Toss with remaining basil. Serve with additional grated cheese on the side.

EACH SERVING: ABOUT 440 CALORIES | 20G PROTEIN | 71G CARBOHYDRATE | 8G TOTAL FAT (4G SATURATED) | 3G FIBER | 24MG CHOLESTEROL | 295MG SODIUM

CREAMY RIGATONI WITH SPINACH

Ricotta is the base for this simple, no-cook pasta sauce. We used part-skim to cut the fat and make a more healthful family meal.

ACTIVE TIME: 5 MINUTES · **TOTAL TIME:** 20 MINUTES
MAKES: 6 MAIN-DISH SERVINGS

1 PACKAGE (16 OUNCES) RIGATONI OR ZITI

1 PACKAGE (10 OUNCES) FROZEN CHOPPED SPINACH

1 CONTAINER (15 OUNCES) PART-SKIM RICOTTA CHEESE

¼ CUP GRATED PARMESAN CHEESE

10 OIL-PACKED SUN-DRIED TOMATOES, DRAINED AND FINELY CHOPPED (¼ CUP; SEE TIP)

¾ TEASPOON SALT

1 In large saucepot, begin cooking pasta as label directs for al dente; when about 10 minutes of cooking time remain, add frozen spinach to the pot. Drain well, reserving ½ cup pasta cooking water.

2 Return pasta, spinach, and reserved cooking water to saucepot. Add ricotta, Parmesan, sun-dried tomatoes, and salt. Heat over medium-low heat, tossing until pasta is evenly coated and heated through.

TIP Save the oil from the sun-dried tomatoes and use it in salad dressings.

EACH SERVING: ABOUT 420 CALORIES | 21G PROTEIN | 64G CARBOHYDRATE | 9G TOTAL FAT (5G SATURATED) | 4G FIBER | 25MG CHOLESTEROL | 580MG SODIUM

CORKSCREWS WITH GOAT CHEESE AND SPRING VEGGIES

For an easy—and yummy—main dish, toss sautéed asparagus and leeks with pasta and creamy goat cheese.

ACTIVE TIME: 20 MINUTES · **TOTAL TIME:** 25 MINUTES

MAKES: 4 MAIN-DISH SERVINGS

---

1   BUNCH (ABOUT 1 POUND) LEEKS (SEE TIP, PAGE 102)

1   PACKAGE (16 OUNCES) CORKSCREW PASTA OR BOW TIES (FARFALLE)

1   TABLESPOON BUTTER OR MARGARINE

1   POUND ASPARAGUS, TRIMMED AND CUT DIAGONALLY INTO 2-INCH PIECES

¾   TEASPOON SALT

COARSELY GROUND BLACK PEPPER

⅓   CUP WATER

1   PACKAGE (4 OUNCES) SOFT GOAT CHEESE, CUT INTO SMALL PIECES

1   Cut off roots and leaf ends from leeks. Discard any tough outer leaves. Cut each leek lengthwise in half, then crosswise into ¼-inch-wide slices. Place leeks in large bowl of cold water; with hand, swish leeks around to remove any sand. Transfer leeks to colander. Repeat process, changing water several times, until all sand is removed. Drain well.

2   In large saucepot, cook pasta as label directs.

3   Meanwhile, in nonstick 12-inch skillet, melt butter over medium heat. Add leeks and cook until almost tender, about 5 minutes, stirring often. Stir in asparagus, salt, and ¼ teaspoon pepper; cook 5 minutes longer, stirring often. Add water; cover and cook 3 to 5 minutes, until asparagus is tender-crisp.

4   Drain pasta, reserving ¾ *cup pasta cooking water*. Return pasta to saucepot. Add asparagus mixture and reserved cooking water; toss well. Spoon into large serving bowl; sprinkle with goat cheese and black pepper.

EACH SERVING: ABOUT 580 CALORIES | 23G PROTEIN | 96G CARBOHYDRATE | 11G TOTAL FAT (5G SATURATED) | 6G FIBER | 13MG CHOLESTEROL | 705MG SODIUM

RICOTTA GNOCCHI WITH BROWN BUTTER AND FRESH HERBS

There's no need to be intimidated—these gnocchi are a snap to make. A simple butter and herb sauce is the only dressing up they need.

ACTIVE TIME: 1 HOUR · **TOTAL TIME:** 1 HOUR 20 MINUTES
MAKES: 4 MAIN-DISH SERVINGS

1	CONTAINER (15 OUNCES) RICOTTA CHEESE	¾	CUP ALL-PURPOSE FLOUR OR AS NEEDED
6	TABLESPOONS FRESHLY GRATED PARMESAN CHEESE	3	TABLESPOONS BUTTER
¾	CUP CHOPPED FRESH PARSLEY	1	TEASPOON CHOPPED FRESH SAGE
¾	TEASPOON SALT	¼	TEASPOON GROUND BLACK PEPPER

1 In medium bowl, combine ricotta, Parmesan, parsley, and ½ teaspoon salt. Sprinkle flour over ricotta mixture and, with your hands, work mixture into soft, smooth dough. If dough is sticky, add some flour. Work dough just until flour is incorporated into cheese mixture; do not overwork.

2 Break off piece of dough; on a lightly floured surface, roll into ¾-inch-thick rope. (If rope doesn't hold together, return to bowl with remaining dough and work in more flour.) Cut dough rope into ¾-inch lengths. Place one piece of dough on inside curve of fork tines, gently pressing on dough with thumb as you roll dough along tines. Allow dough to drop off fork, slightly curling in on itself and forming an oval. One side of gnocchi will have ridges and opposite side will have an indentation. Repeat rolling, cutting, and shaping with remaining dough. (Gnocchi can be made to this point up to 4 hours ahead. Arrange in floured jelly-roll pan; cover and refrigerate.)

3 In 5-quart saucepot, begin heating 4 *quarts water* to boiling over high heat.

4 While water heats, make butter sauce: In 2-quart saucepan, melt butter over medium heat. Continue to cook, stirring, until butter turns golden brown. (If butter gets too dark, it will be bitter.) Remove from heat and add sage, remaining ¼ teaspoon salt, and pepper; set aside.

5 When water boils, add half of gnocchi and cook until gnocchi float to surface, 2 to 3 minutes. With slotted spoon, transfer gnocchi to warm shallow serving bowl. Repeat with remaining gnocchi. To serve, toss gnocchi with sage butter.

EACH SERVING: ABOUT 390 CALORIES | 18G PROTEIN | 22G CARBOHYDRATE | 26G TOTAL FAT (16G SATURATED) | 2G FIBER | 84MG CHOLESTEROL | 788MG SODIUM

CHEESE RAVIOLI WITH RIPE TOMATOES

Who knew you could prepare pasta in a microwave? And the simple, from-scratch sauce uses the perfectly ripe tomatoes of late summer—and doesn't require any cooking. Whipped up fresh and fast and tossed with ricotta ravioli, it's a flavorful send-off to the season.

TOTAL TIME: 25 MINUTES
MAKES: 4 MAIN-DISH SERVINGS

1½ POUNDS RIPE TOMATOES, CHOPPED (4 CUPS)

½ CUP PACKED FRESH BASIL LEAVES, CHOPPED

3 TABLESPOONS OLIVE OIL

¼ TEASPOON FRESHLY GRATED LEMON PEEL

¼ TEASPOON SALT

¼ TEASPOON GROUND BLACK PEPPER

1 BAG (18 OUNCES) MICROWAVABLE CHEESE RAVIOLI

¼ CUP FRESHLY GRATED PARMESAN CHEESE

1 In large bowl, combine tomatoes, basil, olive oil, lemon peel, salt, and pepper. Let stand at room temperature at least 15 minutes or up to 30 minutes to blend flavors.

2 Meanwhile, cook ravioli in microwave as label directs.

3 Add hot pasta to tomato mixture; toss to coat. Sprinkle with Parmesan to serve.

EACH SERVING: ABOUT 375 CALORIES | 14G PROTEIN | 45G CARBOHYDRATE | 16G TOTAL FAT (4G SATURATED) | 4G FIBER | 19MG CHOLESTEROL | 535MG SODIUM

PESTO RAVIOLI AND PEAS

With store-bought pesto and a no-cook tomato sauce, you can have dinner on the table in less than twenty minutes!

ACTIVE TIME: 10 MINUTES · **TOTAL TIME:** 20 MINUTES

MAKES: 4 MAIN-DISH SERVINGS

---

1 POUND REFRIGERATED CHEESE RAVIOLI

2 MEDIUM TOMATOES, CUT INTO ¼-INCH DICE

1 CUP LOOSELY PACKED FRESH BASIL LEAVES, CHOPPED

⅛ TEASPOON SALT

⅛ TEASPOON COARSELY GROUND BLACK PEPPER

1 PACKAGE (10 OUNCES) FROZEN PEAS

¼ CUP BASIL PESTO, STORE-BOUGHT OR HOMEMADE (PAGE 13)

1 In large saucepot, cook ravioli as label directs.

2 Meanwhile, in small bowl, combine tomatoes, basil, salt, and pepper; set aside.

3 Place frozen peas in colander, and drain ravioli over peas. In large serving bowl, toss the ravioli and peas with pesto; top with the tomato mixture.

EACH SERVING: ABOUT 510 CALORIES | 23G PROTEIN | 55G CARBOHYDRATE | 24G TOTAL FAT (9G SATURATED) | 8G FIBER | 43MG CHOLESTEROL | 705MG SODIUM

CAVATELLI WITH RICOTTA AND FRESH TOMATO SAUCE

Fresh, sun-ripened tomatoes bursting with juice are all it takes to make this spectacularly good yet easy Italian sauce.

ACTIVE TIME: 5 MINUTES · **TOTAL TIME:** 20 MINUTES
MAKES: 4 MAIN-DISH SERVINGS

1	BAG (16 OUNCES) FROZEN CAVATELLI (SEE TIP)	½	TEASPOON SALT
1	TABLESPOON OLIVE OIL	¼	TEASPOON COARSELY GROUND BLACK PEPPER
1	GARLIC CLOVE, CRUSHED WITH GARLIC PRESS	¾	CUP PART-SKIM RICOTTA CHEESE
4	MEDIUM TOMATOES (ABOUT 1½ POUNDS), DICED	¼	CUP GRATED PECORINO-ROMANO OR PARMESAN CHEESE

1 In large saucepot, cook cavatelli as label directs.

2 Meanwhile, in nonstick 10-inch skillet, heat olive oil over medium heat. Add garlic and cook 1 minute, stirring. Stir in tomatoes, salt, and pepper; cook, stirring occasionally, 5 minutes or until tomatoes break up slightly.

3 Drain cavatelli; transfer to serving bowl. Stir in ricotta and Romano. Pour tomato mixture on top; toss before serving.

TIP Look for cavatelli, a short, rippled pasta, in the freezer section of the supermarket. If it's not available, use frozen gnocchi.

EACH SERVING: ABOUT 455 CALORIES | 20G PROTEIN | 71G CARBOHYDRATE | 11G TOTAL FAT (5G SATURATED) | 4G FIBER | 40MG CHOLESTEROL | 560MG SODIUM

LASAGNA TOSS WITH SPINACH AND RICOTTA

Here's real lasagna flavor in half the time. Simply boil the noodles while the sauce cooks, then toss with two cheeses and basil.

ACTIVE TIME: 20 MINUTES · **TOTAL TIME:** 35 MINUTES
MAKES: 4 MAIN-DISH SERVINGS

1 TABLESPOON OLIVE OIL

1 MEDIUM ONION (6 TO 8 OUNCES), FINELY CHOPPED

2 GARLIC CLOVES, CRUSHED WITH GARLIC PRESS

1 CAN (28 OUNCES) PLUM TOMATOES IN JUICE

¾ TEASPOON SALT

¼ TEASPOON COARSELY GROUND BLACK PEPPER

1 PACKAGE (10 OUNCES) FROZEN CHOPPED SPINACH

½ CUP LOOSELY PACKED FRESH BASIL LEAVES, CHOPPED

1 PACKAGE (16 OUNCES) LASAGNA NOODLES

¼ CUP FRESHLY GRATED PARMESAN CHEESE PLUS ADDITIONAL FOR SERVING

1 CUP PART-SKIM RICOTTA CHEESE

1 In nonstick 12-inch skillet, heat oil over medium heat until hot. Add onion and cook 10 minutes or until tender, stirring occasionally. Add garlic and cook 30 seconds, stirring.

2 Stir in tomatoes with their juice, salt, and pepper, breaking up tomatoes with side of spoon; heat to boiling over high heat. Reduce heat to medium and cook, uncovered, 8 minutes. Add frozen spinach and cook, covered, 10 minutes or until spinach is tender, stirring occasionally. Stir in the chopped basil.

3 Meanwhile, in large saucepot, cook noodles as label directs but increase cooking time by 2 to 3 minutes so that noodles are al dente.

4 Drain noodles; return to saucepot. Add tomato mixture and Parmesan cheese; toss well. Spoon into pasta bowls; top with dollops of ricotta cheese. Serve with additional Parmesan on the side.

EACH SERVING: ABOUT 620 CALORIES | 28G PROTEIN | 100G CARBOHYDRATE | 12G TOTAL FAT (5G SATURATED) | 8G FIBER | 23MG CHOLESTEROL | 1,640MG SODIUM

MEATY PASTAS

Penne Rigate with Sweet-and-Spicy Picadillo Sauce (page 74)

SPAGHETTI AND MEATBALLS

This hearty favorite never goes out of style. We like to use a combination of beef, veal, and pork for the richest flavor, but ground chuck is good too. For a lower-fat meal, substitute the Lean Meatballs, opposite.

ACTIVE TIME: 20 MINUTES · TOTAL TIME: 1 HOUR

MAKES: 6 MAIN-DISH SERVINGS

MARINARA SAUCE (PAGE 16)

1½ POUNDS GROUND MEAT FOR MEAT LOAF (BEEF, PORK, AND/OR VEAL) OR GROUND BEEF CHUCK

1 CUP FRESH BREAD CRUMBS (FROM ABOUT 2 SLICES BREAD)

1 LARGE EGG

¼ CUP GRATED PECORINO-ROMANO OR PARMESAN CHEESE

¼ CUP CHOPPED FRESH PARSLEY

1 GARLIC CLOVE, FINELY CHOPPED

1 TEASPOON SALT

¼ TEASPOON GROUND BLACK PEPPER

2 TEASPOONS OLIVE OIL

1 PACKAGE (16 OUNCES) SPAGHETTI

1 Prepare marinara sauce, or warm premade sauce, if refrigerated or frozen.

2 Meanwhile, prepare meatballs: In large bowl, combine ground meat, bread crumbs, egg, Romano, parsley, garlic, salt, and pepper just until blended but not overmixed. Shape into twelve 2-inch balls, handling meat as little as possible.

3 In nonstick 10-inch skillet, heat olive oil over medium heat until hot. Add meatballs and cook, gently turning, until browned and just cooked through, about 20 minutes. Stir sauce into meatballs and heat to boiling, stirring to loosen browned bits from the bottom of the skillet.

4 Meanwhile, in large saucepot, cook pasta as label directs. Drain. In warm serving bowl, gently toss pasta with meatballs and sauce.

EACH SERVING: ABOUT 690 CALORIES | 34G PROTEIN | 69G CARBOHYDRATE | 30G TOTAL FAT (10G SATURATED) | 4G FIBER | 129MG CHOLESTEROL | 1,077MG SODIUM

LEAN MEATBALLS

There are two key ingredients here—bread, which makes the meatballs tender, and turkey, which cuts the fat. Serve them with tomato sauce over spaghetti or make a meatball sandwich.

ACTIVE TIME: 25 MINUTES · TOTAL TIME: 40 MINUTES
MAKES: 24 MEATBALLS

3   SLICES FIRM WHITE BREAD, DICED

⅓   CUP WATER

1   POUND LEAN (90%) GROUND BEEF

1   POUND LEAN GROUND TURKEY

2   LARGE EGG WHITES

⅓   CUP GRATED PECORINO-ROMANO OR PARMESAN CHEESE

3   TABLESPOONS GRATED ONION

2   TABLESPOONS MINCED FRESH PARSLEY

1   TEASPOON SALT

¼   TEASPOON COARSELY GROUND BLACK PEPPER

1   GARLIC CLOVE, MINCED

1   Preheat oven to 425°F. Line a 15½" by 10 ½" jelly-roll pan with foil; spray with nonstick cooking spray.

2   In large bowl, combine diced bread and water. Mix with hands until bread is evenly moistened. Add ground beef and turkey, egg whites, cheese, onion, parsley, salt, pepper, and garlic. Combine until ingredients are well incorporated.

3   Shape meat mixture into twenty-four 1½-inch meatballs. (For easier shaping, use slightly wet hands.) Place meatballs in jelly-roll pan and bake 15 to 20 minutes, until cooked through and lightly browned.

TIP To freeze cooked meatballs, let them cool completely in the jelly-roll pan on a wire rack, then place the pan in the freezer for 20 minutes. Transfer the frozen meatballs to a large zip-tight plastic bag and freeze for up to 1 month. To use them, thaw them in the refrigerator overnight. Or remove the meatballs from the bag and place them on a microwave-safe plate. Microwave on Medium (50 percent power) for 2 to 4 minutes, until just thawed.

EACH MEATBALL: ABOUT 70 CALORIES | 9G PROTEIN | 2G CARBOHYDRATE | 3G TOTAL FAT (1G SATURATED) | 0.5G FIBER | 24MG CHOLESTEROL | 140MG SODIUM

PASTA WITH SAUSAGE AND BUTTERNUT SQUASH

Our food editor, Susan Westmoreland, sampled this exquisite combination in Italy—now it's one of our favorite pastas. For a nice complement to the sweet squash, serve with sautéed broccoli rabe flavored with a little garlic.

ACTIVE TIME: 20 MINUTES · **TOTAL TIME:** 30 MINUTES
MAKES: 6 MAIN-DISH SERVINGS

1   MEDIUM BUTTERNUT SQUASH (1¾ POUNDS)

12 OUNCES SWEET ITALIAN SAUSAGE LINKS, CASINGS REMOVED

1   PACKAGE (16 OUNCES) CORKSCREW PASTA

¼   TEASPOON SALT

¼   TEASPOON COARSELY GROUND BLACK PEPPER

⅓   CUP PACKED FRESH BASIL LEAVES, CHOPPED, PLUS ADDITIONAL FOR GARNISH

¼   CUP GRATED PARMESAN CHEESE

1   Cut butternut squash lengthwise in half; discard seeds. Peel squash and cut into ½-inch chunks. Set aside.

2   In nonstick 12-inch skillet, cook sausage over medium-high until browned, about 7 minutes, stirring frequently to break up sausage. With slotted spoon, transfer sausage to bowl; discard all but 2 tablespoon drippings from skillet.

3   Meanwhile, in saucepot, cook pasta as label directs.

4   To drippings in skillet, add butternut squash, salt, and pepper. Cook, covered, over medium heat, about 10 minutes or until the squash is tender, stirring mixture occasionally.

5   Drain pasta, reserving ¾ *cup pasta cooking water*. Return pasta to saucepot; toss with sausage, butternut squash, basil, Parmesan, and reserved cooking water. Garnish with basil leaves.

EACH SERVING: ABOUT 505 CALORIES | 20G PROTEIN | 66G CARBOHYDRATE | 17G TOTAL FAT (6G SATURATED) | 5G FIBER | 40MG CHOLESTEROL | 645MG SODIUM

LASAGNA TOSS BOLOGNESE

Lasagna is a perennial family favorite, but it takes two and a half hours to prep and bake (and that's not counting the 15 minutes it needs once it's out of the oven to settle so it's easier to cut and serve). Our streamlined version clocks in at just 30 minutes, without losing any of the robust flavors of the original. For photo, see page 2.

ACTIVE TIME: 15 MINUTES · **TOTAL TIME:** 30 MINUTES
MAKES: 6 MAIN-DISH SERVINGS

1 PACKAGE (16 OUNCES) LASAGNA NOODLES (SEE TIP)

2 TEASPOONS OLIVE OIL

1 POUND LEAN (90%) GROUND BEEF OR GROUND MEAT FOR MEAT LOAF (BEEF, PORK, AND/OR VEAL)

½ CUP DRY RED WINE

1 JAR (24 OUNCES) PREPARED MARINARA SAUCE, OR 3 CUPS HOMEMADE (SEE PAGE 16)

⅓ CUP WHOLE MILK

¾ CUP PART-SKIM RICOTTA CHEESE

½ CUP FRESH BASIL, CHOPPED

¼ CUP FRESHLY GRATED PECORINO-ROMANO CHEESE

¼ TEASPOON COARSELY GROUND BLACK PEPPER

⅓ CUP SHREDDED PART-SKIM MOZZARELLA CHEESE

1 In large saucepot, cook lasagna noodles as label directs, but increase cooking time by 2 to 3 minutes so that noodles are al dente.

2 Meanwhile, in 12-inch skillet, heat oil on medium-high. Add meat and cook until no longer pink, breaking it up with spoon, about 3 minutes. If using meat-loaf mix, drain off fat. Add wine; cook 2 to 3 minutes or until almost evaporated. Stir in marinara; heat to boiling. Simmer on low 5 minutes, stirring occasionally. Stir in milk; simmer 5 minutes.

3 In bowl, stir ricotta with basil, Romano, and pepper; set aside.

4 Drain noodles; return to saucepot. Add meat sauce and mozzarella; toss well. Spoon onto warm plates; top with dollops of ricotta mixture.

TIP Tempted to cook up no-boil lasagna noodles to save time? Don't: They'll break apart when tossed.

EACH SERVING: ABOUT 655 CALORIES | 32G PROTEIN | 71G CARBOHYDRATE | 26G TOTAL FAT (10G SATURATED) | 5G FIBER | 71MG CHOLESTEROL | 800MG SODIUM

MEATBALL STROGANOFF

This traditional Russian dish usually features pieces of sautéed beef in a sour-cream sauce. Here we've made this classic even more family-friendly by substituting meatballs for the beef and serving them over a heap of egg noodles.

ACTIVE TIME: 10 MINUTES · TOTAL TIME: 30 MINUTES
MAKES: 4 MAIN-DISH SERVINGS

8	OUNCES WIDE EGG NOODLES	3	TABLESPOONS WATER
1	POUND LEAN (90%) GROUND BEEF	1	TABLESPOON ALL-PURPOSE FLOUR
12	SALTINE CRACKERS, CRUSHED	1	TEASPOON PAPRIKA
1	SMALL ONION, FINELY CHOPPED	1	CAN (14½ OUNCES) CHICKEN BROTH
1	LARGE EGG	½	CUP REDUCED-FAT SOUR CREAM
¼	TEASPOON SALT		

1 In covered 4-quart saucepan, heat *3 quarts salted water* to boiling over high heat. Add noodles and cook as label directs.

2 Meanwhile, in medium bowl, combine beef, saltines, onion, egg, salt, and water just until well blended; do not overmix. Shape mixture into 16 meatballs, handling meat as little as possible.

3 Spray nonstick 12-inch skillet with vegetable cooking spray; heat over medium-high heat until hot. Add meatballs and cook, turning frequently, until meat is browned and no longer pink in center, about 12 minutes. Transfer meatballs to plate.

4 Stir flour and paprika into drippings in pan; cook, stirring, 30 seconds. Stir in broth and heat to boiling; boil until thickened, about 2 minutes. Reduce heat to low. Stir in sour cream. Return meatballs to pan; heat through.

5 Drain noodles. To serve, spoon meatball mixture over noodles.

EACH SERVING: ABOUT 560 CALORIES | 36G PROTEIN | 52G CARBOHYDRATE | 22G TOTAL FAT (9G SATURATED FAT) | 1G FIBER | 190MG CHOLESTEROL | 865MG SODIUM

PENNE WITH SAUSAGE AND BROCCOLI RABE

Balancing the bracing bite of broccoli rabe with the savory sweetness of Italian sausage, this Tuscan time saver—it's table-ready in 30 minutes—will become your weekday default dinner.

ACTIVE TIME: 10 MINUTES · **TOTAL TIME:** 30 MINUTES

MAKES: 4 MAIN-DISH SERVINGS

1 BUNCH BROCCOLI RABE (1 POUND)	2 GARLIC CLOVES, CRUSHED WITH PRESS
12 OUNCES PENNE	¼ CUP FRESHLY GRATED PARMESAN CHEESE, PLUS ADDITIONAL FOR GARNISH
1 LINK (4 OUNCES) SWEET ITALIAN SAUSAGE, CASING REMOVED	
2 SHALLOTS, FINELY CHOPPED	

1 Heat large covered saucepot of salted *water* to boiling on high. Meanwhile, trim tough stem ends from broccoli rabe and discard. Cut broccoli rabe into 1-inch pieces and add to boiling water. Cook 4 to 5 minutes or until bright green and just tender. With slotted spoon, transfer broccoli rabe to large colander, leaving water in pot on stove. Rinse broccoli rabe with cold water and drain again.

2 Return broccoli rabe cooking water to boiling and cook penne in it as label directs.

3 Meanwhile, heat deep 12-inch skillet on medium-high until hot. Add sausage in single layer; cook 4 to 5 minutes or until it looses its pink color, turning to brown evenly. (Reduce heat to medium if browning too quickly.) Add shallots and garlic; cook 2 minutes or until tender, stirring. Transfer 1½ *cups pasta cooking water* from saucepot to skillet. Heat to boiling, stirring occasionally.

4 Drain pasta and add to skillet with sausage. Stir in Parmesan, broccoli rabe, salt, and pepper until well mixed. Divide among shallow bowls; sprinkle with additional Parmesan.

EACH SERVING: ABOUT 470 CALORIES | 20G PROTEIN | 70G CARBOHYDRATE | 12G TOTAL FAT (4G SATURATED) | 4G FIBER | 26MG CHOLESTEROL | 765MG SODIUM

PENNE RIGATE WITH SWEET-AND-SPICY PICADILLO SAUCE

Here pasta gets a Spanish twist, with a meat sauce similar to the filling you might find in empanadas. For photo, see page 64.

ACTIVE TIME: 10 MINUTES · TOTAL TIME: 26 MINUTES

MAKES: 6 MAIN-DISH SERVINGS

1   PACKAGE (16 OUNCES) WHOLE-WHEAT PENNE RIGATE, BOW TIES (FARFALLE), OR RADIATORE

2   TEASPOONS OLIVE OIL

1   SMALL ONION (4 TO 6 OUNCES), FINELY CHOPPED

2   GARLIC CLOVES, CRUSHED WITH GARLIC PRESS

¼   TEASPOON GROUND CINNAMON

⅛ TO ¼ TEASPOON GROUND RED PEPPER (CAYENNE)

¾   POUND LEAN (90%) GROUND BEEF

½   TEASPOON SALT

1   CAN (14¼ OUNCES) TOMATOES IN PUREE, PREFERABLY REDUCED SODIUM

½   CUP DARK SEEDLESS RAISINS

¼   CUP SALAD OLIVES OR CHOPPED PIMIENTO-STUFFED OLIVES, DRAINED

CHOPPED FRESH PARSLEY FOR GARNISH

1   In large saucepot, cook pasta as label directs.

2   Meanwhile, in nonstick 12-inch skillet, heat oil over medium heat until hot. Add onion and cook, stirring frequently, until tender, about 5 minutes. Stir in garlic, cinnamon, and ground red pepper; cook 30 seconds. Increase heat to medium-high; add beef and salt and cook, stirring frequently, until beef begins to brown, about 5 minutes. Spoon off any excess fat as necessary. Stir in tomatoes with their puree, raisins, and olives, breaking up tomatoes with side of spoon, and cook until sauce thickens slightly, about 5 minutes longer.

3   When pasta has reached desired doneness, remove 1 *cup pasta cooking water*; set aside. Drain pasta and return to saucepot. Add beef mixture and reserved cooking water; toss well to coat pasta. Season with salt to taste. Garnish with parsley to serve.

EACH SERVING: ABOUT 450 CALORIES | 22G PROTEIN | 67G CARBOHYDRATE | 12G TOTAL FAT (3G SATURATED) | 9G FIBER | 37MG CHOLESTEROL | 175MG SODIUM (IF USING REDUCED-SODIUM TOMATOES)

GNOCCHI WITH HAM AND ASPARAGUS

A luscious mushroom sauce transforms gnocchi into a sumptuous meal—and it takes just 15 minutes to prepare! When buying asparagus, look for tight tips and a bright green color.

TOTAL TIME: 15 MINUTES

MAKES: 6 MAIN-DISH SERVINGS

1   PACKAGE (16 OUNCES) GNOCCHI OR MEDIUM SHELL PASTA (CONCHIGLIE)

2   TABLESPOONS BUTTER OR MARGARINE

1   MEDIUM ONION (6 TO 8 OUNCES), CHOPPED

4   OUNCES SLICED SMOKED HAM, CUT INTO THIN STRIPS

1   PACKAGE (8 OUNCES) SLICED MUSHROOMS

1   POUND ASPARAGUS, TRIMMED AND CUT INTO 2-INCH PIECES

1   CUP REDUCED-SODIUM CHICKEN BROTH

½   CUP HEAVY OR WHIPPING CREAM

⅛   TEASPOON GROUND BLACK PEPPER

GRATED PARMESAN CHEESE (OPTIONAL)

1   In large saucepot, cook pasta as label directs.

2   Meanwhile, in 10-inch skillet, melt butter over medium-high heat. Add onion and ham and cook, stirring occasionally, 5 minutes or until onion is tender.

3   Add mushrooms and cook until mushrooms are tender and liquid has evaporated, about 5 minutes. Stir in asparagus, chicken broth, cream, and pepper; heat to boiling over high heat, stirring. Boil 3 to 5 minutes, until the asparagus is tender.

4   Drain pasta; return to saucepot. Add mushroom mixture; toss well. Serve with Parmesan cheese, if you like.

EACH SERVING: ABOUT 435 CALORIES | 17G PROTEIN | 62G CARBOHYDRATE | 13G TOTAL FAT (6G SATURATED) | 3G FIBER | 38MG CHOLESTEROL | 455MG SODIUM

RUFFLED PASTA WITH LAMB AND MINT

Morocco was the inspiration for the spice mix in this dish. Ruffle-edged mafalda pasta makes a nice change from flat pasta.

ACTIVE TIME: 15 MINUTES · **TOTAL TIME:** 30 MINUTES
MAKES: 6 MAIN-DISH SERVINGS

1   TABLESPOON OLIVE OIL

1   LARGE ONION (12 OUNCES), CUT INTO ¼-INCH DICE

1   MEDIUM RED PEPPER, CUT INTO ¼-INCH DICE

12 OUNCES GROUND LAMB

3   GARLIC CLOVES, MINCED

2   TEASPOONS DRIED MINT

2   TEASPOONS GROUND CORIANDER

¾   TEASPOON SALT

½   TEASPOON GROUND RED PEPPER (CAYENNE)

1   CAN (28 OUNCES) TOMATOES

3   TABLESPOONS TOMATO PASTE

12 OUNCES MAFALDA (RUFFLED) NOODLES OR FETTUCCINE

½   CUP LOOSELY PACKED FRESH PARSLEY LEAVES, CHOPPED, PLUS ADDITIONAL FOR GARNISH

1   In 12-inch skillet, heat oil over medium heat until hot. Add onion and red pepper, and cook 10 minutes or until lightly browned and almost tender, stirring occasionally. Increase heat to medium-high; add lamb, garlic, mint, coriander, salt, and ground red pepper and cook 8 minutes or until browned, stirring occasionally.

2   Stir in tomatoes with their juice and tomato paste, breaking up tomatoes with side of spoon; heat to boiling. Reduce heat to medium and simmer, uncovered, 5 minutes.

3   Meanwhile, in large saucepot, cook mafalda as label directs. Drain mafalda; return to saucepot. Add lamb mixture and chopped parsley, and toss well to coat. Garnish with additional parsley.

EACH SERVING: ABOUT 440 CALORIES | 19G PROTEIN | 55G CARBOHYDRATE | 17G TOTAL FAT (6G SATURATED) | 5G FIBER | 41MG CHOLESTEROL | 780MG SODIUM

SPAGHETTI ALL'AMATRICIANA

A spicy pairing of pancetta and red chiles gives this pasta classic distinctive taste. It's named for the town of Amatrice, near Rome.

ACTIVE TIME: 10 MINUTES · TOTAL TIME: 40 MINUTES
MAKES: 4 MAIN-DISH SERVINGS

1   TABLESPOON OLIVE OIL

4   OUNCES SLICED PANCETTA, CHOPPED (SEE TIP)

1   SMALL ONION (4 TO 6 OUNCES), CHOPPED

1   GARLIC CLOVE, FINELY CHOPPED

¼   TEASPOON CRUSHED RED PEPPER

1   CAN (28 OUNCES) PLUM TOMATOES

½   TEASPOON SALT

1   PACKAGE (16 OUNCES) SPAGHETTI OR BUCATINI

¼   CUP CHOPPED FRESH PARSLEY

1   In nonreactive 5-quart Dutch oven, heat oil over medium heat. Add pancetta and cook, stirring, until lightly browned, about 5 minutes. Stir in onion and cook until tender, about 3 minutes. Stir in garlic and crushed red pepper; cook 15 seconds. Add tomatoes with their juice and salt; heat to boiling, breaking up tomatoes with side of spoon. Reduce heat and simmer, stirring occasionally, 30 minutes.

2   Meanwhile, in large saucepot, cook pasta as label directs. Drain. In warm serving bowl, toss pasta with sauce and parsley.

TIP Pancetta, an Italian bacon, is cured in a mixture of salt and spices. Unlike American bacon, it is not smoked, so its flavor is somewhat milder. Look for it in Italian markets, specialty meat shops, or large supermarkets. If you can't find it, use bacon.

EACH SERVING: ABOUT 635 CALORIES | 20G PROTEIN | 96G CARBOHYDRATE | 17G TOTAL FAT (5G SATURATED) | 7G FIBER | 63MG CHOLESTEROL | 826MG SODIUM

WHOLE-WHEAT SPAGHETTI WITH FONTINA AND HAM

A favorite combination—ham and cheese—tastes great tossed with pasta. If your supermarket doesn't carry Fontina, you can substitute Gruyère.

ACTIVE TIME: 10 MINUTES · TOTAL TIME: 20 MINUTES
MAKES: 4 MAIN-DISH SERVINGS

1   PACKAGE (16 OUNCES) WHOLE-WHEAT SPAGHETTI

2   TABLESPOONS OLIVE OIL

2   BUNCHES GREEN ONIONS, SLICED DIAGONALLY ½ INCH THICK

1   GARLIC CLOVE, CRUSHED WITH GARLIC PRESS

½   TEASPOON SALT

¼   TEASPOON CRUSHED RED PEPPER

1   CUP CHICKEN BROTH

4   OUNCES FONTINA CHEESE, SHREDDED (1 CUP)

4   OUNCES SLICED COOKED HAM (PREFERABLY BAKED), CUT INTO 2" BY ¼" STRIPS

1   In large saucepot, cook pasta as label directs.
2   Meanwhile, in 12-inch skillet, heat oil over medium-high heat until hot. Add green onions and cook 2 to 3 minutes, until lightly golden, stirring occasionally. Add garlic, salt, and crushed red pepper and cook 30 seconds, stirring. Stir in chicken broth and heat to boiling.
3   Drain spaghetti; return to saucepot. Add broth mixture, cheese, and ham, and toss well to coat.

EACH SERVING: ABOUT 640 CALORIES | 31G PROTEIN | 92G CARBOHYDRATE | 20G TOTAL FAT (8G SATURATED) | 11G FIBER | 48 MG CHOLESTEROL | 1,290 MG SODIUM

RADIATORE WITH ARUGULA, TOMATOES, AND PANCETTA

Here's a BLT Italian-style—pasta replaces the bread, arugula replaces the lettuce, and pancetta replaces the bacon. So easy, so good.

TOTAL TIME: 15 MINUTES

MAKES: 4 MAIN-DISH SERVINGS

1 PACKAGE (16 OUNCES) RADIATORE OR CORKSCREW PASTA	½ TEASPOON SALT
4 OUNCES SLICED PANCETTA OR BACON, CUT INTO ¼-INCH PIECES (SEE TIP, PAGE 78)	¼ TEASPOON COARSELY GROUND BLACK PEPPER
	8 OUNCES ARUGULA, RINSED AND DRIED VERY WELL, TOUGH STEMS REMOVED
1 GARLIC CLOVE, CRUSHED WITH GARLIC PRESS	
1 PINT CHERRY TOMATOES, QUARTERED	¼ CUP GRATED PARMESAN CHEESE, PLUS ADDITIONAL FOR GARNISH

1   In large saucepot, cook pasta as label directs.

2   Meanwhile, in 10-inch skillet, cook pancetta over medium heat until lightly browned, stirring occasionally. (If using bacon, discard all but 1 tablespoon fat after browning.) Add garlic; cook 30 seconds, stirring. Add tomatoes, salt, and pepper, and cook 1 to 2 minutes. Remove skillet from heat; cover and keep warm.

3   Drain the pasta; return to saucepot. Add pancetta mixture, arugula, and grated Parmesan; toss well. Garnish with additional Parmesan.

EACH SERVING: ABOUT 560 CALORIES | 22G PROTEIN | 93G CARBOHYDRATE | 12G TOTAL FAT (4G SATURATED) | 6G FIBER | 15MG CHOLESTEROL | 680MG SODIUM

FUSILLI WITH SWISS CHARD, GARBANZO BEANS, AND BACON

Dark-green Swiss chard is loaded with vitamins K, A, and C, as well as minerals; toss it into an already good-for-you bean and whole-grain pasta dish, and you've got a nutrition powerhouse. The single slice of bacon lends flavor without adding much fat.

ACTIVE TIME: 20 MINUTES · **TOTAL TIME:** 30 MINUTES

MAKES: 6 MAIN-DISH SERVINGS

12 OUNCES WHOLE-WHEAT FUSILLI OR ROTINI

1 BUNCH SWISS CHARD (1 POUND), TOUGH ENDS TRIMMED

1 SLICE BACON, CUT INTO ½-INCH-WIDE STRIPS

1 GARLIC CLOVE, CRUSHED WITH GARLIC PRESS

¼ TEASPOON CRUSHED RED PEPPER

1 CAN (15 TO 19 OUNCES) GARBANZO BEANS, RINSED AND DRAINED

½ TEASPOON SALT

2 TABLESPOONS FRESH LEMON JUICE

1 In large saucepot, cook pasta as label directs.

2 Meanwhile, cut ribs and stems from Swiss chard leaves. Cut ribs and stems into 1-inch pieces; cut leaves into 2-inch pieces. Rinse Swiss chard in large bowl of cold water; swish to remove any dirt. Transfer to colander. Do not spin dry.

3 In 12-inch skillet, cook bacon over medium-high heat until browned, tossing occasionally. With slotted spoon, transfer bacon to paper towels to drain. Reduce heat to medium. To bacon fat in skillet, add garlic and crushed red pepper; cook 30 seconds, stirring. Add chard, beans, and salt. Cover and cook until chard begins to wilt, about 2 minutes. Uncover and cook until stems are tender-crisp, about 5 minutes longer.

4 Drain pasta, reserving ¼ cup pasta cooking water. Return pasta to saucepot. Stir in bacon, Swiss chard mixture, and lemon juice until combined. If mixture seems dry, add reserved cooking water.

EACH SERVING: ABOUT 500 CALORIES | 21G PROTEIN | 93G CARBOHYDRATE | 8G TOTAL FAT (2G SATURATED) | 14G FIBER | 6MG CHOLESTEROL | 755MG SODIUM

BOW TIES WITH CHICKEN AND MUSHROOMS

Flavorful and inexpensive chicken thighs are dressed up in a creamy sauce featuring three mushrooms—shiitake, oyster, and white.

ACTIVE TIME: 20 MINUTES · TOTAL TIME: 30 MINUTES
MAKES: 4 MAIN-DISH SERVINGS

---

1   TEASPOON OLIVE OIL

1   POUND SKINLESS, BONELESS CHICKEN THIGHS, CUT INTO 1-INCH PIECES

¾   TEASPOON SALT

¼   TEASPOON COARSELY GROUND BLACK PEPPER

1   TABLESPOON BUTTER OR MARGARINE

8   OUNCES WHITE MUSHROOMS, THINLY SLICED

4   OUNCES SHIITAKE MUSHROOMS, STEMS REMOVED AND CAPS THINLY SLICED

4   OUNCES OYSTER MUSHROOMS, TOUGH STEM ENDS REMOVED AND CAPS THINLY SLICED

1   MEDIUM ONION (6 TO 8 OUNCES), CUT IN HALF, THEN THINLY SLICED CROSSWISE

1   GARLIC CLOVE, CRUSHED WITH GARLIC PRESS

1   CUP FROZEN PEAS

¼   CUP HEAVY OR WHIPPING CREAM

2   TABLESPOONS BRANDY

12 OUNCES BOW TIES (FARFALLE)

---

1 In 12-inch skillet, heat oil over medium-high heat until hot. Add chicken, ½ teaspoon salt, and pepper; cook 5 minutes or just until chicken loses its pink color inside, stirring frequently. Transfer chicken to plate; keep warm.

2 In same skillet, melt butter. Add all mushrooms, onion, garlic, and remaining ¼ teaspoon salt, and cook until vegetables are tender and golden, about 15 minutes, stirring often. Stir in peas, cream, and brandy; heat to boiling. Remove skillet from heat.

3 Meanwhile, in large saucepot, cook pasta as label directs. When pasta has reached desired doneness, remove ½ cup *pasta cooking water*. Drain pasta; return to saucepot. Add mushroom mixture, chicken, and reserved cooking water; toss well.

EACH SERVING: ABOUT 625 CALORIES | 39G PROTEIN | 79G CARBOHYDRATE | 16G TOTAL FAT (6G SATURATED) | 10G FIBER | 114MG CHOLESTEROL | 720MG SODIUM

CHICKEN PASTA PRIMAVERA

Thanks to the addictively rich sauce, thickened with cream and Parmesan cheese, your family will clamor for seconds, while you'll appreciate the abundant veggies they're getting—including red peppers and a generous portion of in-season asparagus.

ACTIVE TIME: 25 MINUTES · **TOTAL TIME:** 30 MINUTES
MAKES: 6 MAIN-DISH SERVINGS

12 OUNCES CAVATAPPI OR FUSILLI PASTA

2 GREEN ONIONS

4 TEASPOONS OLIVE OIL

1½ POUNDS SKINLESS, BONELESS CHICKEN-BREAST HALVES, CUT INTO 1-INCH CHUNKS

½ TEASPOON SALT

¼ TEASPOON FRESHLY GROUND BLACK PEPPER

1 GARLIC CLOVE, CRUSHED WITH PRESS

1 POUND ASPARAGUS, TRIMMED AND CUT INTO 1-INCH PIECES

1 MEDIUM RED PEPPER, THINLY SLICED

½ CUP HEAVY OR WHIPPING CREAM

¼ TEASPOON CRUSHED RED PEPPER

½ CUP FRESHLY GRATED PARMESAN CHEESE

¼ CUP LOOSELY PACKED FRESH BASIL LEAVES, THINLY SLICED

1   In large saucepot, cook pasta as label directs. Drain pasta, reserving ½ *cup pasta cooking water*. Return pasta and reserved cooking water to saucepot.

2   Meanwhile, slice green onions; reserve 2 tablespoons sliced dark green tops for garnish. In 12-inch skillet, heat 2 teaspoons oil on medium-high until hot. Sprinkle chicken with ¼ teaspoon salt and pepper. Add chicken to skillet and cook 7 minutes or until chicken is browned and no longer pink throughout, stirring occasionally. Transfer chicken to medium bowl; set aside.

3   To same skillet, add remaining 2 teaspoons oil; reduce heat to medium. Add green onions and garlic; cook 1 minute, stirring. Add asparagus and red pepper; cook 6 to 7 minutes or until vegetables are tender-crisp, stirring frequently. Stir in cream, crushed red pepper, and remaining ¼ teaspoon salt. Heat to boiling over medium-high heat. Stir in reserved chicken pieces and remove skillet from heat.

4   To saucepot with pasta, add Parmesan, chicken mixture, and basil; stir to combine. Spoon into bowls and garnish with reserved dark green onion.

EACH SERVING: ABOUT 485 CALORIES | 38G PROTEIN | 46G CARBOHYDRATE | 15G TOTAL FAT (7G SATURATED FAT) | 3G FIBER | 98MG CHOLESTEROL | 470MG SODIUM

CHICKEN BOLOGNESE

This delicious twist on a classic dish trims the calories and fat without sacrificing the richly satisfying flavor.

ACTIVE TIME: 25 MINUTES · **TOTAL TIME:** 40 MINUTES
MAKES: 6 MAIN-DISH SERVINGS

12	OUNCES LINGUINE OR FETTUCCINE	1	GARLIC CLOVE, CRUSHED WITH PRESS
4	TEASPOONS OLIVE OIL	1	CAN (28 OUNCES) CRUSHED TOMATOES
1	POUND GROUND CHICKEN BREAST	¼	TEASPOON GROUND BLACK PEPPER
½	TEASPOON SALT	½	CUP REDUCED-FAT (2%) MILK
2	MEDIUM CARROTS, PEELED AND CHOPPED	⅓	CUP FRESHLY GRATED PARMESAN CHEESE
2	MEDIUM STALKS CELERY, CHOPPED	¼	CUP LOOSELY PACKED FRESH PARSLEY LEAVES, CHOPPED
1	LARGE ONION (12 OUNCES), CHOPPED		

1 In large saucepot, cook pasta as label directs.

2 Meanwhile, in 12-inch nonstick skillet, heat 2 teaspoons oil on medium 1 minute. Add ground chicken to skillet; sprinkle with ¼ teaspoon salt. Cook chicken 8 to 9 minutes, or until it is no longer pink, stirring occasionally. Transfer chicken along with any juices to medium bowl.

3 To same skillet, add remaining 2 teaspoons oil with carrots, celery, onion, and garlic; cook 10 to 12 minutes or until vegetables are lightly browned and tender, stirring occasionally. Stir in tomatoes with their juice, remaining ¼ teaspoon salt, and pepper; heat to boiling. Reduce heat to medium-low and simmer, uncovered, 10 minutes, stirring occasionally. Stir in cooked chicken and milk; heat through.

4 Reserve ¼ cup pasta cooking water. Drain pasta and return to saucepot; stir in sauce from skillet, Parmesan, parsley, and reserved cooking water, and toss to coat.

EACH SERVING: ABOUT 410 CALORIES | 29G PROTEIN | 59G CARBOHYDRATE | 6G TOTAL FAT (2G SATURATED) | 5G FIBER | 49MG CHOLESTEROL | 800MG SODIUM

ASIAN CHICKEN-NOODLE STIR-FRY

These dark, slender soba noodles, made from buckwheat flour, are a specialty of Japan. We love their nutty flavor combined with stir-fried strips of chicken breasts, bok choy, and red pepper.

ACTIVE TIME: 15 MINUTES · **TOTAL TIME:** 30 MINUTES
MAKES: 4 MAIN-DISH SERVINGS

1 PACKAGE (ABOUT 8 OUNCES) SOBA NOODLES

2 TABLESPOONS VEGETABLE OIL

1 POUND BONELESS, SKINLESS CHICKEN BREASTS, CUT LENGTHWISE INTO ½-INCH-WIDE STRIPS

2 TABLESPOONS SOY SAUCE, PLUS ADDITIONAL FOR SERVING

3 GREEN ONIONS, THINLY SLICED

1 LARGE RED PEPPER, CUT LENGTHWISE INTO ¼-INCH-WIDE STRIPS

1 MEDIUM HEAD BOK CHOY (ABOUT 1½ POUNDS), CUT CROSSWISE INTO ½-INCH-WIDE RIBBONS

1 CUP CHICKEN BROTH

2 GARLIC CLOVES, CRUSHED WITH GARLIC PRESS

1 TABLESPOON GRATED, PEELED FRESH GINGER (SEE TIP, PAGE 99)

1 TABLESPOON SEASONED RICE VINEGAR

2 TEASPOONS CORNSTARCH

1 TEASPOON SUGAR

1 In large saucepot, cook soba noodles as label directs. Drain noodles; rinse under cold running water and drain again. Set aside.

2 Meanwhile, in 12-inch skillet, heat 1 tablespoon oil over medium-high heat until hot. Add chicken and 1 tablespoon soy sauce, and cook, stirring often, until chicken loses its pink color throughout, about 5 minutes. Transfer chicken to plate.

3 Add remaining 1 tablespoon oil to skillet; add green onions and red pepper, and cook 3 minutes, stirring often. Add bok choy and cook until vegetables are tender-crisp, about 3 minutes longer.

4 Meanwhile, in 2-cup glass measuring cup, whisk together broth, garlic, ginger, vinegar, cornstarch, sugar, and remaining 1 tablespoon soy sauce.

5 Add noodles and sauce mixture to vegetable mixture and heat to boiling; cook 1 minute, stirring to coat noodles. Add chicken and toss just until heated through. Serve with extra soy sauce on the side.

EACH SERVING: ABOUT 440 CALORIES | 38G PROTEIN | 55G CARBOHYDRATE | 10G TOTAL FAT (1G SATURATED) | 5G FIBER | 66MG CHOLESTEROL | 1,505MG SODIUM

SEAFOOD PASTAS

Trattoria-Style Shrimp Fettuccine (page 97)

PASTA WITH TUNA PUTTANESCA

We've used tuna instead of anchovies in this tasty no-cook twist on traditional puttanesca sauce. For best flavor use extra-virgin olive oil.

TOTAL TIME: 15 MINUTES

MAKES: 6 MAIN-DISH SERVINGS

1 PACKAGE (16 OUNCES) FUSILLI OR CORKSCREW PASTA

3 TABLESPOONS CAPERS, DRAINED AND CHOPPED

3 TABLESPOONS MINCED SHALLOT

2 TABLESPOONS RED WINE VINEGAR

1 TABLESPOON OLIVE OIL

½ TEASPOON GRATED LEMON PEEL

½ TEASPOON SALT

¼ TEASPOON COARSELY GROUND BLACK PEPPER

1 CAN (6 OUNCES) LIGHT TUNA IN OLIVE OIL

2 MEDIUM BUNCHES WATERCRESS, TOUGH STEMS REMOVED

½ CUP LOOSELY PACKED FRESH BASIL LEAVES, CHOPPED

1 In large saucepot, cook pasta as label directs.

2 Meanwhile, in a large bowl, with fork, stir capers, shallot, red wine vinegar, olive oil, lemon peel, salt, and black pepper until well mixed. Add undrained tuna and watercress; toss well.

3 When pasta has reached desired doneness, remove ½ *cup pasta cooking water*. Drain pasta and return to saucepot. Add tuna mixture, reserved cooking water, and basil; toss well.

EACH SERVING: ABOUT 375 CALORIES | 17G PROTEIN | 58G CARBOHYDRATE | 8G TOTAL FAT (1G SATURATED) | 3G FIBER | 4MG CHOLESTEROL | 540MG SODIUM

PENNE WITH SALMON AND ASPARAGUS

A spring evening, during the time of year when the first asparagus appear in the market, is the perfect time to make this enticing dish. Serve a dessert of fresh strawberries topped with brown-sugar-sweetened and vanilla-flavored sour cream.

TOTAL TIME: 15 MINUTES

MAKES: 6 MAIN-DISH SERVINGS

1   PACKAGE (16 OUNCES) PENNE RIGATE OR BOW TIES (FARFALLE)

3   TEASPOONS OLIVE OIL

1   POUND ASPARAGUS, TRIMMED AND CUT INTO 2-INCH PIECES

½   TEASPOON SALT

¼   TEASPOON COARSELY GROUND BLACK PEPPER

1   LARGE SHALLOT, FINELY CHOPPED (¼ CUP)

⅓   CUP DRY WHITE WINE

1   CUP LOW-SODIUM CHICKEN BROTH

1   SKINLESS SALMON FILLET (1 POUND), CUT CROSSWISE INTO THIRDS, THEN LENGTHWISE INTO ¼-INCH-THICK SLICES

1   TABLESPOON CHOPPED FRESH TARRAGON

1   In large saucepot, cook pasta as label directs. Drain.

2   Meanwhile, in 12-inch skillet, heat 2 teaspoons oil over medium-high heat. Add asparagus, salt, and pepper, and cook until asparagus is almost tender-crisp, about 5 minutes. Add shallot and remaining 1 teaspoon oil; cook, stirring constantly, 2 minutes longer. Add wine; heat to boiling over high heat. Stir in broth and heat to boiling. Place salmon slices in skillet; cover and cook until just opaque throughout, 2 to 3 minutes. Remove skillet from heat; stir in tarragon.

3   In warm serving bowl, toss pasta with asparagus mixture.

EACH SERVING: ABOUT 460 CALORIES | 27G PROTEIN | 60G CARBOHYDRATE | 12G TOTAL FAT (2G SATURATED) | 3G FIBER | 45MG CHOLESTEROL | 404MG SODIUM

MULTIGRAIN PASTA WITH MAHI-MAHI, TOMATOES, AND BASIL

Mahi-mahi is a wonderfully versatile fish, rich in niacin and B$_6$ vitamins. It takes well to grilling, broiling, baking, and steaming—here it's pan-seared in a tasty combination with fresh tomatoes, garlic slices, and basil.

ACTIVE TIME: 10 MINUTES · **TOTAL TIME:** 30 MINUTES
MAKES: 4 MAIN-DISH SERVINGS

½ PACKAGE (8 OUNCES) MULTIGRAIN ROTINI PASTA

2 TEASPOONS PLUS 1 TABLESPOON EXTRA-VIRGIN OLIVE OIL

1 POUND SKINLESS MAHI-MAHI, CUT INTO 1-INCH CHUNKS

½ TEASPOON SALT

¼ TEASPOON GROUND BLACK PEPPER

2 GARLIC CLOVES, THINLY SLICED

3 CUPS GRAPE TOMATOES (1½ PINTS)

½ CUP DRY WHITE WINE

½ CUP FIRMLY PACKED SMALL FRESH BASIL LEAVES

1 Heat large covered saucepot of *salted water* to boiling over high heat. Add pasta and cook as label directs.

2 Meanwhile, in deep nonstick 12-inch skillet, heat 2 teaspoons oil over medium-high heat until hot. Add mahi-mahi; sprinkle with ¼ teaspoon salt and ⅛ teaspoon pepper and cook just until mahi-mahi turns opaque in center, 3 to 4 minutes, gently stirring. Transfer mahi-mahi to plate; set aside.

3 In same skillet, heat remaining 1 tablespoon oil over medium heat until hot. Add garlic and cook until golden, about 1 minute, stirring constantly. Add tomatoes; cover and cook until they burst, 4 to 5 minutes, stirring occasionally. Stir in wine, half of basil, remaining ¼ teaspoon salt, and remaining ⅛ teaspoon pepper; cook, uncovered, 1 minute to blend flavors.

4 Reserve ¼ cup *pasta cooking water*, then drain pasta. Add pasta, reserved cooking water, mahi-mahi, and remaining basil to tomato mixture in skillet; toss until well combined.

EACH SERVING: ABOUT 380 CALORIES | 33G PROTEIN | 45G CARBOHYDRATE | 8G TOTAL FAT (1G SATURATED) | 6G FIBER | 83MG CHOLESTEROL | 500MG SODIUM

GREEK LASAGNA TOSS WITH TOMATOES, SHRIMP, AND FETA

The saltiness of the feta and brininess of the shrimp contrast with the sweet tomatoes in this Mediterranean-inspired dish.

ACTIVE TIME: 15 MINUTES · **TOTAL TIME:** 30 MINUTES

MAKES: 4 MAIN-DISH SERVINGS

1 PACKAGE (16 OUNCES) LASAGNA NOODLES

2 TEASPOONS OLIVE OIL

1 MEDIUM ONION (6 TO 8 OUNCES), CHOPPED

1 CAN (28 OUNCES) PLUM TOMATOES

¼ TEASPOONS CRUSHED RED PEPPER

¼ TEASPOON DRIED OREGANO

1 POUND LARGE SHRIMP, SHELLED AND DEVEINED, WITH TAIL PART OF SHELL LEFT ON IF YOU LIKE

¼ CUP LOOSELY PACKED FRESH PARSLEY LEAVES, CHOPPED

½ CUP FETA CHEESE, CRUMBLED (2 OUNCES), PLUS ADDITIONAL FOR SERVING

1 In large saucepot, cook pasta as label directs but add about 2 minutes to cooking time, so that noodles are al dente.

2 Meanwhile, in 12-inch skillet, heat oil over medium heat until hot. Add onion and cook 5 to 7 minutes or until tender and lightly browned. Stir in tomatoes with their juice, crushed red pepper, and oregano; heat to boiling over high heat, breaking up tomatoes with side of spoon. Reduce heat to medium and cook 7 minutes to thicken slightly. Stir in shrimp, and cook 3 to 4 minutes or until shrimp turn opaque throughout. Remove skillet from heat; stir in chopped parsley and ½ cup crumbled feta.

3 Drain pasta; return to saucepot. Add shrimp mixture to noodles in saucepot and toss to coat. Spoon pasta mixture into large serving bowl; serve additional feta on the side for sprinkling.

EACH SERVING: ABOUT 630 CALORIES | 37G PROTEIN | 98G CARBOHYDRATE | 9G TOTAL FAT (3G SATURATED) | 5G FIBER | 153MG CHOLESTEROL | 590MG SODIUM

PAD THAI

Go to a Thai restaurant and you're certain to find pad Thai—a tasty mix of noodles, shrimp, peanuts, and eggs. It's surprisingly easy to make at home. Just be sure to have everything in place before you start because it cooks quickly.

ACTIVE TIME: 25 MINUTES · **TOTAL TIME:** 35 MINUTES
MAKES: 4 MAIN-DISH SERVINGS

1   PACKAGE (7 OR 8 OUNCES) FLAT RICE STICK NOODLES OR 8 OUNCES ANGEL HAIR PASTA (CAPELLINI)

½   POUND MEDIUM SHRIMP, SHELLED AND DEVEINED

¼   CUP FRESH LIME JUICE

¼   CUP ASIAN FISH SAUCE (SEE TIP)

2   TABLESPOONS SUGAR

1   TABLESPOON VEGETABLE OIL

2   GARLIC CLOVES, CRUSHED WITH GARLIC PRESS

¼   TEASPOON CRUSHED RED PEPPER

2   LARGE EGGS, LIGHTLY BEATEN

6   OUNCES FRESH BEAN SPROUTS (ABOUT 2 CUPS), RINSED

2   TABLESPOONS UNSALTED ROASTED PEANUTS, COARSELY CHOPPED

3   GREEN ONIONS, THINLY SLICED

½   CUP LOOSELY PACKED CILANTRO LEAVES

LIME WEDGES

1   Break pasta strands in half. In large bowl, soak rice stick noodles in *hot water* to cover 20 minutes. (If using angel hair pasta, cook as label directs and rinse with cold running water.)

2   Meanwhile, cut each shrimp horizontally in half. In small bowl, combine lime juice, fish sauce, and sugar. Measure all remaining ingredients before beginning to cook and set out within reach.

3   Drain noodles. In a wok or 12-inch skillet, heat vegetable oil over high heat until hot but not smoking. Add shrimp, garlic, and crushed red pepper and cook, stirring, 1 minute. Add eggs and cook, stirring, 20 seconds. Add drained noodles and cook, stirring, 2 minutes. Add fish-sauce mixture, half of bean sprouts, half of peanuts, and half of green onions; cook, stirring, 1 minute.

4   Transfer noodle mixture to platter; top with remaining bean sprouts, peanuts, and green onions. Sprinkle with cilantro leaves. Serve with lime wedges.

EACH SERVING: ABOUT 395 CALORIES | 19G PROTEIN | 59G CARBOHYDRATE | 9G TOTAL FAT (2G SATURATED) | 3G FIBER | 172MG CHOLESTEROL | 1,400MG SODIUM

TIP An integral flavoring in Southeast Asian cooking, fish sauce is made from fermented fish. It is known as *nam pla* in Thailand and *nuoc nam* in Vietnam. Store at room temperature in a dark place; it will keep for about one year.

VERMICELLI WITH SHRIMP AND BROCCOLI

For a delicious change of pace, shrimp and broccoli are stir-fried with one of our favorite Asian spice combinations—garlic, hot red pepper, and soy sauce. Add pasta and serve.

ACTIVE TIME: 15 MINUTES · **TOTAL TIME:** 25 MINUTES

MAKES: 6 MAIN-DISH SERVINGS

1 PACKAGE (16 OUNCES) VERMICELLI OR THIN SPAGHETTI (SPAGHETTINI)

1 TABLESPOON VEGETABLE OIL

1 POUND MEDIUM SHRIMP, SHELLED AND DEVEINED, WITH TAIL PART OF SHELL LEFT ON IF YOU LIKE

1 TABLESPOON GRATED, PEELED FRESH GINGER (SEE TIP, PAGE 99)

2 GARLIC CLOVES, CRUSHED WITH GARLIC PRESS

¼ TEASPOON CRUSHED RED PEPPER

2 PACKAGES (12 OUNCES EACH) BROCCOLI FLOWERETS

1 CUP REDUCED-SODIUM CHICKEN BROTH

2 TABLESPOONS SOY SAUCE

1 TEASPOON ASIAN SESAME OIL

1 In large saucepot, cook pasta as label directs.

2 Meanwhile, in 10-inch skillet, heat vegetable oil over medium-high heat until hot. Add shrimp, ginger, garlic, and crushed red pepper. Cook, stirring, 2 minutes or just until shrimp turn opaque throughout. Transfer shrimp to bowl.

3 Add broccoli to skillet and cook, stirring, 1 minute. Stir in chicken broth and heat to boiling over high heat. Cook, uncovered, stirring often, until broccoli is just tender, about 3 minutes. Stir in soy sauce, sesame oil, and shrimp; heat through.

4 Drain pasta; return to saucepot. Add shrimp mixture; toss well.

EACH SERVING: ABOUT 415 CALORIES | 26G PROTEIN | 65G CARBOHYDRATE | 6G TOTAL FAT (1G SATURATED) | 6G FIBER | 95MG CHOLESTEROL | 655MG SODIUM

TRATTORIA-STYLE SHRIMP FETTUCCINE

Loaded with good-for-you spinach, this slimmer version of the high-calorie restaurant classic swaps diet-derailing cream for a savory broth of wine and clam juice. For photo, see page 88.

ACTIVE TIME: 20 MINUTES · **TOTAL TIME:** 30 MINUTES

MAKES: 6 MAIN-DISH SERVINGS

12 OUNCES FETTUCCINE OR SPAGHETTI

2 TABLESPOONS OLIVE OIL

1 MEDIUM ONION (6 TO 8 OUNCES), CHOPPED

2 GARLIC CLOVES, THINLY SLICED

½ CUP WHITE WINE

1 BOTTLE (8 OUNCES) CLAM JUICE

½ TEASPOON SALT

1 POUND SHELLED AND DEVEINED LARGE SHRIMP, WITH TAIL PART OF SHELL LEFT ON IF YOU LIKE

1 BAG (5 TO 6 OUNCES) BABY SPINACH

⅓ CUP LOOSELY PACKED FRESH PARSLEY LEAVES, CHOPPED

1 In large saucepot, cook pasta as label directs.

2 Meanwhile, in 12-inch skillet, heat oil on medium until hot. Add onion and garlic, and cook 10 minutes or until golden and tender, stirring often. Add wine; increase heat to medium-high and cook 1 minute. Stir in clam juice and salt; heat to boiling. Stir in shrimp, and cook 2 to 3 minutes or until shrimp turn opaque throughout.

3 Drain pasta and add to skillet with spinach and parsley; toss to coat.

EACH SERVING: ABOUT 350 CALORIES | 24G PROTEIN | 46G CARBOHYDRATE | 7G TOTAL FAT (1G SATURATED) | 4G FIBER | 115MG CHOLESTEROL | 505MG SODIUM

SOBA NOODLES WITH SHRIMP, SNOW PEAS, AND CARROTS

This dish couldn't be easier to make. The shrimp, peas, and carrots are cooked in the same water as the noodles, then tossed with a delicious peanut sauce that takes just a couple of minutes to put together.

ACTIVE TIME: 15 MINUTES · **TOTAL TIME:** 35 MINUTES
MAKES: 4 MAIN-DISH SERVINGS

¼ CUP CREAMY PEANUT BUTTER

2 TEASPOONS GRATED, PEELED FRESH GINGER (SEE TIP)

2 TABLESPOONS LOW-SODIUM SOY SAUCE

1 TABLESPOON DISTILLED WHITE VINEGAR

1 TEASPOON ASIAN SESAME OIL

½ TEASPOON HOT PEPPER SAUCE

1 TEASPOON SALT

1 PACKAGE (8 OUNCES) SOBA NOODLES

½ BAG (10 OUNCES) SHREDDED OR MATCHSTICK CARROTS (ABOUT 1½ CUPS)

1 POUND LARGE SHRIMP, SHELLED AND DEVEINED, WITH TAIL PART LEFT ON IF YOU LIKE

4 OUNCES SNOW PEAS, STRINGS REMOVED

½ CUP LOOSELY PACKED FRESH CILANTRO LEAVES, CHOPPED, PLUS ADDITIONAL SPRIGS FOR GARNISH

1 In small bowl, place peanut butter, ginger, soy sauce, vinegar, sesame oil, and hot pepper sauce; set aside.

2 Heat covered 5- to 6-quart saucepot of *water* and salt to boiling over high heat. Add noodles and cook 4 minutes. Add carrots and cook 1 minute. Add shrimp and snow peas and cook 2 minutes more. Reserve ½ *cup cooking water*. Drain noodles, shrimp, and vegetables into large colander. Transfer mixture to large bowl.

3 With wire whisk, beat peanut-butter mixture until well blended. Add peanut sauce, reserved cooking water, and chopped cilantro to noodle mixture in bowl and toss until evenly coated.

4 To serve, spoon into large bowls; garnish each serving with a cilantro sprig.

TIP Use a vegetable peeler to peel ginger, and be careful to remove only the very top layer of skin because the flesh directly beneath is the most delicate. Then, chop, slice, or shred the ginger as directed using a sharp knife or box grater. A ginger grater (a relatively inexpensive tool) works best for fine grating because it yields plenty of juice with minimal fibers.

EACH SERVING: ABOUT 430 CALORIES | 33G PROTEIN | 53G CARBOHYDRATE | 12G TOTAL FAT (2G SATURATED) | 6G FIBER | 140MG CHOLESTEROL | 960MG SODIUM

LINGUINE WITH WHITE CLAM SAUCE

Fresh clams are surprisingly easy to prepare. And they taste fabulous tossed with sautéed garlic, parsley, and pasta with a hint of red pepper.

ACTIVE TIME: 25 MINUTES · **TOTAL TIME:** 30 MINUTES

MAKES: 6 MAIN-DISH SERVINGS

½ CUP DRY WHITE WINE

2 DOZEN LITTLENECK CLAMS, SCRUBBED (SEE TIP)

1 PACKAGE (16 OUNCES) LINGUINE OR SPAGHETTI

¼ CUP OLIVE OIL

1 LARGE GARLIC CLOVE, FINELY CHOPPED

¼ TEASPOON CRUSHED RED PEPPER

¼ CUP CHOPPED FRESH PARSLEY

1 In nonreactive 5-quart Dutch oven, heat wine to boiling over high heat. Add clams; cover and cook until clams open, 5 to 10 minutes, transferring clams to bowl as they open. Discard any clams that have not opened by end of cooking time.

2 Strain clam broth remaining in Dutch oven through sieve lined with paper towels; set aside. When cool enough to handle, remove clams from shells and coarsely chop. Discard shells.

3 Meanwhile, in large saucepot, cook pasta as label directs. Drain.

4 Add oil, garlic, and crushed red pepper to same clean Dutch oven. Cook over medium heat, stirring occasionally, just until garlic turns golden. Stir in parsley, clams, and clam broth; heat just to simmering. Add pasta to Dutch oven and toss until combined.

TIP With a stiff-bristled brush or other sturdy scrubber, clean clams well under cold running water to remove sand.

EACH SERVING: ABOUT 425 CALORIES | 19G PROTEIN | 59G CARBOHYDRATE | 11G TOTAL FAT (1G SATURATED) | 2G FIBER | 24MG CHOLESTEROL | 111MG SODIUM

LINGUINE WITH RED CLAM SAUCE

If you can't make it to the fish market for fresh clams, substitute two 10-ounce cans of whole baby clams plus one-fourth of the clam liquid.

ACTIVE TIME: 20 MINUTES · **TOTAL TIME:** 1 HOUR
MAKES: 6 MAIN-DISH SERVINGS

MARINARA SAUCE (PAGE 16)

½ CUP DRY WHITE WINE

2 DOZEN LITTLENECK CLAMS, SCRUBBED (SEE TIP)

1 PACKAGE (16 OUNCES) LINGUINE

1 TABLESPOON BUTTER OR MARGARINE, CUT INTO PIECES (OPTIONAL)

¼ CUP CHOPPED FRESH PARSLEY

1 Prepare marinara sauce or defrost premade frozen sauce.

2 In nonreactive 12-inch skillet, heat wine to boiling over high heat. Add clams; cover and cook until clams open, 5 to 10 minutes, transferring clams to bowl as they open. Discard any clams that have not opened by end of cooking time. Strain clam broth from skillet through sieve lined with paper towels; reserve ¼ cup. When cool enough to handle, remove clams from shells and coarsely chop. Discard shells.

3 Meanwhile, in large saucepot, cook the pasta as label directs. Drain.

4 In same clean 12-inch skillet, combine marinara sauce, reserved broth, and clams; cook over low heat until heated through. In warm serving bowl, toss pasta with sauce and butter, if using. Sprinkle with parsley and serve.

TIP With a stiff-bristled brush or other sturdy scrubber, clean clams well under cold running water to remove sand.

EACH SERVING: ABOUT 430 CALORIES | 20G PROTEIN | 67G CARBOHYDRATE | 9G TOTAL FAT (2G SATURATED) | 3G FIBER | 29MG CHOLESTEROL | 582MG SODIUM

LINGUINE WITH SCALLOPS AND SAFFRON

Sweet, tender scallops in saffron-flavored cream. When buying sea scallops, choose those with a very pale beige or pink color and a fresh aroma. Keep them refrigerated and use them within two days.

ACTIVE TIME: 20 MINUTES · **TOTAL TIME:** 25 MINUTES
MAKES: 6 MAIN-DISH SERVINGS

3 MEDIUM LEEKS (ABOUT 1 POUND; SEE TIP)

2 TABLESPOONS BUTTER OR MARGARINE

¾ TEASPOON SALT

¼ TEASPOON COARSELY GROUND BLACK PEPPER

½ TEASPOON GRATED ORANGE PEEL

LARGE PINCH SAFFRON THREADS, CRUMBLED

¼ CUP DRY WHITE WINE

1 BOTTLE (8 OUNCES) CLAM JUICE

1 POUND SEA SCALLOPS, RINSED AND EACH CUT HORIZONTALLY IN HALF

¼ CUP HEAVY OR WHIPPING CREAM

1 PACKAGE (16 OUNCES) LINGUINE OR SPAGHETTI

½ CUP LOOSELY PACKED FRESH PARSLEY LEAVES

1 Cut off roots and tough green tops from leeks. Cut each leek lengthwise in half, then crosswise into ½-inch-wide slices. Rinse leeks in large bowl of cold water to remove sand; drain well.

2 In 12-inch skillet, melt butter over medium heat. Add leeks, salt, and pepper, and cook until leeks are soft, about 8 minutes, stirring frequently. Add orange peel and saffron and cook 2 minutes, stirring. Add wine; cook 1 minute longer. Increase heat to medium-high; add clam juice; heat to boiling. Add scallops and cook 3 to 4 minutes until opaque. Stir in cream and heat through.

3 Meanwhile, in large saucepot, cook pasta as label directs.

4 Drain pasta; return to saucepot. Add leek mixture; toss well. Sprinkle with parsley just before serving.

TIP Leeks can harbor sand among their layers. Swish them thoroughly in the cleaning water to be sure all sand is removed. Transfer the cleaned leeks from the water with a slotted spoon to make certain that any sand stays at the bottom of the bowl.

EACH SERVING: ABOUT 440 CALORIES | 24G PROTEIN | 66G CARBOHYDRATE | 9G TOTAL FAT (3G SATURATED) | 3G FIBER | 40MG CHOLESTEROL | 635MG SODIUM

SEAFOOD-STUFFED SHELLS

Easy to serve and easy to eat, these shrimp-and-scrod-filled shells make a terrific party dish.

ACTIVE TIME: 1 HOUR 15 MINUTES · **TOTAL TIME:** 1 HOUR 30 MINUTES
MAKES: 10 MAIN-DISH SERVINGS

30	JUMBO PASTA SHELLS	¼	TEASPOON CRUSHED RED PEPPER
3	GARLIC CLOVES	⅓	CUP HEAVY OR WHIPPING CREAM
2	TABLESPOONS OLIVE OIL	1	POUND MEDIUM SHRIMP, SHELLED, DEVEINED, AND COARSELY CHOPPED
1	SMALL ONION (4 TO 6 OUNCES), CHOPPED	1	POUND SCROD FILLET, COARSELY CHOPPED
1	BOTTLE (8 OUNCES) CLAM JUICE		
1	CAN (28 OUNCES) TOMATOES IN PUREE	1	PACKAGE (10 OUNCES) FROZEN PEAS
2	TABLESPOONS TOMATO PASTE	2	SLICES FIRM WHITE BREAD, TORN INTO ¼-INCH PIECES
1	TEASPOON SUGAR		

1 In large saucepot, cook pasta as label directs. Drain pasta and rinse with cold running water to stop cooking; drain again. Arrange shells in single layer on waxed paper and set aside. Mince 2 garlic cloves; set the third aside.

2 Meanwhile, in 4-quart saucepan, heat 1 tablespoon olive oil over medium heat until hot. Add onion and cook until tender, about 5 minutes. Add minced garlic and cook 1 minute longer, stirring frequently. Add clam juice and cook 7 minutes over high heat until reduced to ½ cup. Stir in tomatoes with their puree, breaking up tomatoes with side of spoon. Add tomato paste, sugar, and crushed red pepper; heat to boiling. Reduce heat to low; partially cover and simmer about 20 minutes, stirring occasionally. Stir in cream and cook 2 minutes longer; remove saucepan from heat.

3 Transfer 1 cup tomato sauce to 3-quart saucepan. Add shrimp and scrod, and cook over medium-high heat until seafood just turns opaque throughout, about 5 minutes, gently stirring occasionally. Remove from heat; stir equal amounts of frozen peas into both saucepans.

4 Preheat oven to 400°F. Fill each pasta shell with 2 heaping tablespoons seafood mixture and place in 13" by 9" glass baking dish. Pour tomato sauce over stuffed shells.

5 In nonstick 10-inch skillet, heat remaining 1 tablespoon olive oil over medium heat. Crush remaining clove garlic with side of chef's knife and add garlic to pan. Add bread and cook until golden, about 5 minutes, stirring often. Discard garlic.

6 Spoon bread crumbs over stuffed shells. Bake 20 minutes or until hot and bubbly.

EACH SERVING: ABOUT 325 CALORIES | 23G PROTEIN | 38G CARBOHYDRATE | 9G TOTAL FAT (3G SATURATED) | 3G FIBER | 87MG CHOLESTEROL | 450MG SODIUM

SEAFOOD FRA DIAVOLO

A tempting mix of squid, mussels, and shrimp in a robust tomato sauce. Simply add garlic bread and a green salad, and dinner is ready.

ACTIVE TIME: 25 MINUTES · **TOTAL TIME:** 1 HOUR

MAKES: 6 MAIN-DISH SERVINGS

8 OUNCES CLEANED SQUID	1 DOZEN MUSSELS, SCRUBBED AND DEBEARDED (SEE TIP)
1 TABLESPOON OLIVE OIL	
1 LARGE GARLIC CLOVE, FINELY CHOPPED	8 OUNCES MEDIUM SHRIMP, SHELLED AND DEVEINED
¼ TEASPOON CRUSHED RED PEPPER	1 PACKAGE (16 OUNCES) LINGUINE OR SPAGHETTI
1 CAN (28 OUNCES) PLUM TOMATOES	¼ CUP CHOPPED FRESH PARSLEY
½ TEASPOON SALT	

1 Rinse squid and pat dry with paper towels. Slice squid bodies crosswise into ¼-inch rings. Cut tentacles into several pieces if they are large.

2 In nonreactive 4-quart saucepan, heat oil over medium heat. Add garlic and crushed red pepper; cook just until fragrant, about 30 seconds. Stir in tomatoes with their juice and salt, breaking up tomatoes with side of spoon. Heat to boiling over high heat. Add squid and return to boiling. Reduce heat; cover and simmer 30 minutes, then simmer uncovered 15 minutes longer.

3 Increase heat to high. Add mussels; cover and cook 3 minutes. Stir in shrimp; cover and cook until mussels open and shrimp are opaque throughout, about 2 minutes longer. Discard any mussels that have not opened.

4 Meanwhile, in large saucepot, cook pasta as label directs. Drain. In warm serving bowl, toss pasta with seafood mixture and parsley.

TIP To clean mussels, scrub them well under cold running water. Cultivated mussels usually do not have beards, but if you need to debeard the mussels, grasp the hairlike beard with your thumb and forefinger and pull it away from the shell, or scrape it off with a knife.

EACH SERVING: ABOUT 410 CALORIES | 25G PROTEIN | 65G CARBOHYDRATE | 5G TOTAL FAT (1G SATURATED) | 3G FIBER | 140MG CHOLESTEROL | 588MG SODIUM

BAKED PASTAS

Sunday Baked Ziti and Meatball Casserole (page 118)

CURLY MAC 'N' CHEESE

Kids will absolutely love the curly corkscrew pasta in this ever-popular supper dish.

ACTIVE TIME: 30 MINUTES · **TOTAL TIME:** 55 MINUTES

MAKES: 6 MAIN-DISH SERVINGS

---

1 PACKAGE (16 OUNCES) ROTINI

6 CUPS MILK

3 TABLESPOONS CORNSTARCH

¾ TEASPOON SALT

⅛ TEASPOON NUTMEG (SEE TIP, PAGE 133)

½ CUP FRESHLY GRATED PARMESAN CHEESE

8 OUNCES SHARP CHEDDAR CHEESE, SHREDDED (2 CUPS)

1 Preheat oven to 375°F. In large saucepot, cook pasta as label directs. Drain.

2 Meanwhile, in 4-quart saucepan, with wire whisk, mix milk, cornstarch, salt, and nutmeg until smooth. Cook over medium heat, whisking frequently, until mixture has thickened slightly and boils. Boil, whisking constantly, 1 minute. Remove pan from heat. Gradually whisk in Parmesan until cheese has melted and sauce is smooth.

3 Spoon pasta into shallow 3½-quart or 13" by 9" baking dish. Pour sauce over pasta and stir to thoroughly mix. Sprinkle Cheddar over top. Bake until Cheddar has melted and mixture is hot and bubbling, about 25 minutes.

EACH SERVING: ABOUT 475 CALORIES | 23G PROTEIN | 54G CARBOHYDRATE | 18G TOTAL FAT (11G SATURATED) | 2G FIBER | 60MG CHOLESTEROL | 650MG SODIUM

DRESS UP YOUR MAC 'N' CHEESE

Prepare as directed above, but replace the Cheddar with:

- 4 ounces each **Fontina** and **Gorgonzola**
- 4 ounces each **fresh goat cheese** and **Monterey Jack**
- 3 ounces each **sharp Cheddar, Asiago,** and **dry Jack cheese**
- 4 ounces each **sharp white Cheddar** and **Asiago**

REDUCED-FAT MACARONI AND CHEESE

This recipe adds low-fat cottage cheese to the mix for old-fashioned goodness without the guilt.

ACTIVE TIME: 20 MINUTES · **TOTAL TIME:** 45 MINUTES

MAKES: 8 SIDE-DISH OR 4 MAIN-DISH SERVINGS

---

8 OUNCES ELBOW MACARONI TWISTS

1 CONTAINER (16 OUNCES) LOW-FAT (1%) COTTAGE CHEESE

2 TABLESPOONS ALL-PURPOSE FLOUR

2 CUPS SKIM MILK

4 OUNCES SHARP CHEDDAR CHEESE, SHREDDED (1 CUP)

1 TEASPOON SALT

¼ TEASPOON GROUND BLACK PEPPER

PINCH GROUND NUTMEG (SEE TIP, PAGE 133)

¼ CUP FRESHLY GRATED PARMESAN CHEESE

1 Preheat oven to 375°F. Grease broiler-safe shallow 2½-quart casserole. In medium saucepot, cook macaroni as label directs, but do not add salt to water. Drain.

2 In food processor with knife blade attached or in blender, puree cottage cheese with ¼ cup milk until smooth.

3 In 2-quart saucepan, blend flour with ¼ cup milk until smooth. With wire whisk, slowly stir in remaining milk until blended. Cook over medium heat, stirring, until mixture has thickened slightly and boils. Remove from heat; stir in cottage cheese mixture, Cheddar, salt, pepper, and nutmeg.

4 Spoon macaroni into prepared casserole and cover with cheese sauce. Bake 20 minutes. Remove from oven; sprinkle with Parmesan. Turn oven control to broil.

5 Place casserole in broiler at closest position to heat source; broil until top is golden brown, 2 to 3 minutes.

EACH SIDE-DISH SERVING: ABOUT 250 CALORIES | 18G PROTEIN | 28G CARBOHYDRATE 7G TOTAL FAT (4G SATURATED) | 1G FIBER | 21MG CHOLESTEROL | 724MG SODIUM

MACARONI AND CHEESE DELUXE

A great dish gets even better with the addition of blue cheese, crunchy toasted nuts, and Parmesan-dusted tomatoes. A terrific choice for casual entertaining.

ACTIVE TIME: 30 MINUTES · **TOTAL TIME:** 55 MINUTES
MAKES: 6 MAIN-DISH SERVINGS

1   PACKAGE (16 OUNCES) CAMPANELLE OR PENNE PASTA

3   TABLESPOONS BUTTER OR MARGARINE

1   MEDIUM ONION (6 TO 8 OUNCES), DICED

2   TABLESPOONS ALL-PURPOSE FLOUR

¼   TEASPOON COARSELY GROUND BLACK PEPPER

¼   TEASPOON GROUND RED PEPPER (CAYENNE)

¼   TEASPOON GROUND NUTMEG

¼   TEASPOON SALT

4   CUPS LOW-FAT (1%) MILK

½   CUP GRATED PARMESAN CHEESE

1   CUP FROZEN PEAS

4   OUNCES CREAMY BLUE CHEESE, SUCH AS GORGONZOLA, CUT UP OR CRUMBLED INTO PIECES

½   PINT PEAR-SHAPED OR ROUND CHERRY TOMATOES, HALVED

½   CUP WALNUTS, TOASTED (SEE TIP)

1   In large saucepot, cook pasta as label directs. Preheat oven to 400°F.

2   Meanwhile, in 3-quart saucepan, melt butter over medium heat; add onion and cook 8 to 10 minutes until tender, stirring occasionally. With wire whisk, stir in flour, black pepper, ground red pepper, nutmeg, and salt, and cook 1 minute, stirring constantly. Gradually whisk in milk and cook over medium-high heat, stirring frequently, until sauce boils and thickens slightly. Boil 1 minute, stirring. Stir in ¼ cup Parmesan cheese. Remove the saucepan from heat.

3   Place frozen peas in colander; drain pasta over peas and return pasta mixture to saucepot. Stir in sauce and blue cheese. Transfer pasta mixture to deep 3-quart casserole.

4   In small bowl, toss tomato halves with remaining ¼ cup Parmesan cheese. Top casserole with tomato halves. Bake, uncovered, 20 minutes, or until hot and bubbly and top is lightly browned. Sprinkle with walnuts before serving.

FREEZING AND REHEATING BAKED PASTAS

Cool the baked pasta in casserole pan, uncovered, at least 30 minutes in refrigerator or until just warm. Wrap tightly with heavy-duty foil; label and freeze up to 3 months.

At least 24 hours but no more than 2 days before reheating, place your frozen casserole in the refrigerator to thaw slightly.

To reheat in a conventional oven, unwrap the casserole. Loosely cover it with foil and bake according to the recipe's reheating instructions until the center of the casserole reaches 160°F (check with an instant-read thermometer).

To reheat in a microwave, unwrap the casserole; cover the top with waxed paper, tucking it under the dish (make sure it's microwave-safe) to keep in place, or use plastic wrap and turn back a corner to vent. Heat in microwave according to the recipe's heating instructions, first on Low until ice crystals are gone and you can easily insert knife into center of casserole. Then cook on High until food is heated through and the internal temperature of your casserole is 160°F on an instant-read thermometer.

TIP To toast walnuts, spread them in a single layer on a baking sheet, then bake in a 350°F oven, stirring occasionally, for about 10 minutes, or until lightly browned and fragrant.

EACH SERVING: ABOUT 610 CALORIES | 26G PROTEIN | 76G CARBOHYDRATE | 23G TOTAL FAT (6G SATURATED) | 5G FIBER | 43MG CHOLESTEROL | 965MG SODIUM

MULTIGRAIN MAC AND CHEESE WITH CREAMY TOMATO-BASIL SAUCE

We top our casserole with panko, bread crumbs traditionally used in Japanese cooking as a coating for fried foods. Much coarser than the ones Americans are familiar with, these jagged-edged crumbs produce a crispier, crunchier coating. Look for panko in the Asian section of your supermarket.

ACTIVE TIME: 40 MINUTES · **TOTAL TIME:** 1 HOUR

MAKES: 6 MAIN-DISH SERVINGS

1 PACKAGE (16 OUNCES) MULTIGRAIN OR WHOLE-WHEAT ROTINI OR PENNE PASTA

1 CAN (14½ OUNCES) DICED TOMATOES, DRAINED

2 TABLESPOONS BUTTER OR MARGARINE

1 CUP PANKO (JAPANESE-STYLE BREAD CRUMBS) OR CRACKER CRUMBS

¾ CUP FRESHLY GRATED PECORINO-ROMANO CHEESE

1 SMALL ONION (4 TO 6 OUNCES), CHOPPED

1 GARLIC CLOVE, FINELY CHOPPED

3 TABLESPOONS CORNSTARCH

4 CUPS REDUCED-FAT MILK (2%)

½ TEASPOON SALT

¼ TEASPOON GROUND BLACK PEPPER

10 OUNCES REDUCED-FAT SHARP CHEDDAR CHEESE (2%), SHREDDED (2½ CUPS)

1 CUP LOOSELY PACKED FRESH BASIL LEAVES, CHOPPED

1 In large saucepot, prepare pasta, cooking 2 minutes less than label directs. Drain pasta; transfer to large bowl. Stir in tomatoes; set aside.

2 Preheat oven to 375°F.

3 In microwave-safe small bowl, heat 1 tablespoon butter in microwave on High 20 seconds or until melted. Stir in panko and ¼ cup Romano until blended; set aside.

4 Meanwhile, in 4-quart saucepan, melt remaining 1 tablespoon butter over medium heat; add onion and cook until tender and lightly browned, 6 to 8 minutes, stirring occasionally. Add garlic and cook 1 minute, stirring.

5 In medium bowl, whisk cornstarch into milk until blended. Whisk milk mixture, salt, and pepper into onion mixture in saucepan; heat to boiling over medium-high heat, stirring frequently. Boil sauce 1 minute to thicken slightly. Remove saucepan from heat and stir in Cheddar, basil, and remaining ½ cup Romano until cheeses melt. Stir cheese mixture into pasta mixture.

6 Transfer pasta mixture to individual-serving (1½-cup) au gratin dishes or one 13" by 9" glass baking dish; top with panko mixture. Bake until center is hot and top is lightly browned, about 20 minutes.

EACH SERVING: ABOUT 645 CALORIES | 34G PROTEIN | 82G CARBOHYDRATE | 21G TOTAL FAT (11G SATURATED) | 7G FIBER | 56MG CHOLESTEROL | 1,055MG SODIUM

SAUSAGE-AND-PEPPER BAKED ZITI

This new twist on baked ziti will please kids as well as adults. You can assemble it up to a day ahead, refrigerate, and bake just before serving.

ACTIVE TIME: 40 MINUTES · **TOTAL TIME:** 1 HOUR PLUS STANDING
MAKES: 10 MAIN-DISH SERVINGS

1½ POUNDS SWEET AND/OR HOT ITALIAN-SAUSAGE LINKS, CUT CROSSWISE INTO 1-INCH-THICK PIECES

4 GARLIC CLOVES, THINLY SLICED

2 LARGE GREEN, YELLOW, AND/OR RED PEPPERS, CUT INTO ¼-INCH-THICK SLICES

1 JUMBO ONION (1 POUND), CUT IN HALF, THEN CUT CROSSWISE INTO ¼-INCH-THICK SLICES

1 CAN (28 OUNCES) TOMATOES IN PUREE

1 TEASPOON SALT

1 PACKAGE (16 OUNCES) ZITI OR PENNE

1 PACKAGE (8 OUNCES) PART-SKIM MOZZARELLA CHEESE, CUT INTO ½-INCH CUBES

½ CUP FRESHLY GRATED PECORINO-ROMANO CHEESE

1 Prepare sauce: In deep nonstick 12-inch skillet, cook sausage over medium-high heat, stirring occasionally, until browned on all sides, about 5 minutes.

2 Reduce heat to medium. Discard all but 2 tablespoons sausage drippings from skillet. Add garlic, peppers, and onion to sausage and cook, covered, until vegetables are tender, about 10 minutes, stirring occasionally. Stir in tomatoes with their puree and salt; heat to boiling over medium heat, breaking up tomatoes with side of spoon. Reduce heat to low; cover and simmer 10 minutes.

3 Meanwhile, preheat oven to 400°F. In large saucepot, prepare pasta, cooking 2 minutes less than label directs. Drain pasta; return to saucepot. Add sauce and stir until pasta is evenly coated. Add mozzarella; toss to combine.

4 Transfer pasta mixture to 13" by 9" baking dish and spread evenly; sprinkle with Romano. Bake, uncovered, until hot and bubbling and top is brown, 20 to 25 minutes. Let stand 10 minutes for easier serving.

EACH SERVING: ABOUT 520 CALORIES | 25G PROTEIN | 49G CARBOHYDRATE | 23G FAT (10G SATURATED) | 4G FIBER | 65MG CHOLESTEROL | 1,190 SODIUM

BAKED ZITI WITH VEGETABLES

This meatless version of baked ziti is chock-full of vegetables.

ACTIVE TIME: 20 MINUTES · TOTAL TIME: 1 HOUR
MAKES: 6 MAIN-DISH SERVINGS

---

1   PACKAGE (16 OUNCES) ZITI OR PENNE

2   MEDIUM GREEN PEPPERS

2   MEDIUM CARROTS, PEELED

2   MEDIUM STALKS CELERY

1   MEDIUM ONION (6 TO 8 OUNCES), PEELED

1   TABLESPOON VEGETABLE OIL

¼   CUP WATER

1   CAN (28 OUNCES) CRUSHED TOMATOES

3   CUPS SPICY HOT OR REGULAR VEGETABLE JUICE

1   TABLESPOON SUGAR

1½ TEASPOONS SALT

½   TEASPOON DRIED OREGANO

8   OUNCES REDUCED-FAT MOZZARELLA CHEESE, SHREDDED (2 CUPS)

2   TABLESPOONS FRESHLY GRATED PARMESAN CHEESE

1   In large saucepot, cook ziti as label directs.

2   Meanwhile, cut green peppers, carrots, celery, and onion into ½-inch pieces. In 12-inch skillet, heat oil over medium-high heat until hot. Add vegetables and cook until lightly browned.

3   Stir in water; continue cooking over medium heat until vegetables are tender-crisp.

4   Preheat oven to 375°F.

5   Drain ziti in colander; set aside. To same saucepot, add cooked vegetables; stir in tomatoes, juice, sugar, salt, and oregano; heat to boiling over high heat. Remove saucepot from heat; stir in ziti.

6   Reserve 1 cup mozzarella for topping. Into ziti mixture in saucepot, stir Parmesan and remaining mozzarella. Spoon mixture into shallow 4-quart casserole; sprinkle with reserved mozzarella. Cover casserole and bake until mozzarella melts and mixture is hot and bubbly, about 30 minutes.

EACH SERVING: ABOUT 490 CALORIES | 25G PROTEIN | 82G CARBOHYDRATE | 8G TOTAL FAT (3G SATURATED) | 8G FIBER | 15MG CHOLESTEROL | 1,430MG SODIUM

SUNDAY BAKED ZITI AND MEATBALL CASSEROLE

A crowd-pleaser that's easy to prepare. If you're in a time crunch, use four cups of your favorite jarred tomato sauce. For photo, see page 108.

ACTIVE TIME: 30 MINUTES · **TOTAL TIME:** 1 HOUR

MAKES: 8 MAIN-DISH SERVINGS

1   PACKAGE (16 OUNCES) ZITI OR PENNE

4   CUPS BIG-BATCH TOMATO SAUCE (PAGE 17)

1   LARGE EGG

1   CONTAINER (15 OUNCES) PART-SKIM RICOTTA CHEESE

2   TABLESPOONS GRATED PARMESAN CHEESE

1   TABLESPOON CHOPPED FRESH PARSLEY

½   TEASPOON SALT

¼   TEASPOON COARSELY GROUND BLACK PEPPER

8   LEAN MEATBALLS (PAGE 67), THAWED IF FROZEN, SLICED

1   PACKAGE (4 OUNCES) SHREDDED PART-SKIM MOZZARELLA CHEESE (1 CUP)

1   In saucepot, cook pasta as label directs; drain. Return pasta to saucepot.

2   Meanwhile, in 3-quart saucepan, heat tomato sauce, covered, over medium-low heat. (If tomato sauce is frozen, add 2 tablespoons water to saucepan to prevent scorching.) When sauce is hot, add 3 cups to pasta; toss well. Reserve remaining 1 cup sauce.

3   In medium bowl, stir together egg, ricotta cheese, Parmesan cheese, parsley, salt, and pepper.

4   Preheat oven to 400°F. Into 3½- to 4-quart shallow casserole or 13" by 9" glass baking dish, spoon half the pasta mixture; top with all meatball slices. Drop ricotta-cheese mixture by spoonfuls evenly over meatball layer. Spoon remaining pasta mixture over cheese layer, then spoon remaining 1 cup sauce over pasta. Sprinkle with shredded mozzarella.

5   Bake, uncovered, 25 minutes or until very hot and cheese browns slightly.

EACH SERVING: ABOUT 470 CALORIES | 29G PROTEIN | 55G CARBOHYDRATE | 13G TOTAL FAT (5G SATURATED) | 4G FIBER | 79MG CHOLESTEROL | 1,040MG SODIUM

BAKED RIGATONI AND PEAS FOR A CROWD

With this easy make-ahead, the cook can enjoy the party. The pasta is baked in two dishes so one can stay warm in the oven while guests help themselves to the other at the buffet table.

ACTIVE TIME: 45 MINUTES · **TOTAL TIME:** 1 HOUR 10 MINUTES
MAKES: 16 SIDE-DISH SERVINGS

8 TABLESPOONS BUTTER OR MARGARINE (1 STICK)	1 BAG (20 OUNCES) FROZEN PEAS, THAWED
½ CUP ALL-PURPOSE FLOUR	2 CANS (14½ OUNCES EACH) DICED TOMATOES
7 CUPS MILK, WARMED	
2 CUPS GRATED PARMESAN CHEESE	1 CUP LOOSELY PACKED FRESH BASIL LEAVES, THINLY SLICED
2 TEASPOONS SALT	
2 PACKAGES (16 OUNCES EACH) RIGATONI OR ZITI	½ CUP PLAIN DRIED BREAD CRUMBS

1 Prepare cheese sauce: In heavy 4-quart saucepan, melt 6 tablespoons butter over low heat. Add flour and cook, stirring, 2 minutes. With wire whisk, gradually whisk in warm milk. Cook over medium heat, stirring constantly with wooden spoon, until sauce has thickened and boils. Reduce heat and simmer, stirring frequently, about 5 minutes. Stir in 1½ cups Parmesan and salt. Remove from heat.

2 Meanwhile, in 12-quart saucepot, cook pasta as label directs; drain. Return rigatoni to saucepot.

3 Preheat oven to 350°F. Pour cheese sauce over rigatoni in saucepot, stirring to combine. Stir in peas, tomatoes with their juice, and basil. Spoon pasta mixture into two shallow 3½- to 4-quart casseroles or two 13" by 9" baking dishes.

4 In small saucepan, melt remaining 2 tablespoons butter over low heat. Remove from heat and stir in bread crumbs and remaining ½ cup Parmesan. Sprinkle topping over pasta. Bake until casserole is bubbling and topping is golden, 30 to 35 minutes.

EACH SERVING: ABOUT 450 CALORIES | 19G PROTEIN | 60G CARBOHYDRATE | 15G TOTAL FAT (9G SATURATED) | 4G FIBER | 41MG CHOLESTEROL | 970MG SODIUM

BAKED ZITI WITH EGGPLANT AND RICOTTA

If you want to prepare this dish ahead, roast the eggplant, make the sauce, and refrigerate separately. When ready to bake, cook the pasta and assemble; add about 10 minutes to the baking time to compensate for the chilled ingredients.

ACTIVE TIME: 40 MINUTES · **TOTAL TIME:** 1 HOUR
MAKES: 6 MAIN-DISH SERVINGS

1   MEDIUM EGGPLANT (1½ TO 2 POUNDS), CUT INTO 1-INCH PIECES

3   TABLESPOONS OLIVE OIL

¾   TEASPOON SALT

1   SMALL ONION (4 TO 6 OUNCES), FINELY CHOPPED

2   GARLIC CLOVES, MINCED

1   CAN (28 OUNCES) PLUM TOMATOES

2   TABLESPOONS TOMATO PASTE

¼   TEASPOON GROUND BLACK PEPPER

3   TABLESPOONS CHOPPED FRESH BASIL

1   PACKAGE (16 OUNCES) ZITI OR PENNE

¼   CUP FRESHLY GRATED PARMESAN CHEESE

1   CUP RICOTTA CHEESE

1   Preheat oven to 450°F. In large bowl, toss eggplant, 2 tablespoons oil, and ¼ teaspoon salt until evenly coated. Arrange eggplant in single layer in two 15½" by 10½" jelly-roll pans or large baking sheets. Place pans in oven and roast eggplant until tender and golden, about 30 minutes, rotating pans between upper and lower racks halfway through cooking and stirring twice. Set pans aside to cool. Turn oven control to 400°F.

2   Meanwhile, in 3-quart saucepan, heat remaining 1 tablespoon oil over medium heat until hot. Add onion and cook until tender, about 5 minutes, stirring occasionally. Add garlic and cook 1 minute longer, stirring frequently. Stir in tomatoes with their juice, tomato paste, pepper, and remaining ½ teaspoon salt, breaking up tomatoes with side of spoon; heat to boiling over high heat. Reduce heat to low and simmer until sauce thickens slightly, about 10 minutes. Stir in 2 tablespoons basil.

3   In large saucepot, prepare pasta as label directs. Drain; return pasta to saucepot.

4 To pasta in saucepot, add roasted eggplant, tomato sauce, and Parmesan; toss until evenly mixed. Spoon mixture into individual-serving (2-cup) gratin dishes or shallow casseroles; top with dollops of ricotta. Cover casseroles with foil and bake until hot and bubbly, about 20 minutes.

5 To serve, sprinkle tops with remaining 1 tablespoon basil.

EACH SERVING: ABOUT 500 CALORIES | 19G PROTEIN | 73G CARBOHYDRATE | 15G TOTAL FAT (5G SATURATED) | 2G FIBER | 24MG CHOLESTEROL | 695MG SODIUM

SPAGHETTI CARBONARA PIE

Try this for brunch or on a chilly evening—it takes just minutes to assemble before popping it into the oven.

ACTIVE TIME: 15 MINUTES · **TOTAL TIME:** 50 MINUTES PLUS STANDING

MAKES: 6 MAIN-DISH SERVINGS

---

12 OUNCES SPAGHETTI

4 OUNCES BACON (ABOUT 6 SLICES), CUT INTO ¼-INCH PIECES

1 CONTAINER (15 OUNCES) PART-SKIM RICOTTA CHEESE

½ CUP GRATED PECORINO-ROMANO CHEESE

2 LARGE EGGS

1 LARGE EGG YOLK

½ TEASPOON COARSELY GROUND BLACK PEPPER

½ TEASPOON SALT

PINCH GROUND NUTMEG (SEE TIP, PAGE 133)

2 CUPS MILK

---

1 Preheat oven to 375°F. In large saucepot, cook spaghetti as label directs.

2 Meanwhile, in nonstick 10-inch skillet, cook the bacon over medium heat until browned, about 12 minutes. With slotted spoon, transfer bacon to paper towels to drain; set aside.

3 In blender at low speed, blend ricotta, Romano, eggs, egg yolk, pepper, salt, nutmeg, and ½ cup milk until smooth.

4 Drain pasta and return to saucepot. Add ricotta mixture, bacon, and remaining 1½ cups milk, stirring to combine.

5 Transfer pasta mixture to round 2½-quart baking dish about 2 inches deep. Bake 35 to 40 minutes, until golden around edges and almost set but still slightly liquid in center. Let pie stand 10 minutes before serving (liquid will be absorbed during standing). Cut into wedges to serve.

EACH SERVING: ABOUT 470 CALORIES | 25G PROTEIN | 50G CARBOHYDRATE | 18G TOTAL FAT (9G SATURATED) | 2G FIBER | 154MG CHOLESTEROL | 595MG SODIUM

PASTA E FAGIOLI BAKE

We turned the much-loved Italian pasta-and-bean soup into a casserole by adding a little extra pasta and Romano cheese, and topping it with bread crumbs. Serve a tossed green salad on the side.

ACTIVE TIME: 35 MINUTES · **TOTAL TIME:** 50 MINUTES

MAKES: 6 MAIN-DISH SERVINGS

8 OUNCES DITALINI PASTA (1¾ CUPS)	1 CAN (16 OUNCES) PLUM TOMATOES
2 SLICES BACON, CUT INTO ½-INCH PIECES	¾ CUP CHICKEN BROTH
1 MEDIUM ONION (6 TO 8 OUNCES), DICED	¼ TEASPOON COARSELY GROUND BLACK PEPPER
2 TEASPOONS PLUS 1 TABLESPOON OLIVE OIL	¼ CUP PLUS 2 TABLESPOONS GRATED PECORINO-ROMANO CHEESE
3 GARLIC CLOVES, MINCED	2 SLICES FIRM WHITE BREAD, TORN INTO ¼-INCH PIECES
2 CANS (15½ TO 19 OUNCES EACH) WHITE KIDNEY BEANS (CANNELLINI), RINSED AND DRAINED	1 TABLESPOON CHOPPED FRESH PARSLEY LEAVES

1 Preheat oven to 400°F. In large saucepot, cook pasta as label directs. Drain well, reserving ½ cup pasta cooking water. Return the pasta to saucepot.

2 Meanwhile, in 4-quart saucepan, cook bacon over medium heat until browned, stirring occasionally. Transfer bacon to paper towels to drain.

3 Pour off all but 1 teaspoon bacon fat from saucepan. Reduce heat to medium-low. Add onion and 2 teaspoons olive oil, and cook 5 minutes or until onion is tender, stirring occasionally. Stir in 1 teaspoon minced garlic, and cook 1 minute, stirring. Stir in beans, tomatoes with their juice, chicken broth, pepper, and cooked bacon, breaking up tomatoes with side of spoon; heat to boiling over high heat. Reduce heat to medium and simmer mixture, uncovered, 5 minutes, stirring occasionally.

4 To pasta in saucepot, add bean mixture, ¼ cup Romano, and reserved cooking water; toss well. Transfer mixture to 3-quart casserole.

5 In small bowl, toss bread pieces with parsley, remaining olive oil, remaining minced garlic, and remaining 2 tablespoons Romano until evenly coated. Sprinkle bread mixture over pasta. Bake pasta 15 minutes, uncovered, until hot and bubbly and top is golden.

EACH SERVING: ABOUT 405 CALORIES | 19G PROTEIN | 63G CARBOHYDRATE | 9G TOTAL FAT (3G SATURATED) | 9G FIBER | 9MG CHOLESTEROL | 815MG SODIUM

CLASSIC LASAGNA WITH MEAT SAUCE

Guys with big appetites—and just about everyone else—will love this hearty dish. We use both beef and Italian sausage to double the flavor and call for no-boil noodles to save time. If your package contains fifteen noodles (rather than twelve, like the brand we used), put an extra noodle in each of the first three layers when assembling the lasagna.

ACTIVE TIME: 45 MINUTES · **TOTAL TIME:** 1 HOUR 15 MINUTES PLUS STANDING
MAKES: 10 MAIN-DISH SERVINGS

8 OUNCES SWEET ITALIAN-SAUSAGE LINKS, CASINGS REMOVED

8 OUNCES LEAN GROUND BEEF

1 SMALL ONION (4 TO 6 OUNCES), DICED

2 GARLIC CLOVES, MINCED

1 CAN (28 OUNCES) PLUS 1 CAN (14½ TO 16 OUNCES) TOMATOES

2 TABLESPOONS TOMATO PASTE

½ TEASPOON SALT

2 TABLESPOONS CHOPPED FRESH BASIL

1 LARGE EGG

¼ TEASPOON COARSELY GROUND BLACK PEPPER

1 CONTAINER (15 OUNCES) PART-SKIM RICOTTA CHEESE

4 OUNCES PART-SKIM MOZZARELLA CHEESE, SHREDDED (1 CUP)

¾ CUP GRATED PARMESAN CHEESE

1 PACKAGE (8 OUNCES) NO-BOIL LASAGNA NOODLES (12 NOODLES)

1 Heat 4-quart saucepan over medium-high heat until hot. Add sausage and ground beef, and cook, stirring, 1 minute. Add onion and cook until meat is browned and onion is tender, about 5 minutes, stirring occasionally and breaking up sausage with side of spoon. Pour off drippings from saucepan. Add garlic to meat mixture in saucepan and cook 1 minute.
2 Stir in tomatoes with their juice, tomato paste, and salt, breaking up tomatoes with spoon; heat to boiling. Reduce heat to medium and cook, uncovered, 20 minutes, stirring occasionally. Stir in basil.
3 While sauce simmers, in a medium bowl, mix egg, pepper, ricotta, ½ cup mozzarella, and ½ cup Parmesan until blended.
4 Preheat oven to 350°F. Into 13" by 9" glass baking dish, evenly spoon 2 cups sauce. Arrange 3 noodles over sauce, making sure noodles do not touch sides of dish (they will expand). Top with 1¼ cups ricotta mixture,

LASAGNA NOODLE BASICS

Classic lasagna noodles must be boiled before you assemble and bake your lasagna. Choose from domestic noodles, which are on the thick side, or imported ones, which are thinner and more delicate.

No-boil noodles are convenient because they have been pre-cooked, then dried before packaging. During baking, they soak up liquid from the other ingredients and soften.

For best results, always use the type of lasagna noodle specified in the recipe. But if you are short on time and want to substitute no-boil noodles for classic, stir about 1 cup additional water or tomato juice into the sauce. Alternatively, you can reconstitute sheets of no-boil lasagna before using: Let them soak in enough water to cover until supple, 5 to 10 minutes, then drain the noodles and assemble the dish.

3 noodles, and 2 cups sauce. Arrange 3 noodles on top; spread with remaining ricotta mixture. Top with remaining noodles and remaining sauce. Sprinkle with remaining ½ cup mozzarella and ¼ cup Parmesan. (If making a day ahead, cover and refrigerate.)

5 Cover lasagna with foil and bake 30 minutes (1 hour if refrigerated) or until hot and bubbly. Let lasagna stand 10 minutes for easier serving.

EACH SERVING: ABOUT 350 CALORIES | 24G PROTEIN | 27G CARBOHYDRATE | 16G TOTAL FAT (8G SATURATED) | 2G FIBER | 78MG CHOLESTEROL | 775MG SODIUM

TURKEY AND VEGGIE LASAGNA

Leftover turkey never had it so good in this hearty, satisfying take on lasagna.

ACTIVE TIME: 25 MINUTES · **TOTAL TIME:** 1 HOUR 10 MINUTES PLUS STANDING
MAKES: 6 MAIN-DISH SERVINGS

4   TABLESPOONS BUTTER OR MARGARINE

1   PACKAGE (10 OUNCES) SLICED MUSHROOMS

1   SMALL ONION (4 TO 6 OUNCES), FINELY CHOPPED

1   GARLIC CLOVE, CRUSHED WITH GARLIC PRESS

⅓   CUP ALL-PURPOSE FLOUR

2   CUPS LOW-FAT (1%) MILK, WARMED

1   CAN (14½ OUNCES) CHICKEN BROTH

8   NO-BOIL LASAGNA NOODLES

1   PACKAGE (10 OUNCES) FROZEN CHOPPED SPINACH, THAWED AND SQUEEZED DRY

2   CUPS ½-INCH PIECES LEFTOVER COOKED TURKEY (10 OUNCES)

¾   CUP FRESHLY GRATED PARMESAN CHEESE

1   CUP SHREDDED PART-SKIM MOZZARELLA CHEESE (4 OUNCES)

1   In nonstick 12-inch skillet, melt 1 tablespoon butter over medium heat. Add mushrooms, onion, and garlic, and cook until mushrooms are lightly browned, about 8 minutes, stirring occasionally. Set aside.

2   Meanwhile, in 4-quart saucepan, melt remaining 3 tablespoons butter over medium heat. Whisk in flour and cook 1 minute. Gradually whisk in milk and broth until well blended; cook until sauce thickens and boils, stirring frequently. Boil 2 minutes. Set sauce aside.

3   Preheat oven to 375°F. Spray 8-inch glass or ceramic baking dish with nonstick cooking spray. Pour ½ cup sauce in bottom of baking dish; arrange 2 noodles over sauce, overlapping to fit. Top evenly with half of spinach, half of turkey, then ½ cup sauce; sprinkle with ¼ cup Parmesan. Top with 2 noodles, mushroom mixture, ¾ cup mozzarella, then ½ cup sauce. Top with 2 noodles, remaining spinach and turkey, then ¾ cup sauce, and ¼ cup Parmesan. Arrange remaining noodles on top; spoon remaining sauce over noodles to cover. Sprinkle with remaining mozzarella and Parmesan.

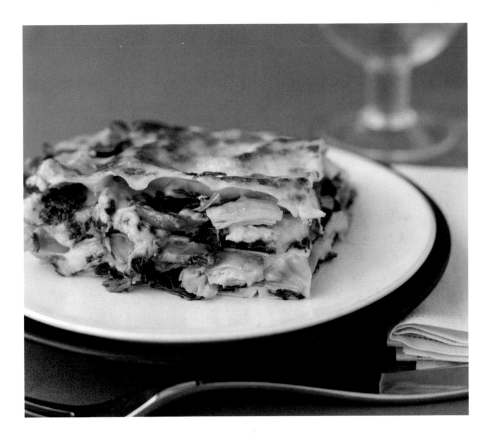

4   Cover baking dish with foil. Bake lasagna 30 minutes. Remove foil and bake until hot and bubbly in the center and lightly browned on top, about 15 minutes longer. Let stand 15 minutes for easier serving.

EACH SERVING: ABOUT 445 CALORIES | 33G PROTEIN | 36G CARBOHYDRATE | 18G TOTAL FAT (7G SATURATED) | 3G FIBER | 57MG CHOLESTEROL | 740MG SODIUM

VEGETABLE LASAGNA

So chock-full of vegetables and cheese, you'll never miss the meat. We recommend using our homemade Marinara Sauce, but if you're in a rush, you can substitute 3½ cups of jarred sauce.

ACTIVE TIME: 1 HOUR · **TOTAL TIME:** 1 HOUR 40 MINUTES PLUS STANDING
MAKES: 10 MAIN-DISH SERVINGS

MARINARA SAUCE (PAGE 16)

12 LASAGNA NOODLES (10 OUNCES)

2 MEDIUM ZUCCHINI (8 OUNCES EACH), CUT INTO ¼-INCH-THICK SLICES

2 TABLESPOONS OLIVE OIL

¾ TEASPOON SALT

¼ TEASPOON GROUND BLACK PEPPER

1 GARLIC CLOVE, FINELY CHOPPED

⅛ TEASPOON CRUSHED RED PEPPER

2 TABLESPOONS ALL-PURPOSE FLOUR

⅔ CUP MILK, WARMED

2 PACKAGES (10 OUNCES EACH) FROZEN CHOPPED SPINACH, THAWED AND SQUEEZED DRY

2 TABLESPOONS PLUS ¼ CUP GRATED PARMESAN CHEESE

1 CONTAINER (15 OUNCES) PART-SKIM RICOTTA CHEESE

2 TABLESPOONS CHOPPED FRESH PARSLEY

4 OUNCES MOZZARELLA CHEESE, SHREDDED (1 CUP)

1 Prepare marinara sauce or defrost frozen sauce, if needed. Preheat oven to 450°F.

2 In large saucepot, cook lasagna noodles as label directs. Drain and rinse with cold running water. Return noodles to saucepot with enough *cold water* to cover.

3 In large bowl, toss zucchini with 1 tablespoon oil, ¼ teaspoon salt, and ⅛ teaspoon black pepper. Arrange zucchini slices on large cookie sheet and bake, turning once, until tender, about 12 minutes. Reduce oven control to 350°F.

4 While zucchini bakes, in nonstick 12-inch skillet, heat remaining 1 tablespoon oil over medium heat. Add garlic and crushed red pepper; cook until garlic is golden. Stir in flour until blended. With wire whisk, gradually whisk in warm milk with wooden spoon. Cook, stirring constantly, until sauce has thickened and boils, about 2 minutes. Remove from heat and stir in spinach, 2 tablespoons Parmesan, and ¼ teaspoon salt.

5 In medium bowl, stir ricotta, parsley, remaining ¼ cup Parmesan, remaining ¼ teaspoon salt, and remaining ⅛ teaspoon black pepper until combined.

6 Drain lasagna noodles on clean kitchen towels.

7 In 13" by 9" baking dish, spread about 1 cup marinara sauce. Arrange 4 lasagna noodles over sauce, overlapping to fit. Spread ricotta mixture on top of noodles. Arrange 4 more noodles over ricotta and top with all of zucchini, overlapping slices to fit. Spread with 1 cup sauce and sprinkle with half of mozzarella; top with all of spinach mixture. Arrange remaining 4 noodles on top and spread with remaining marinara sauce. Sprinkle with remaining mozzarella.

8 Cover lasagna with foil and bake 30 minutes. Remove foil and bake until cheese is lightly golden, about 10 minutes longer. Let stand 15 minutes for easier serving.

EACH SERVING: ABOUT 220 CALORIES | 13G PROTEIN | 14G CARBOHYDRATE | 13G TOTAL FAT (5G SATURATED) | 4G FIBER | 27MG CHOLESTEROL | 687MG SODIUM

BUTTERNUT-SQUASH LASAGNA

Celebrate autumn with this luscious roasted squash and Swiss chard main dish.

ACTIVE TIME: 1 HOUR 15 MINUTES · TOTAL TIME: 1 HOUR 55 MINUTES PLUS STANDING
MAKES: 10 MAIN-DISH SERVINGS

12 LASAGNA NOODLES (10 OUNCES)	2 TABLESPOONS BUTTER OR MARGARINE
1 LARGE BUTTERNUT SQUASH (3 POUNDS), PEELED, SEEDED, AND CUT INTO 1-INCH CHUNKS	⅓ CUP ALL-PURPOSE FLOUR
	¼ TEASPOON COARSELY GROUND BLACK PEPPER
2 TABLESPOONS OLIVE OIL	
1 TEASPOON SALT	¼ TEASPOON GROUND NUTMEG (SEE TIP)
1 JUMBO ONION (1 POUND), CUT IN HALF AND THINLY SLICED	¼ TEASPOON DRIED THYME
	4 CUPS LOW-FAT (1%) MILK
1 LARGE BUNCH SWISS CHARD (ABOUT 1½ POUNDS), COARSELY CHOPPED, WITH TOUGH STEMS DISCARDED	¾ CUP GRATED PARMESAN CHEESE

1 In saucepot, cook lasagna noodles as label directs. Drain noodles and rinse with cold running water; drain again. Layer noodles between sheets of waxed paper.

2 Meanwhile, preheat oven to 450°F. In large bowl, toss butternut squash chunks with 1 tablespoon olive oil and ½ teaspoon salt. Place squash on 15½" by 10½" jelly-roll pan or large cookie sheet. Roast squash 30 minutes or until fork-tender, stirring halfway through cooking. Remove from oven and, with fork or potato masher, mash squash until almost smooth; set aside. Reduce oven temperature to 375°F.

3 Meanwhile, in 5-quart Dutch oven, heat remaining 1 tablespoon olive oil over medium heat until hot. Add onion and ¼ teaspoon salt, and cook about 25 minutes or until golden, stirring often. Add chard; cook until wilted and liquid evaporates, about 7 minutes. Remove Dutch oven from heat; set aside.

4 In 3-quart saucepan, melt butter over medium heat. With wire whisk, stir in flour, pepper, remaining ¼ teaspoon salt, nutmeg, and thyme, and cook 1 minute, stirring constantly. Gradually whisk in milk and cook over medium-high heat, stirring frequently, until sauce boils and thickens slightly. Boil 1 minute, stirring. Whisk in all but 2 tablespoons Parmesan. Remove saucepan from heat.

5 In 13" by 9" glass baking dish, spoon about ½ cup white sauce to evenly cover bottom of dish. Arrange 4 lasagna noodles over sauce, overlapping to fit. Evenly spread all Swiss chard mixture over noodles and top with about 1 cup white sauce. Arrange 4 lasagna noodles on top, then about 1 cup white sauce and all butternut squash. Top with remaining lasagna noodles and remaining white sauce. Sprinkle with remaining 2 tablespoons Parmesan cheese.

6 Cover lasagna with foil and bake 30 minutes; remove foil and bake 10 minutes longer or until hot and bubbly. Let lasagna stand 10 minutes for easier serving.

TIP Nutmeg is a natural in milk-based dishes. For the best flavor, buy a whole nutmeg and grate it yourself just before using.

EACH SERVING: ABOUT 315 CALORIES | 13G PROTEIN | 47G CARBOHYDRATE | 9G TOTAL FAT (3G SATURATED) | 6G FIBER | 10MG CHOLESTEROL | 575MG SODIUM

TUSCAN LASAGNA SPIRALS

Spinach, bacon, and Fontina cheese make a spectacular filling for this creatively assembled lasagna. Both filling and sauce can be made a day ahead and refrigerated. Fill, roll, and bake as directed, but add about 15 minutes to the final baking time.

ACTIVE TIME: 1 HOUR · **TOTAL TIME:** 1 HOUR 55 MINUTES
MAKES: 6 MAIN-DISH SERVINGS

---

12 LASAGNA NOODLES (10 OUNCES)

1 TABLESPOON OLIVE OIL

1 JUMBO ONION (ABOUT 1 POUND), FINELY CHOPPED

4 GARLIC CLOVES, CRUSHED WITH GARLIC PRESS

4 SLICES BACON (ABOUT 3 OUNCES), CUT INTO ¼-INCH PIECES

1 POUND WHITE MUSHROOMS, FINELY CHOPPED

1 POUND PORTOBELLO MUSHROOMS, STEMS REMOVED AND CAPS FINELY CHOPPED

1 PACKAGE (10 OUNCES) FROZEN CHOPPED SPINACH, THAWED AND SQUEEZED DRY

4 OUNCES FONTINA CHEESE, SHREDDED (1 CUP)

½ CUP GRATED PARMESAN CHEESE

½ TEASPOON SALT

¼ TEASPOON COARSELY GROUND BLACK PEPPER

1 CAN (28 OUNCES) PLUS 1 CAN (14½ TO 16 OUNCES) TOMATOES IN PUREE

⅓ CUP WATER

1 In large saucepot, cook lasagna noodles as label directs. Drain noodles and rinse with cold running water; drain again. Layer noodles between sheets of waxed paper.

2 Preheat oven to 450°F. In nonstick 12-inch skillet, heat oil over medium heat until hot. Add onion and cook 12 to 15 minutes, until golden. Add garlic; cook 2 minutes longer, stirring frequently. Reserve ½ cup onion mixture for sauce; transfer remaining mixture to large bowl.

3 Add bacon to skillet and cook until browned, 7 to 8 minutes, stirring occasionally. With slotted spoon, transfer bacon to bowl with onion mixture.

4 Into each of two 15½" by 10½" jelly-roll pans, spoon 2 teaspoons bacon fat from skillet. Discard any remaining fat; do not clean skillet. Place pans in oven; heat 3 minutes. Add white mushrooms to 1 pan; toss to coat. Add portobello mushrooms to other pan; toss to coat. Bake mushrooms, uncovered, 25 minutes or until lightly browned, rotating pans between upper and lower racks halfway through cooking time. Transfer all mushrooms to bowl with onion mixture; stir in spinach, Fontina, Parmesan, salt, and pepper. Turn oven control to 350°F.

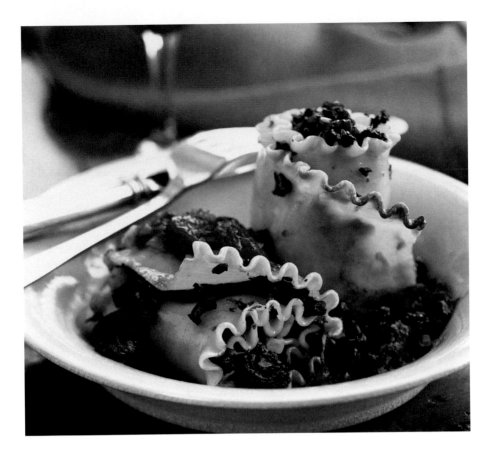

5   In same skillet, heat both cans of tomatoes with their puree, water, and reserved onion mixture to boiling over medium-high heat, stirring occasionally and breaking up tomatoes with side of spoon. Reduce heat to low; cover and simmer sauce 10 minutes. Stir ½ cup sauce into mushroom mixture in bowl. Spoon remaining sauce into 13" by 9" glass baking dish.

6   On work surface, place 6 lasagna noodles. Spoon scant ½ cup mushroom filling down center of each noodle. Roll each noodle, jelly-roll fashion; place rolled noodles, ruffled side up, in dish with sauce. Repeat with remaining noodles and filling.

7   Cover and bake 30 minutes or until heated through.

EACH SERVING: ABOUT 500 CALORIES | 24G PROTEIN | 66G CARBOHYDRATE | 18G TOTAL FAT (8G SATURATED) | 8G FIBER | 35MG CHOLESTEROL | 1,360MG SODIUM

PASTA SALADS

Rice Noodles with Many Herbs (page 153)

PENNE WITH GREEN BEANS AND BASIL

Your blender will help you make this tasty sauce in a snap.

ACTIVE TIME: 15 MINUTES · **TOTAL TIME:** 30 MINUTES
MAKES: 4 MAIN-DISH SERVINGS

8 OUNCES PENNE OR BOW TIES (FARFALLE)

1 POUND GREEN BEANS, TRIMMED AND HALVED

1½ TEASPOONS SALT

1 CUP LOOSELY PACKED FRESH BASIL LEAVES, PLUS ADDITIONAL SMALL LEAVES FOR GARNISH

¼ CUP EXTRA-VIRGIN OLIVE OIL

1 TABLESPOON WATER

½ TEASPOON COARSELY GROUND BLACK PEPPER

1 MEDIUM TOMATO, DICED

1 In large saucepot, cook pasta as label directs.

2 Meanwhile, in 12-inch skillet, heat *1 inch water* to boiling over high heat. Add beans and ½ teaspoon salt; heat to boiling. Cook, uncovered, 8 to 10 minutes, until tender-crisp. Drain. Rinse beans under cold running water to cool slightly; drain again.

3 In blender at high speed, blend basil, oil, and water until almost smooth, stopping blender occasionally and scraping down sides with rubber spatula. Transfer the basil puree to a large bowl; stir in pepper and 1 teaspoon salt.

4 Drain pasta; rinse under cold running water and drain again. Toss pasta, beans, and tomato with basil puree. Garnish with basil leaves.

EACH SERVING: ABOUT 370 CALORIES | 10G PROTEIN | 52G CARBOHYDRATE | 15G TOTAL FAT (2G SATURATED) | 6G FIBER | 0MG CHOLESTEROL | 680MG SODIUM

PROVENÇAL PASTA SALAD

The signature flavors of southern France—garlic, tomatoes, peppers, and olive oil—are featured in this robust salad. For an authentic finishing touch, drizzle with a little extra-virgin olive oil before serving.

ACTIVE TIME: 30 MINUTES · **TOTAL TIME:** 45 MINUTES
MAKES: 6 MAIN-DISH SERVINGS

1 PACKAGE (16 OUNCES) BOW TIES (FARFALLE)

2 MEDIUM RED PEPPERS, ROASTED (SEE TIP), OR 1 JAR (7 OUNCES) ROASTED RED PEPPERS, DRAINED

2 TABLESPOONS OLIVE OIL

1 MEDIUM ONION (6 TO 8 OUNCES), CHOPPED

1 SMALL EGGPLANT (ABOUT ¾ POUND), CUT INTO ½-INCH CHUNKS

2 GARLIC CLOVES, MINCED

¾ TEASPOON SALT

¼ TEASPOON COARSELY GROUND BLACK PEPPER

1 PINT CHERRY TOMATOES, HALVED

1 CUP LOOSELY PACKED FRESH BASIL LEAVES, COARSELY CHOPPED

⅓ CUP KALAMATA OLIVES, PITTED AND COARSELY CHOPPED

1 In large saucepot, cook pasta as label directs. Reserve ¼ cup pasta cooking water. Drain and rinse pasta under cold running water; drain again. Cut roasted peppers into ½-inch pieces.

2 In 12-inch skillet, heat oil over medium heat until hot. Add onion and cook about 10 minutes or until tender and golden, stirring often. Increase heat to medium-high. Add eggplant, garlic, salt, and pepper and cook 8 minutes longer or until eggplant is tender and golden, stirring often.

3 To pasta, add roasted peppers, onion mixture, tomatoes, basil, olives, and reserved cooking water; toss gently. Transfer pasta mixture to serving bowl. Cover and refrigerate if not serving right away.

TIP To roast peppers, preheat the broiler. Line a broiling pan (without rack) with foil. Cut each pepper lengthwise in half, and discard the stems and seeds. Place the pepper halves in the pan, cut side down, flattening each with your hand. Broil them 5 to 6 inches from the heat source until the skins are charred and blistered, 10 to 15 minutes. Wrap foil around the peppers and allow them to steam at room temperature for 15 minutes or until they are cool enough to handle. Peel off and discard the skins, then proceed with your recipe.

EACH SERVING: ABOUT 375 CALORIES | 11G PROTEIN | 67G CARBOHYDRATE | 7G TOTAL FAT (1G SATURATED) | 3G FIBER | 0MG CHOLESTEROL | 460MG SODIUM

PASTA NIÇOISE

The classic French composed salad that features tuna, tomatoes, and green beans—salade niçoise—is the inspiration for this dish. With the addition of cavatappi, a short spiral pasta, it becomes a wonderfully easy one-dish meal. You can serve it warm or at room temperature.

ACTIVE TIME: 15 MINUTES · **TOTAL TIME:** 25 MINUTES

MAKES: 6 MAIN-DISH SERVINGS

1 PACKAGE (16 OUNCES) CAVATAPPI OR RADIATORE PASTA	½ TEASPOON GROUND BLACK PEPPER
1 POUND RED POTATOES, CUT INTO ¾-INCH CHUNKS	2 ANCHOVIES, MINCED
	1 GARLIC CLOVE, CRUSHED WITH GARLIC PRESS
1 POUND GREEN BEANS, TRIMMED AND EACH CUT CROSSWISE IN HALF	1 CAN (12 OUNCES) SOLID WHITE TUNA PACKED IN WATER, DRAINED
1 TO 2 LEMONS	1 CUP LOOSELY PACKED FRESH PARSLEY LEAVES, CHOPPED
¾ CUP CHICKEN BROTH	
¼ CUP OLIVE OIL	⅔ CUP GRATED PARMESAN CHEESE
2 TEASPOONS DIJON MUSTARD	

1 Heat large saucepot of salted *water* to boiling over high heat. Add pasta and potatoes; heat to boiling. Cook 2 minutes; add green beans and cook 6 minutes longer or until pasta and vegetables are tender. Drain well.

2 Meanwhile, from lemons, grate 1 teaspoon peel and squeeze 3 table-spoons juice.

3 In small bowl, with wire whisk or fork, mix lemon peel, lemon juice, broth, oil, mustard, pepper, anchovies, and garlic.

4 Arrange pasta, potatoes, beans, and tuna on platter. Drizzle with dressing; sprinkle with parsley and Parmesan.

EACH SERVING: ABOUT 570 CALORIES | 31G PROTEIN | 78G CARBOHYDRATE | 15G TOTAL FAT (4G SATURATED) | 6G FIBER | 31MG CHOLESTEROL | 745MG SODIUM

PASTA SALAD WITH TOMATO AND BOCCONCINI

Sweet cherry tomatoes, mozzarella, and a shower of chopped fresh parsley and basil make this summer salad as colorful as it is delicious. Chill after preparing to meld the flavors if you like, but bring the pasta to room temperature before serving.

ACTIVE TIME: 15 MINUTES · **TOTAL TIME:** 30 MINUTES
MAKES: 6 MAIN-DISH SERVINGS

2 PINTS CHERRY TOMATOES, HALVED

½ CUP LOOSELY PACKED FRESH FLAT-LEAF PARSLEY LEAVES, CHOPPED

½ CUP LOOSELY PACKED FRESH BASIL LEAVES, THINLY SLICED

¼ CUP OLIVE OIL

1 TEASPOON SALT

¼ TEASPOON COARSELY GROUND BLACK PEPPER

1 GARLIC CLOVE, CRUSHED WITH GARLIC PRESS

1 PACKAGE (16 OUNCES) PENNE OR CORKSCREW PASTA 12 OUNCES

SMALL MOZZARELLA BALLS (BOCCONCINI), HALVED (SEE TIP)

1 In large serving bowl, stir cherry tomatoes, parsley, basil, oil, salt, pepper, and garlic. Let stand at room temperature at least 1 hour or up to 4 hours to blend flavors.

2 In large saucepot, cook pasta as label directs. Drain well.

3 Add pasta to tomato mixture; toss with bocconcini.

TIP Bocconcini (Italian for "little mouthfuls") are small balls of mozzarella that can be found in gourmet shops and in the dairy case of some supermarkets. They are packed in whey or water and are sometimes tossed with herbs and spices, such as basil, black pepper, and crushed red pepper. If you buy the kind with flavorings, adjust the seasonings that are called for accordingly.

EACH SERVING: ABOUT 545 CALORIES | 21G PROTEIN | 64G CARBOHYDRATE | 23G TOTAL FAT (9G SATURATED) | 2G FIBER | 44MG CHOLESTEROL | 540MG SODIUM

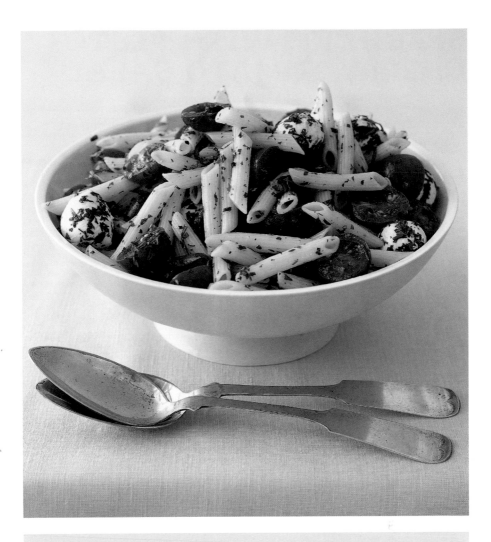

HOW TO CHOP FRESH HERBS

There's nothing like a sprinkling of fresh herbs to brighten a dish. To chop parsley, cilantro, mint, or other small leaves, strip the leaves from the stems and pile them on a cutting board. Cut the herbs into small pieces by holding the tip of the blade against the board and rocking the handle up and down. Continue until the herbs are chopped as coarsely or finely as you want.

To slice basil, sage, or other large leaves, stack the leaves, then tightly roll them up lengthwise, cigar style. Place on a cutting board and cut crosswise with a large sharp knife into thin or thick slice. This technique is sometimes referred to as chiffonade.

SPAGHETTI WITH PESTO– CHERRY TOMATO SALAD

Two old favorites add up to one great meal when spaghetti with pesto is topped with a cherry tomato salad. If you're in a hurry, you can substitute prepared pesto—you need about 4 ounces.

ACTIVE TIME: 20 MINUTES · **TOTAL TIME:** 30 MINUTES
MAKES: 6 MAIN-DISH SERVINGS

HOMEMADE PESTO, PAGE 13

1½ PINTS RED AND/OR YELLOW CHERRY TOMATOES, HALVED (ABOUT 3½ CUPS)

½ SMALL RED ONION, THINLY SLICED (ABOUT ½ CUP)

⅓ CUP PACKED FRESH BASIL LEAVES, CUT INTO STRIPS, PLUS SPRIGS FOR GARNISH

1 TABLESPOON EXTRA-VIRGIN OLIVE OIL

1½ TEASPOONS RED WINE VINEGAR

½ TEASPOON SALT

¼ TEASPOON GROUND BLACK PEPPER

1 PACKAGE (16 OUNCES) THIN SPAGHETTI (SUCH AS SPAGHETTINI)

1 Prepare pesto and transfer to small bowl. Place plastic wrap directly on pesto surface to prevent browning; set aside.
2 Prepare cherry-tomato salad: In medium bowl, mix tomatoes, onion, basil strips, oil, vinegar, salt, and pepper. Set aside.
3 In large saucepot, cook spaghetti as label directs.
4 When spaghetti has reached desired doneness, remove ¼ cup *pasta cooking water* and reserve. Drain spaghetti and return to saucepot. Add pesto and reserved cooking water; toss well.
5 To serve, spoon spaghetti mixture into serving bowls; top with tomato salad. Garnish with basil sprigs.

EACH SERVING: ABOUT 680 CALORIES | 22G PROTEIN | 95G CARBOHYDRATE | 24G TOTAL FAT (5G SATURATED) | 6G FIBER | 8MG CHOLESTEROL | 1,225MG SODIUM

PASTA WITH FETA, MINT, AND OLIVES

The tantalizing flavors of a Greek salad—feta cheese, mint, and olives—are perfect with pasta. Taste your olives before making the sauce: If they're very briny, you may want to omit the lemon juice or reduce the amount you use.

ACTIVE TIME: 15 MINUTES · **TOTAL TIME:** 25 MINUTES

MAKES: 4 MAIN-DISH OR 8 SIDE-DISH SERVINGS

1 PACKAGE (16 OUNCES) GEMELLI OR PENNE	2 TABLESPOONS EXTRA-VIRGIN OLIVE OIL
4 OUNCES FETA CHEESE, CRUMBLED (1 CUP)	1 TABLESPOON FRESH LEMON JUICE
¼ CUP KALAMATA OLIVES, PITTED AND SLICED	⅛ TEASPOON GROUND BLACK PEPPER
¼ CUP CHOPPED FRESH MINT LEAVES	1 BUNCH (10 TO 12 OUNCES) SPINACH, RINSED AND DRAINED VERY WELL, TOUGH STEMS REMOVED AND LEAVES TORN

1 In large saucepot, cook pasta as label directs.

2 Meanwhile, in medium bowl, combine feta, olives, mint, olive oil, lemon juice, and pepper.

3 Drain pasta; return to saucepot. Add feta mixture and spinach; toss well.

EACH MAIN-DISH SERVING: ABOUT 595 CALORIES | 20G PROTEIN | 90G CARBOHYDRATE 17G TOTAL FAT (6G SATURATED) | 5G FIBER | 25MG CHOLESTEROL | 640MG SODIUM

PASTA SALAD WITH LEMON AND PEAS

This super-simple salad makes a nice change from potato salad at picnics. Try it with anything from chicken to grilled steak.

ACTIVE TIME: 20 MINUTES · **TOTAL TIME:** 30 MINUTES
MAKES: 12 SIDE-DISH SERVINGS

1   PACKAGE (16 OUNCES) BOW TIES (FARFALLE) OR SMALL SHELL PASTA

1   PACKAGE (10 OUNCES) FROZEN BABY PEAS

2   LEMONS

⅔   CUP MILK

½   CUP LIGHT MAYONNAISE

1   TEASPOON SALT

¼   TEASPOON COARSELY GROUND BLACK PEPPER

1   CUP LOOSELY PACKED FRESH BASIL LEAVES, CHOPPED

4   GREEN ONIONS, THINLY SLICED

1   In large saucepot, cook pasta as label directs, adding peas during last 2 minutes of cooking time. Drain pasta and peas; rinse with cold water and drain well.

2   Meanwhile, from lemons, grate 1 tablespoon peel and squeeze 3 table-spoons juice. In large bowl, with wire whisk, mix lemon peel and juice with milk, mayonnaise, salt, pepper, basil, and green onions until blended.

3   Add pasta and peas to mayonnaise dressing; toss to coat well. Cover and refrigerate up to two days if not serving right away.

EACH SERVING: ABOUT 205 CALORIES | 7G PROTEIN | 33G CARBOHYDRATE | 4G TOTAL FAT (1G SATURATED) | 4G FIBER | 5MG CHOLESTEROL | 327MG SODIUM

PASTA AND PEPPER TOSS WITH SUMMER BASIL

This colorful mix of sweet yellow and red peppers, tomatoes, eggplant, and zucchini can be served at room temperature. It's a natural for picnics and potlucks.

ACTIVE TIME: 45 MINUTES · **TOTAL TIME:** 55 MINUTES

MAKES: 12 SIDE-DISH SERVINGS

---

1 PACKAGE (16 OUNCES) PENNE, RADIATORE, OR FUSILLI

3 MEDIUM RED PEPPERS, ROASTED (SEE TIP, PAGE 140)

2 MEDIUM YELLOW PEPPERS, ROASTED (SEE TIP, PAGE 140)

4 TABLESPOONS OLIVE OIL

1 MEDIUM RED ONION, CHOPPED

3 MEDIUM ZUCCHINI (6 OUNCES EACH), EACH CUT LENGTHWISE IN HALF THEN THINLY SLICED CROSSWISE

1 MEDIUM EGGPLANT (1¼ POUNDS), CUT INTO ½-INCH CHUNKS

SALT

3 MEDIUM RIPE TOMATOES (1 POUND), CHOPPED

1 CUP LOOSELY PACKED FRESH BASIL LEAVES

2 TABLESPOONS CAPERS, DRAINED

1 Roast peppers and cut them into ½-inch pieces. Set aside.

2 Meanwhile in large saucepot, cook pasta as label directs; drain. Rinse with cold water, and drain again. Set aside.

3 In nonstick 12-inch skillet, heat 1 tablespoon oil over medium heat until hot. Add onion and cook 6 minutes or until tender, stirring occasionally. Add zucchini and 1 tablespoon oil, and cook 7 minutes or until zucchini are tender-crisp, stirring frequently. Add eggplant, a sprinkling of salt, and remaining 2 tablespoons oil, and cook 8 minutes or until eggplant is tender, stirring frequently.

4 Transfer vegetables to large bowl; stir in tomatoes, basil, capers, and ½ teaspoon salt. Add pasta; toss well. Serve salad warm, or cover and refrigerate until ready to serve.

EACH SERVING: ABOUT 225 CALORIES | 7G PROTEIN | 38G CARBOHYDRATE | 6G TOTAL FAT (1G SATURATED) | 4G FIBER | 0MG CHOLESTEROL | 285MG SODIUM

TOMATO AND ORZO SALAD

This perfect pasta toss requires little cooking but yields big flavor.

ACTIVE TIME: 20 MINUTES · **TOTAL TIME:** 30 MINUTES
MAKES: 4 MAIN-DISH SERVINGS

1¼ CUPS ORZO PASTA

½ POUND GREEN BEANS, TRIMMED AND EACH CUT INTO THIRDS

2 LARGE LEMONS

2 TABLESPOONS EXTRA-VIRGIN OLIVE OIL

2 TEASPOONS FRESH OREGANO LEAVES, CHOPPED

¾ TEASPOON SALT

¼ TEASPOON COARSELY GROUND BLACK PEPPER

1 POUND RIPE TOMATOES (3 MEDIUM), CUT INTO ½-INCH PIECES

4 OUNCES RICOTTA SALATA CHEESE, CRUMBLED, OR PARMESAN CHEESE, SHAVED

1 In 4-quart saucepan, heat 3 *quarts salted water* to boiling over high heat. Add orzo; return to boiling and cook 4 minutes. Add green beans and cook until orzo and beans are tender, about 4 minutes longer. Drain well.

2 Meanwhile, from lemons, grate 1 teaspoon peel and squeeze ¼ cup juice. In large bowl, with wire whisk or fork, mix oil, oregano, ¾ teaspoon salt, pepper, and lemon peel and juice until blended.

3 Add warm orzo and beans to dressing in bowl and toss well. Gently stir in tomatoes and ricotta salata.

EACH SERVING: ABOUT 340 CALORIES | 12G PROTEIN | 44G CARBOHYDRATE | 14G TOTAL FAT (6G SATURATED) | 5G FIBER | 26MG CHOLESTEROL | 1,010MG SODIUM

GAZPACHO-STYLE PASTA SALAD

Classic gazpacho soup ingredients get pulsed in the food processor while the small seashell pasta cooks. Toss them together, and you have a colorful summer salad.

ACTIVE TIME: 15 MINUTES · **TOTAL TIME:** 30 MINUTES PLUS CHILLING
MAKES: 4 MAIN-DISH SERVINGS

1 PACKAGE (16 OUNCES) SMALL SHELL OR ORECCHIETTE PASTA

1 ENGLISH (SEEDLESS) CUCUMBER (1 POUND), UNPEELED AND CUT INTO 2-INCH PIECES

½ MEDIUM YELLOW PEPPER, CUT INTO 1-INCH PIECES

½ MEDIUM RED PEPPER, CUT INTO 1-INCH PIECES

1 JALAPEÑO CHILE, SEEDED AND CUT INTO ½-INCH PIECES

1 GARLIC CLOVE, CUT INTO THIRDS

1½ POUNDS TOMATOES (5 MEDIUM), CUT INTO ½-INCH PIECES

2 TABLESPOONS OLIVE OIL

2 TABLESPOONS SHERRY VINEGAR OR RED WINE VINEGAR

1½ TEASPOONS SALT

1 SMALL BUNCH FRESH PARSLEY, STEMS DISCARDED

CUCUMBER SLICES AND CHERRY TOMATOES FOR GARNISH

1 In large saucepot, cook pasta as label directs. Drain.

2 Meanwhile, in food processor, with knife blade attached, finely chop cucumber, peppers, onion, chile, and garlic. Do not puree.

3 In large serving bowl, toss vegetable mixture with tomatoes, oil, vinegar, and salt until well mixed. Set aside 4 parsley leaves for garnish; chop remaining parsley.

4 Add pasta and chopped parsley to vegetable mixture; toss well to combine. Chill salad for about 1 hour and toss again before serving. Garnish each serving with cucumber slices, cherry tomatoes, and reserved parsley leaves.

EACH SERVING: ABOUT 555 CALORIES | 18G PROTEIN | 100G CARBOHYDRATE | 9G TOTAL FAT (1G SATURATED) | 8G FIBER | 0MG CHOLESTEROL | 1,045MG SODIUM

SZECHUAN PEANUT-NOODLE SALAD

A tasty pasta salad packed with great Asian flavors. To serve cold, chill the pasta and toss it with the vegetables just before serving.

ACTIVE TIME: 25 MINUTES · **TOTAL TIME:** 30 MINUTES
MAKES: 5 MAIN-DISH SERVINGS

1 PACKAGE (16 OUNCES) LINGUINE OR SPAGHETTI

2½ TEASPOONS SALT

4 OUNCES SNOW PEAS, STRINGS REMOVED

½ CUP CREAMY PEANUT BUTTER

1 TABLESPOON GRATED, PEELED FRESH GINGER (SEE TIP, PAGE 99)

¼ CUP SOY SAUCE

2 TABLESPOONS DISTILLED WHITE VINEGAR

2 TEASPOONS ASIAN SESAME OIL

¼ TEASPOON HOT PEPPER SAUCE

1 SMALL CUCUMBER (6 OUNCES), PEELED, SEEDED, AND CUT INTO 2" by ¼" MATCHSTICK STRIPS

¼ CUP DRY-ROASTED PEANUTS

1 GREEN ONION, TRIMMED AND CHOPPED

1 In large saucepot, cook linguine as label directs, using 2 teaspoons salt.

2 Meanwhile, in 3-quart saucepan, heat 1 *inch water* to boiling; add snow peas. Reduce heat and simmer 2 minutes; drain. Rinse with cold running water; drain. Cut snow peas lengthwise into ¼-inch-wide matchstick strips; set aside.

3 Drain linguine, reserving 1 *cup pasta cooking water*.

4 Prepare dressing: In large bowl, with wire whisk, mix peanut butter, ginger, reserved cooking water, soy sauce, vinegar, sesame oil, hot pepper sauce, and remaining ½ teaspoon salt until smooth.

5 Add linguine to dressing in bowl and toss to coat. Add snow peas and cucumber; toss to combine. Sprinkle with peanuts and green onion.

EACH SERVING: ABOUT 570 CALORIES | 22G PROTEIN | 78G CARBOHYDRATE | 20G TOTAL FAT (3G SATURATED) | 5G FIBER | 0MG CHOLESTEROL | 1,794MG SODIUM

RICE NOODLES WITH MANY HERBS

Whip up this light summer main dish with fast-cooking noodles, carrots, cucumber, herbs, and our delicious Asian dressing. Serve warm or at room temperature. For photo, see page 136.

TOTAL TIME: 20 MINUTES

MAKES: 4 MAIN-DISH SERVINGS

3   SMALL CARROTS, PEELED AND CUT INTO 2" by ¼" MATCHSTICK STRIPS (1⅓ CUPS)

⅓   CUP SEASONED RICE VINEGAR

1   PACKAGE (16 OUNCES) ½-INCH-WIDE FLAT RICE NOODLES

⅓   ENGLISH (SEEDLESS) CUCUMBER, UNPEELED AND CUT INTO 2" by ¼" MATCHSTICK STRIPS (1 CUP)

1   CUP LOOSELY PACKED FRESH CILANTRO LEAVES

½   CUP LOOSELY PACKED FRESH MINT LEAVES

⅓   CUP LOOSELY PACKED SMALL FRESH BASIL LEAVES

⅓   CUP SNIPPED CHIVES

2   TEASPOONS ASIAN SESAME OIL

1   In small bowl, stir carrots with vinegar. Let stand at room temperature while preparing noodles.

2   In 8-quart saucepot, heat 5 *quarts water* to boiling over high heat. Add noodles and cook just until cooked through, about 3 minutes. Drain noodles; rinse under cold running water and drain again.

3   Transfer noodles to large shallow serving bowl. Add carrots with their liquid, cucumber, cilantro, mint, basil, chives, and sesame oil; toss well.

EACH SERVING: ABOUT 470 CALORIES | 7G PROTEIN | 105G CARBOHYDRATE | 3G TOTAL FAT (0G SATURATED) | 6G FIBER | 0MG CHOLESTEROL | 550MG SODIUM

INDEX

Note: Page numbers in *italics* include photographs/captions.

PHOTOGRAPHY CREDITS

Antonis Achilleos: 38
James Baigrie: 2, 12, 53, 143
Richard Bowditch: 57
Monica Buck: 99, 133
Tara Donne: 120
Brian Hagiwara: 9, 23, 60, 69, 103, 106, 108, 147, 151
Lisa Hubbard: 44
iStock: Carla Guastella: 19, Alex Kotlov: 15, Laura Stanley: 16, Kais Tolmats: 13
Con Poulos: 125
Rita Maas: 64
Kate Mathis: 72
Kate Sears: 20, 58, 85, 88
Alan Richardson: 31, 37, 41, 49, 63, 77, 95
Ann Stratton: 6, 80, 103
Studio D: Philip Friedman: 7
Mark Thomas: 24, 105, 122, 135, 136
Jonelle Weaver: 139
Cheryl Zibisky: 115

Front Cover: James Baigrie
Spine: Brian Hagiwara
Back Cover (clockwise from top left): Alan Richardson, James Baigrie, Mark Thomas

METRIC EQUIVALENTS

The recipes that appear in this cookbook use the standard United States method for measuring liquid and dry or solid ingredients (teaspoons, tablespoons, and cups). The information on this chart is provided to help cooks outside the U.S. successfully use these recipes. All equivalents are approximate.

METRIC EQUIVALENTS FOR DIFFERENT TYPES OF INGREDIENTS

A standard cup measure of a dry or solid ingredient will vary in weight depending on the type of ingredient. A standard cup of liquid is the same volume for any type of liquid. Use the following chart when converting standard cup measures to grams (weight) or milliliters (volume).

Standard Cup	Fine Powder (e.g. flour)	Grain (e.g. rice)	Granular (e.g. sugar)	Liquid Solids (e.g. butter)	Liquid (e.g. milk)
1	140 g	150 g	190 g	200 g	240 ml
¾	105 g	113 g	143 g	150 g	180 ml
⅔	93 g	100 g	125 g	133 g	160 ml
½	70 g	75 g	95 g	100 g	120 ml
⅓	47 g	50 g	63 g	67 g	80 ml
¼	35 g	38 g	48 g	50 g	60 ml
⅛	18 g	19 g	24 g	25 g	30 ml

USEFUL EQUIVALENTS FOR LIQUID INGREDIENTS BY VOLUME

¼ tsp	=					1 ml	
½ tsp	=					2 ml	
1 tsp	=					5 ml	
3 tsp	=	1 tbls	=		½ fl oz	=	15 ml
		2 tbls	=	⅛ cup	=	1 fl oz	=	30 ml
		4 tbls	=	¼ cup	=	2 fl oz	=	60 ml
		5⅓ tbls	=	⅓ cup	=	3 fl oz	=	80 ml
		8 tbls	=	½ cup	=	4 fl oz	=	120 ml
		10⅔ tbls	=	⅔ cup	=	5 fl oz	=	160 ml
		12 tbls	=	¾ cup	=	6 fl oz	=	180 ml
		16 tbls	=	1 cup	=	8 fl oz	=	240 ml
		1 pt	=	2 cups	=	16 fl oz	=	480 ml
		1 qt	=	4 cups	=	32 fl oz	=	960 ml
					33 fl oz	=	1000 ml = 1 L

USEFUL EQUIVALENTS FOR COOKING/OVEN TEMPERATURES

	Fahrenheit	Celsius	Gas Mark
Freeze Water	32° F	0° C	
Room Temperature	68° F	20° C	
Boil Water	212° F	100° C	
Bake	325° F	160° C	3
	350° F	180° C	4
	375° F	190° C	5
	400° F	200° C	6
	425° F	220° C	7
	450° F	230° C	8
Broil			Grill

USEFUL EQUIVALENTS FOR DRY INGREDIENTS BY WEIGHT

(To convert ounces to grams, multiply the number of ounces by 30.)

1 oz	=	⅟₁₆ lb	=	30 g
2 oz	=	¼ lb	=	120 g
4 oz	=	½ lb	=	240 g
8 oz	=	¾ lb	=	360 g
16 oz	=	1 lb	=	480 g

USEFUL EQUIVALENTS LENGTH

(To convert inches to centimeters, multiply the number of inches by 2.5.)

1 in	=		2.5 cm
6 in	= ½ ft	=	15 cm
12 in	= 1 ft	=	30 cm
36 in	= 3 ft	= 1 yd	= 90 cm
40 in	=		100 cm = 1 m

THE GOOD HOUSEKEEPING TRIPLE-TEST PROMISE

At *Good Housekeeping*, we want to make sure that every recipe we print works in any oven, with any brand of ingredient, no matter what. That's why, in our test kitchens at the **Good Housekeeping Research Institute**, we go all out: We test each recipe at least three times—and, often, several more times after that.

When a recipe is first developed, one member of our team prepares the dish and we judge it on these criteria: It must be **delicious, family-friendly, healthy,** and **easy to make.**

1. The recipe is then tested several more times to fine-tune the flavor and ease of preparation, always by the same team member, using the same equipment.

2. Next, another team member follows the recipe as written, **varying the brands of ingredients** and **kinds of equipment.** Even the types of stoves we use are changed.

3. A third team member repeats the whole process **using yet another set of equipment** and **alternative ingredients.**

By the time the recipes appear on these pages, they are guaranteed to work in any kitchen, including yours. WE PROMISE.